SALADS AND SUMMER DISHES

SALADS AND SUMMER DISHES

Grange BOOKS

Published by Grange Books
An imprint of Books & Toys Limited
The Grange
Grange Yard
London SE1 3AG
By arrangement with Ebury Press

ISBN 1 85627 186 2

This edition reprinted 1992

Consultant editor: Jeni Wright
Editors: Veronica Sperling and Barbara Croxford
Design: Mike Leaman
Illustrations: John Woodcock and Kate Simunek
Photography: David Johnson
Cookery: Susanna Tee, Maxine Clark, Janet Smith

Filmset by Advanced Filmsetters (Glasgow) Ltd

Printed and bound in Italy by
New Interlitho, S.p.a., Milan

Contents

Cookery Notes

Follow either metric or imperial measures for the recipes in this book as they are not interchangeable. Sets of spoon measures are available in both metric and imperial size to give accurate measurement of small quantities. All spoon measures are level unless otherwise stated. When measuring milk we have used the exact conversion of 568 ml (1 pint).

* Size 4 eggs should be used except when otherwise stated.

† Granulated sugar is used unless otherwise stated.

● All recipes in this book serve six people unless otherwise stated.

OVEN TEMPERATURE CHART

°C	°F	*Gas mark*
110	225	$\frac{1}{4}$
130	250	$\frac{1}{2}$
140	275	1
150	300	2
170	325	3
180	350	4
190	375	5
200	400	6
220	425	7
230	450	8
240	475	9

KEY TO SYMBOLS

1.00* Indicates minimum preparation and cooking times in hours and minutes. They do not include prepared items in the list of ingredients; calculated times apply only to the method. An asterisk * indicates extra time should be allowed, so check the note immediately below the symbols.

Chef's hats indicate degree of difficulty of a recipe: no hat means it is straightforward; one hat slightly more complicated; two hats indicates that it is for more advanced cooks.

£ Indicates a recipe which is good value for money; £ £ indicates an expensive recipe.

✳ Indicates that a recipe will freeze. If there is no symbol, the recipe is unsuitable for freezing. An asterisk * indicates special freezer instructions so check the note immediately below the symbols.

309 cals Indicates calories per serving, including any serving suggestions (e.g. pitta bread, to serve) given in the list of ingredients.

METRIC CONVERSION SCALE

LIQUID

Imperial	*Exact conversion*	*Recommended ml*
$\frac{1}{4}$ pint	142 ml	150 ml
$\frac{1}{2}$ pint	284 ml	300 ml
1 pint	568 ml	600 ml
$1\frac{1}{2}$ pints	851 ml	900 ml
$1\frac{3}{4}$ pints	992 ml	1 litre

For quantities of $1\frac{3}{4}$ pints and over, litres and fractions of a litre have been used.

SOLID

Imperial	*Exact conversion*	*Recommended g*
1 oz	28.35 g	25 g
2 oz	56.7 g	50 g
4 oz	113.4 g	100 g
8 oz	226.8 g	225 g
12 oz	340.2 g	350 g
14 oz	397.0 g	400 g
16 oz (1 lb)	453.6 g	450 g

1 kilogram (kg) equals 2.2 lb.

Salads and Summer Dishes

Say goodbye to boring salads when you open up this book. Turn the pages and see how to add interest and zest to the fabulous ingredients of summer—there is no better time of the year for creating wonderful food for family and friends. The choice of fresh, seasonal ingredients is virtually limitless in summertime: crisp and crunchy vegetables, freshly dug and picked, plus the most colourful array of soft fruits just waiting for eating—they are all cheap and plentiful for you to enjoy.

There is something for every occasion in *Salads and Summer Dishes*: sunny starters from Spain and Greece, exotic side salads from the Middle East and Indonesia, hot and spicy barbecues from India and the USA, appetising main courses from Italy and France—not to mention England—and the crispiest and freshest vegetable ideas from all over the world. PLUS the most eye-catching and mouth-watering display of desserts you've ever seen in your life!

And as if the recipes aren't enough, at the back of the book, you'll find a huge section of information to help with all aspects of summer eating: an A–Z of summer produce, basic recipes for sauces, salads and dressings, plus relishes and drinks; how to cope successfully with eating outdoors, and masses of freezing information to help you prolong summer.

With this book to hand in the kitchen, you'll never be stuck for interesting and unusual eating ideas all the summer long. In fact, there is such a tempting number and variety of different dishes, you will hardly know where to start. . . .

Starters

Summer starters for dinner parties and lunches should be light and refreshing. Just enough to set the mouth watering and the taste buds tingling. Choose from this selection of Middle Eastern dips, chilled vegetable soups, crisp, fresh salads and light summer pâtés. And don't miss out on two of summer's most delicate and delicious ingredients – asparagus and salmon. Their seasons are short, so enjoy them while you can.

ARTICHOKE HEARTS À LA GRÈCQUE

0.30 £ £ 103 cals

Serves 6

75 ml (5 tbsp) olive oil
15 ml (1 tbsp) white wine vinegar
10 ml (2 tsp) tomato purée
1 large garlic clove, skinned and crushed
7.5 ml ($1\frac{1}{2}$ tsp) chopped fresh thyme or basil
salt and freshly ground pepper
175 g (6 oz) button onions, skinned
5 ml (1 tsp) caster sugar
225 g (8 oz) small button mushrooms, wiped
two 400-g (14-oz) cans artichoke hearts

1 Make the dressing. Place 45 ml (3 tbsp) oil, vinegar, tomato purée, garlic, thyme and seasoning in a bowl and whisk together.

2 Blanch onions in boiling water for 5 minutes; drain well. Heat remaining oil; add onions and sugar and cook for 2 minutes.

3 Add mushrooms and toss over a high heat for a few seconds. Tip contents of pan into dressing. Drain artichoke hearts, rinse and dry. Add hearts to dressing and toss together. Cover and chill.

Menu Suggestion
Serve with Pissaladière (page 30) and Fresh Peach Ice Cream (page 128).

HUMMUS

2.30* £ 252 cals

* Begin ahead if soaking dried peas. Using canned peas, total preparation time is 30 minutes

Serves 8

225 g (8 oz) dried chick peas, soaked overnight, or two 400-g (14-oz) cans chick peas

juice of 2 large lemons

150 ml (¼ pint) tahini (paste of finely ground sesame seeds)

60 ml (4 tbsp) olive oil

1–2 garlic cloves, crushed

salt and freshly ground pepper

black olives and chopped fresh parsley, to garnish

warm pitta bread, to serve

1 If using dried chick peas, drain, place in a saucepan and cover with cold water. Bring to the boil and simmer gently for 2 hours or until tender.

2 Drain the peas, reserving a little of the liquid. Put them in a blender or food processor, reserving a few for garnish, and gradually add the reserved liquid and the lemon juice, blending well after each addition in order to form a smooth purée.

3 Add the tahini paste, oil (reserving 10 ml [2 tbsp]) and garlic and season to taste. Blend again until smooth.

4 Spoon into a serving dish and sprinkle with the reserved oil, chick peas, and the olives and chopped parsley.

Menu Suggestion
Serve with Spicy Lamb Kebabs (page 99), Lemon Sautéed Courgettes (page 73) and Iced Strawberry Meringues (page 126).

HUMMUS
Hummus – or as it is more correctly called – *hummus bi tahina* – is a traditional dip from the Middle East, where it is served as part of the *mezze*.

The *mezze* course is similar to the French *hors d'oeuvre*, a collection of savoury titbits designed to titillate the appetite before the main meal is served. In this country you can serve hummus on its own as a starter.

ORIENTAL SEAFOOD SALAD

0.15 £ £ 405 cals

Serves 4

- 30 ml (2 tbsp) sesame oil
- ½ small onion, peeled and very finely chopped
- 2.5-cm (1-inch) piece fresh root ginger, peeled and crushed
- 10 ml (2 tsp) soy sauce, or to taste
- 120 ml (8 tbsp) thick homemade mayonnaise (see page 145)
- salt and freshly ground pepper
- 225 g (8 oz) peeled prawns
- 225 g (8 oz) white crabmeat, flaked
- 1 red pepper, cored, seeded and diced
- ¼ cucumber, diced
- 50 g (2 oz) fresh beansprouts
- few Chinese leaves or lettuce leaves
- juice of 1 lime
- lime slices and unpeeled prawns, to garnish

1 Heat the oil in a small pan, add the onion and ginger and fry gently until soft. Remove from the heat, transfer to a large bowl and leave to cool.

2 Stir in the soy sauce and mayonnaise, with salt and freshly ground pepper to taste.

3 Fold prawns and crabmeat gently into mayonnaise mixture, then fold in red pepper, cucumber and beansprouts. Adjust seasoning, remembering that soy sauce is itself quite salty.

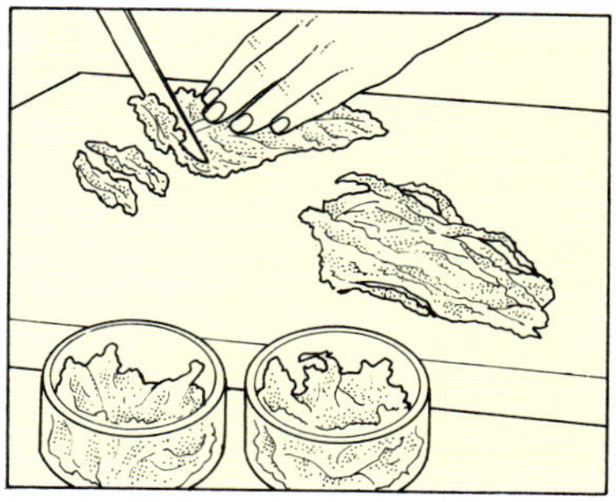

4 Meanwhile, shred the Chinese leaves or lettuce and use to line four glass dishes. To serve, pile the cocktail in the centre, then squeeze a little lime juice over each serving. Serve garnished with lime slices and unpeeled prawns.

Menu Suggestion
Serve with Chicken and Beef Satay (page 104) and Fresh Peach Ice Cream (page 128).

TARAMASALATA

1.30* £ 283 cals

* includes 1 hour chilling

Serves 6

225 g (8 oz) smoked cod's roe

1 garlic clove, skinned

50 g (2 oz) fresh white breadcrumbs

1 small onion, skinned and finely chopped

grated rind and juice of 1 lemon

150 ml ($\frac{1}{4}$ pint) olive oil

90 ml (6 tbsp) hot water

freshly ground pepper

lemon slices, to garnish

pitta bread or toast, to serve (optional)

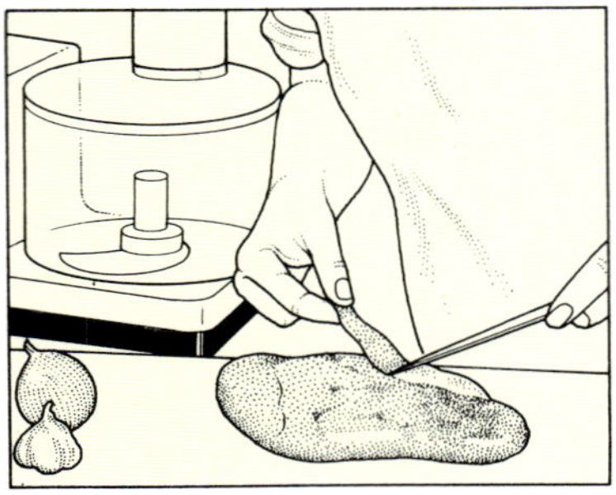

1 Skin the smoked cod's roe and break it up into pieces. Place in a blender or food processor, and blend to form a purée.

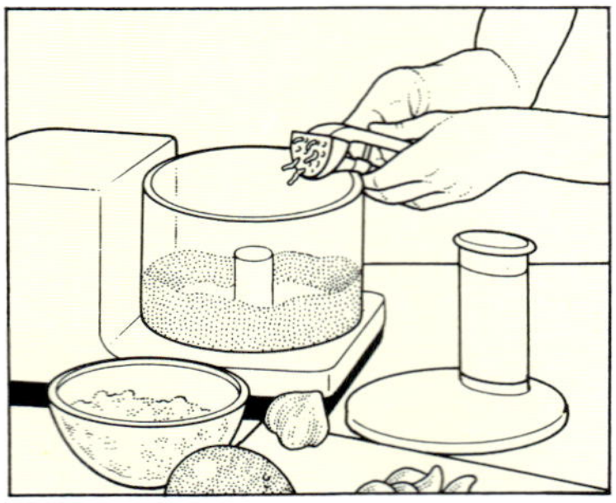

2 Crush the garlic, then add to the cod's roe with the breadcrumbs, onion and lemon rind and juice and blend for a few more seconds.

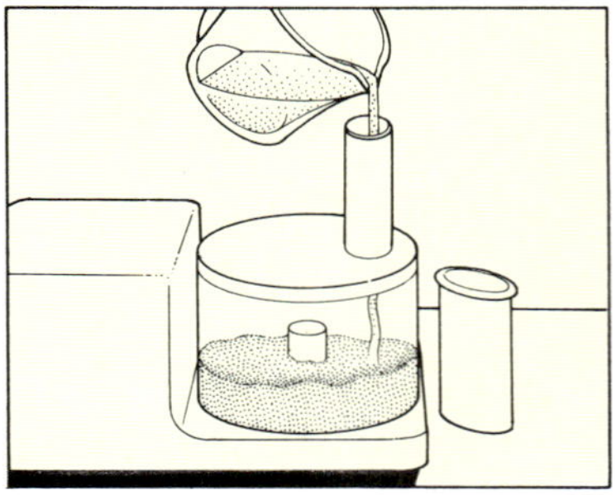

3 Gradually add the oil and blend well after each addition until smooth. Blend in hot water with the pepper.

4 Spoon into a serving dish and chill for at least 1 hour. To serve, garnish with lemon slices. Serve with pitta bread or toast, if liked.

Menu Suggestion
Serve with Greek Salad (page 61) and Hot Apricot Soufflé (page 124).

TARAMASALATA
Taramasalata is a creamy dip with a subtle flavour of smoked fish. From the Greek words *tarama*, meaning dried and salted mullet roe, and *salata* meaning salad, it is eaten all over Greece and Turkey – like hummus (page 10) as part of the *mezze* before a meal. Salted mullet roe is not so easy to obtain as it was when the recipe was first made, so these days taramasalata is most often made with smoked cod's roe, which is very similar. Many supermarkets and delicatessens sell taramasalata (often labelled 'smoked cod's roe pâté') by the kg (lb) or ready-packed in cartons. Most brands have artificial colouring added to them which gives them an unnatural bright pink colour; they also taste very strongly of fish. Homemade taramasalata tastes so much better than these commercial varieties, and it is very simple and quick to make.

CHILLED PEA AND MINT SOUP

1.30* £ ✳ 224 cals

* plus 2–3 hours chilling

Serves 6

900 g (2 lb) fresh peas

50 g (2 oz) butter or margarine

1 onion, skinned and roughly chopped

568 ml (1 pint) milk

600 ml (1 pint) chicken stock

2 large sprigs of fresh mint and mint sprigs to garnish

pinch of caster sugar

salt and freshly ground pepper

150 ml (5 fl oz) single cream

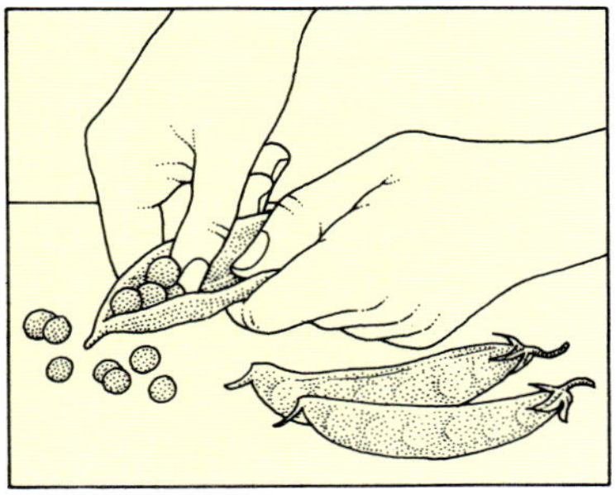

1 Shell the peas. Then melt the butter in a saucepan, add the onion, cover and cook gently for about 15 minutes until it is soft but not brown.

2 Remove from the heat and stir in the milk, stock, peas, the two mint sprigs, sugar and seasoning. Bring to the boil, stirring.

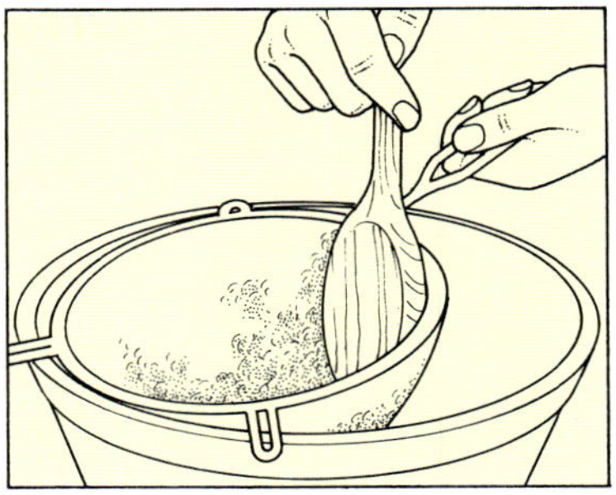

3 Cover and simmer gently for about 30 minutes, until the peas are really tender. Cool slightly, reserving about 45 ml (3 tbsp) peas to garnish and rub the remaining peas through a sieve or place in a blender or food processor and blend to form a smooth purée.

4 Pour into a large bowl. Adjust seasoning, cool. Stir in the fresh cream and chill for 2–3 hours before serving. To serve, garnish with the reserved boiled peas and sprigs of mint.

Menu Suggestion
Serve with Smoked Fish Timbale (page 35), Cucumber Raita (page 82) and Almond and Cherry Flan (page 122).

USING FRESH PEAS

This recipe for Chilled Pea and Mint Soup uses fresh peas – perfect for early summer when you can pick fresh peas from the garden or buy them easily at local farms and markets. There is nothing like the sweet, fragrant flavour of freshly picked peas in summer, so it is a good idea to make at least a double quantity of this soup and freeze some to remind you of the summer. If you want to make this soup at other times of year, it can also be made with frozen peas, in which case you will need half the weight specified in the recipe for fresh. There is no need to defrost them – just add them straight from the packet after adding the milk and stock in step 2 and cook as fresh peas.

SALMON MOUSSE

1.10* ⊟ ⊟ £ £ ✳* 290 cals

* plus 2 hours refrigeration; freeze without aspic and garnish

Serves 8

350 g (12 oz) salmon steaks
1 onion, skinned and sliced
75 g (3 oz) carrots, peeled and sliced
2 bay leaves
10 black peppercorns
salt and freshly ground pepper
150 ml (¼ pint) white wine
240 ml (16 tbsp) water
22.5 ml (4½ tsp) gelatine
300 ml (½ pint) milk
25 g (1 oz) butter or margarine
30 ml (2 tbsp) plain flour
75 ml (5 tbsp) lemon mayonnaise (see page 145)
150 ml (5 fl oz) whipping cream
red food colouring (optional)
1 egg white
15 ml (1 tbsp) medium sherry
5 ml (1 tsp) rosemary vinegar
10-cm (4-inch) piece of cucumber
Melba toast, to serve

1 Place the salmon steaks in a small shallow pan. Add half the onions and carrots, one bay leaf, five peppercorns and a good pinch of salt.

2 Spoon over 75 ml (5 tbsp) wine with 75 ml (5 tbsp) water and bring slowly to the boil. Cover and simmer gently for 10–15 minutes.

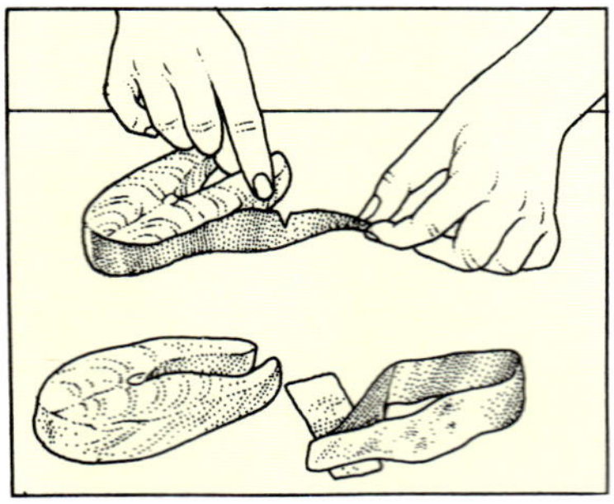

3 Remove salmon pieces (reserve the liquor). Carefully ease off the skin.

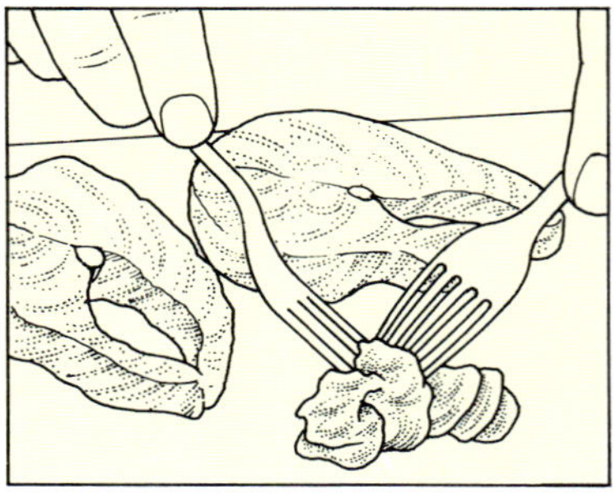

4 Using two forks, roughly flake the fish, being careful to remove any bones. Place the fish in a small bowl and keep on one side. Bubble down the cooking liquor until reduced by half, strain off and reserve.

5 Make the mousse. Spoon 45 ml (3 tbsp) water into a small basin or cup. Carefully sprinkle 15 ml (3 tsp) gelatine over the surface; leave for 10 minutes.

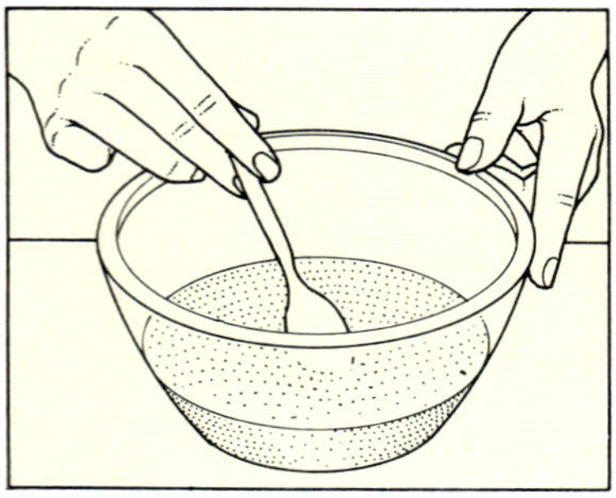

6 Prod any dry grains gently to submerge. Don't stir violently or grains of gelatine will stick to the sides of the bowl and won't soak properly.

7 Bring the milk to the boil with the remaining sliced onion, carrot, bay leaf and peppercorns; pour into a jug and leave to infuse for 10 minutes. Melt butter and off the heat blend in the flour and strained milk. Season, bring to the boil, bubble for 2–3 minutes, stirring. Pour into a bowl and while still warm stir in the soaked gelatine until dissolved.

8 Stir the fish into the cool sauce with the reserved cooking juices. Spoon half at a time into a blender or food processor and switch on for a few seconds only; the fish should retain a little of its texture. Pour into a large mixing bowl.

9 Stir the mayonnaise gently into the salmon mixture. Lightly whip the cream and fold through the mousse, adjust seasoning and add a little red food colouring if necessary.

10 Lastly, whisk the egg white until stiff but not dry, and fold lightly through mousse until no traces of white are visible.

11 Pour the mousse into an oiled 18-cm (7-inch) soufflé dish, smooth the surface, cover and refrigerate for about 2 hours to set.

12 Meanwhile, make aspic by soaking the remaining gelatine in 30 ml (2 tbsp) water and dissolving it in the usual way. Stir in the remaining white wine, the sherry, vinegar, 90 ml (6 tbsp) water and seasoning. Refrigerate for 1 hour to set.

13 Turn mousse out on to a flat platter and gently dab with absorbent kitchen paper to absorb any oil. Turn the aspic out on to a sheet of damp greaseproof or non-stick paper and chop roughly.

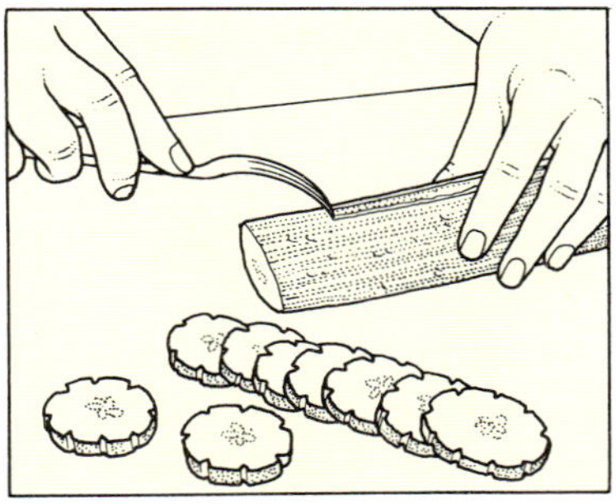

14 Run a fork down cucumber to form grooves, slice thinly. Garnish mousse with a cucumber twist and aspic; serve with Melba toast.

Menu Suggestion
Serve with Fennel and Tomato Salad (page 84) and Mixed Berry Sorbet (page 121).

VARIATION

To make this mousse slightly less expensive, ask your fishmonger for the end or tail pieces of salmon – these are usually sold cheaper than salmon steaks, and as long as you have the same weight of salmon flesh as specified in the recipe you will not notice any difference. End pieces of salmon are a good buy for dishes such as mousses.

MOZZARELLA, AVOCADO AND TOMATO SALAD

0.20 £ 283 cals

Serves 4

2 ripe avocados

120 ml (8 tbsp) basic vinaigrette (see page 143)

175 g (6 oz) Mozzarella cheese, thinly sliced

4 medium tomatoes, thinly sliced

chopped fresh parsley and mint, to garnish

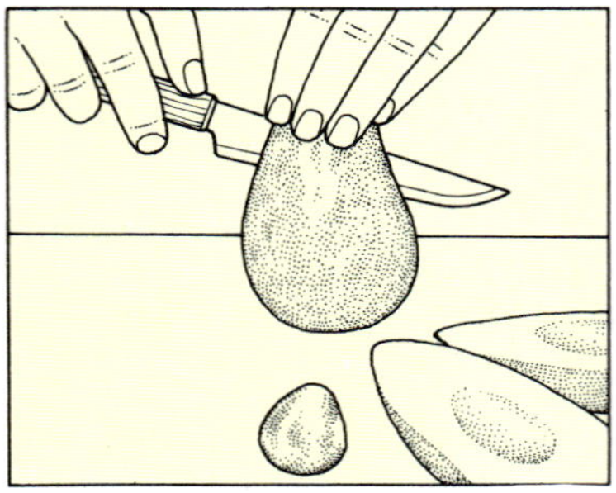

1 Halve the avocados lengthways and carefully remove the stones. Then peel and cut the avocados into slices.

2 Pour the vinaigrette over the avocado slices. Stir to coat the avocado slices thoroughly and prevent discoloration.

3 Arrange slices of Mozzarella, tomato and avocado on four individual serving plates. Spoon over the dressing and garnish with chopped parsley and a sprig of mint.

Menu Suggestion
Serve with Lamb Cutlets en Croûte (page 46) and Iced Raspberry Mousse (page 115).

Feta, Avocado and Tomato Salad

0.20	£	536 cals

Serves 4

2 ripe avocados

120 ml (8 tbsp) garlic vinaigrette (see page 143)

4 medium tomatoes

50 g (2 oz) black olives or green stuffed olives

225 g (8 oz) Feta cheese

30 ml (2 tbsp) chopped fresh marjoram

1 Halve the avocados lengthways and remove the stones, then peel and cut the avocados into slices.

2 Pour the vinaigrette over the avocado slices. Stir gently to coat the slices thoroughly.

3 Cut each tomato into eight. Stone the black olives, if used. Dice the cheese.

4 Arrange the avocados, tomatoes, olives and cheese in a salad bowl. Spoon over the dressing and sprinkle with chopped marjoram.

Menu Suggestion
Serve with Lamb with Cucumber and Mint Stuffing (page 48) and Blackcurrant Sorbet (page 120).

GAZPACHO

0.30* £ ✳ 154 cals

* plus 2 hours chilling

Serves 4

100 g (4 oz) green pepper
1 medium cucumber
450 g (1 lb) fully ripened tomatoes
50–100 g (2–4 oz) onions, skinned
1 garlic clove, skinned
45 ml (3 tbsp) vegetable oil
45 ml (3 tbsp) white wine vinegar
425-g (15-oz) can tomato juice
30 ml (2 tbsp) tomato purée
1.25 ml ($\frac{1}{4}$ tsp) salt
green pepper, ice cubes and croûtons, to serve

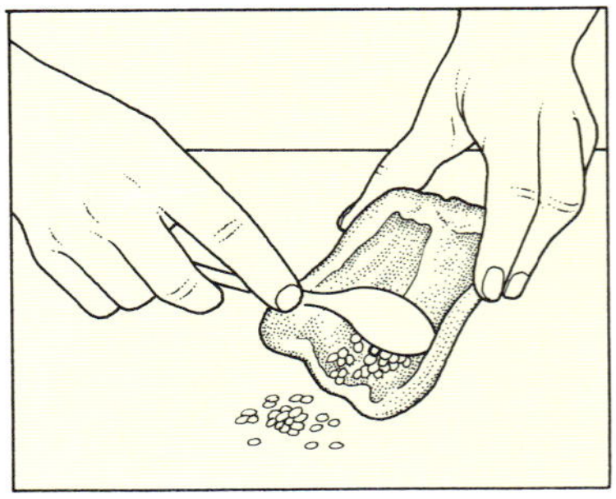

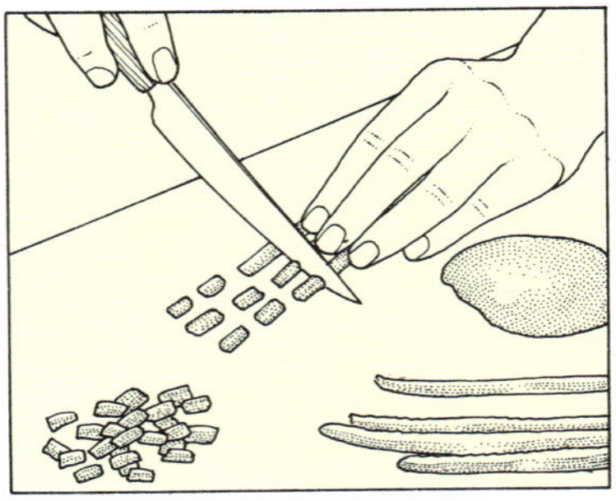

1 Remove the core and seeds from the green pepper and chop roughly with the cucumber, tomatoes, onion and garlic.

2 Mix the ingredients together in a bowl. Place in a blender or food processor in small portions and blend to form a smooth purée. Chill for 2 hours.

3 To serve. Core and seed the green pepper; dice very finely. Pour purée into bowl and add a few ice cubes. Serve garnished with diced pepper and croûtons.

Menu Suggestion
Serve with Cold Beef in Soured Cream (page 34) and Frosted Mint Cheesecake (page 111).

CHICKEN LIVER PÂTÉ WITH GREEN PEPPERCORNS

0.45* £ ✳ 152–189 cals

* plus 3 hours chilling and 30 minutes standing time

Serves 4

100 g (4 oz) butter

1 onion, skinned and chopped

450 g (1 lb) chicken livers

1 garlic clove, skinned and crushed

2.5 ml ($\frac{1}{2}$ tsp) dried marjoram

freshly ground pepper

7.5 ml ($1\frac{1}{2}$ tsp) salt

5 ml (1 tsp) lemon juice

15 ml (1 tbsp) dry sherry

10 ml (2 tsp) crushed green peppercorns

whole green peppercorns and fresh coriander, to garnish

1 Melt half the butter in a frying pan and add the onion. Fry gently for 10 minutes.

2 Add the chicken livers and the rest of the ingredients except for the crushed green peppercorns and the remaining butter. Cook the mixture over a gentle heat for about 10 minutes or until the chicken livers become firm and change colour.

3 Place in a blender or food processor and blend to form a smooth purée or push the mixture through a metal sieve. Stir in the green peppercorns. Adjust seasoning, turn into a serving dish. The mixture should come to just below rim. Refrigerate for at least 2 hours until firm.

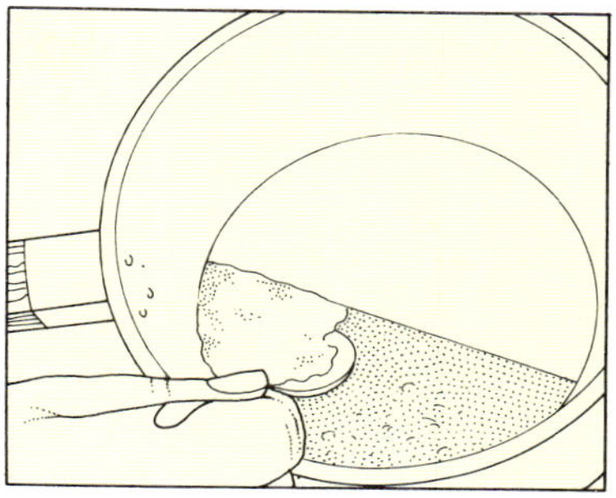

4 Melt remaining butter, skim and spoon over pâté. Refrigerate for about 1 hour to set. Leave at room temperature for 30 minutes then serve garnished with peppercorns and coriander.

Menu Suggestion

Serve with Ceviche (page 50) and Strawberry and Orange Mousse (page 119).

ASPARAGUS MALTAISE

0.30 £ £ 220 cals

Serves 6

450 g (1 lb) asparagus, washed and trimmed

3 egg yolks

grated rind and juice of 1 orange

salt and freshly ground white pepper

100 g (4 oz) unsalted butter, softened

15 ml (1 tbsp) lemon juice

30–45 ml (2–3 tbsp) double cream

orange twists, to garnish

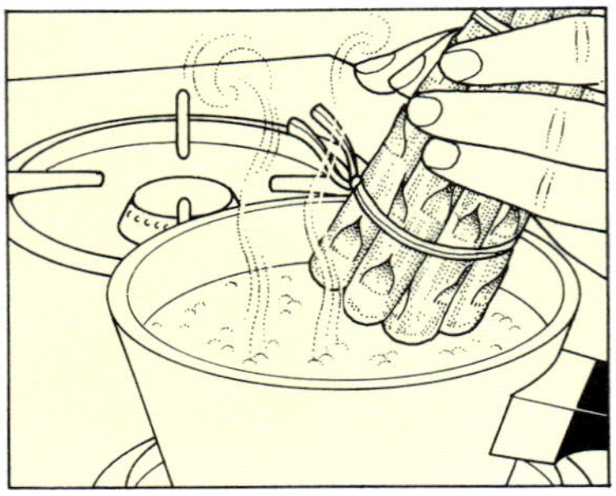

1 Tie the asparagus in bundles of six to eight stalks. Standing them upright in a pan of boiling water, cook for 10–15 minutes until tender.

2 Meanwhile, make the sauce. Beat together the egg yolks, orange rind and seasoning in a bowl with a knob of the softened butter.

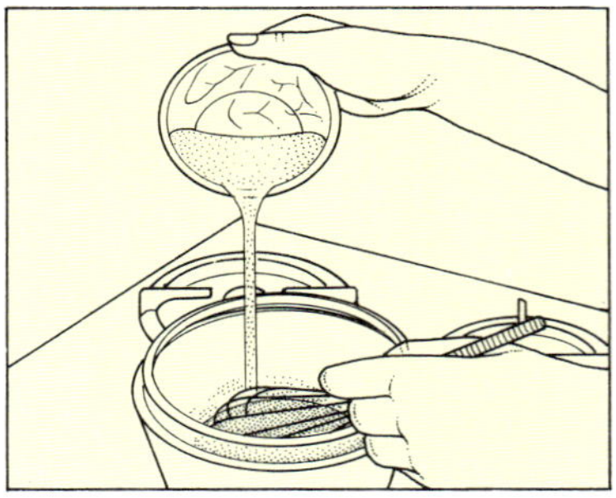

3 Place the bowl over a pan of hot water and whisk in the orange and lemon juice. Cook over a gentle heat and gradually beat in remaining butter, a little at a time.

4 Once the sauce begins to thicken, remove from the heat and continue beating for 1 minute. Adjust seasoning to taste. Stir in the cream.

5 Remove the asparagus from the pan and drain well. To serve, remove the string, garnish and serve immediately with the orange butter sauce handed separately.

Menu Suggestion
Serve with Salmon Trout with Prawns (page 57) and Late Summer Pudding (page 114).

SAUCE MALTAISE

This simple recipe for fresh asparagus served with sauce maltaise is a version of a classic French dish. Sauce maltaise is in fact a variation of hollandaise sauce – grated orange rind and juice is added to make the sauce a delicate shade of pink. Traditionally, a blood orange should be used, but this is not absolutely essential. This sauce can also be served with broccoli or fish.

Hollandaise sauce is not difficult to make, but it does require patience – if you want to make a perfect sauce there are no cutting corners! From the same family of sauces as mayonnaise – it is in fact a cooked emulsion of egg yolks and butter as opposed to the uncooked emulsion of egg yolks and oil – the skill lies in the whisking in of the butter. This should be added a little at a time: if you rush this stage and whisk in more butter before the first amount has emulsified, the resulting sauce will be curdled.

POTTED PRAWN PÂTÉ

0.20* ✳ 100 cals

* plus 1 hour chilling

Serves 8

175 g (6 oz) peeled prawns

75 g (3 oz) butter, softened

10 ml (2 tsp) lemon juice

20 ml (4 tsp) chopped fresh parsley

salt and freshly ground pepper

prawn and lemon, to garnish

French bread, to serve

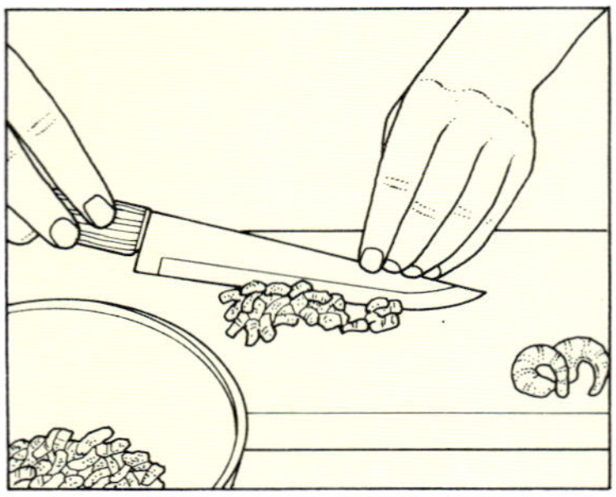

1 Finely chop the prawns. Beat into 50 g (2 oz) butter with the lemon juice, parsley and seasoning.

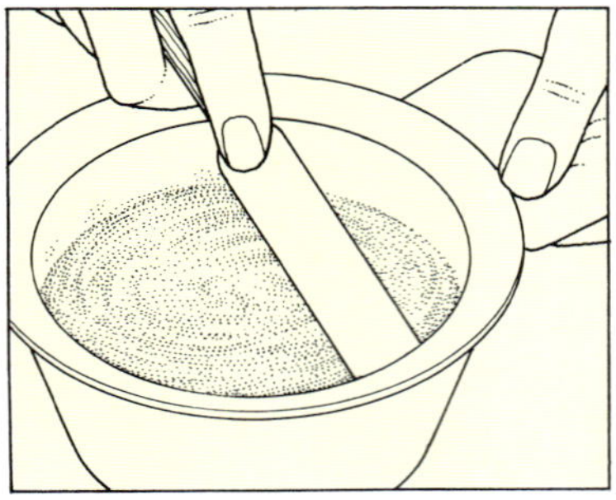

2 Spoon into a serving dish and level the surface. Melt the remaining butter and pour over the prawn mixture. Refrigerate for 1 hour. Garnish with prawn and lemon. Serve with French bread.

Menu Suggestion
Serve with Jellied Tomato Ring (page 36) and Coeurs à la Crème (page 112).

POTTED SHRIMPS

0.10* ✳ 520 cals

* plus 1 hour chilling

Serves 4

150 g (5 oz) peeled shrimps

225 g (8 oz) butter

pinch of ground mace

pinch of cayenne pepper

pinch of ground nutmeg

lemon wedges, to garnish

brown bread or melba toast

1 Melt half the butter in a saucepan. Add the shrimps and heat very gently without boiling. Add the seasonings.

2 Pour the shrimps into ramekin dishes or small pots. Leave them to cool.

3 Gently heat the remaining butter in a pan until it melts, then continue to heat slowly, without browning. Remove from the heat and leave to stand for a few minutes for the salt and sediment to settle, then carefully pour a little clarified butter over the shrimps to cover. Leave until set.

4 Unless the pots are really attractive, turn the shrimps out on to individual plates lined with a few lettuce leaves, but try to retain the shape of the pot. Before serving, remove from the refrigerator and leave at room temperature for about 30 minutes. Serve with lemon wedges and brown bread or melba toast.

CLARIFIED BUTTER

Cooked fish or meat will keep for a longer period if stored under a seal of clarified butter. The seal excludes air and moisture which encourage the growth of bacteria.

Store in the refrigerator and use within 2–3 days. Once the seal has been broken, the fish or meat should be eaten within 7 days.

CRUDITÉS WITH AÏOLI

0.45	£	464–698 cals

Serves 4–6

4 garlic cloves, skinned
1 egg yolk
300 ml ($\frac{1}{2}$ pint) olive oil
lemon juice, to taste
salt and freshly ground pepper
6 celery sticks, trimmed
4 carrots, peeled
$\frac{1}{2}$ cucumber
1 large red pepper, washed, cored, seeded and cut into strips
1 large green pepper, washed, cored, seeded and cut into strips
175 g (6 oz) button mushrooms, wiped
1 small cauliflower, cut into florets
1 bunch radishes, trimmed
6 spring onions, trimmed

1 First make the aïoli. Pound the garlic in a mortar and pestle. Stir in the egg yolk. Add the oil a drop at a time, beating until the mixture begins to thicken. This may happen quite suddenly.

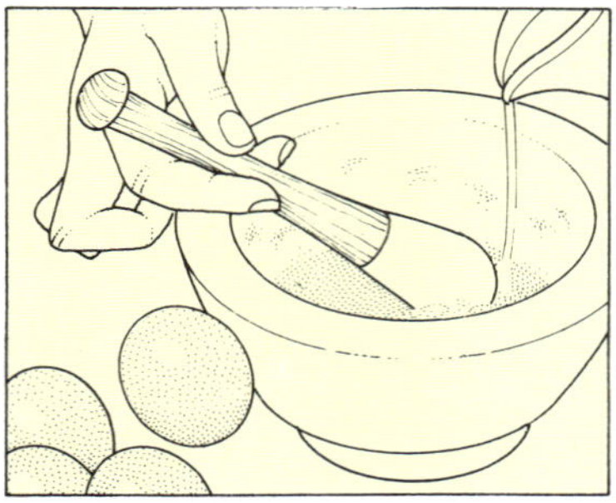

2 Continue adding the oil in a thin, steady stream to make a smooth, thick mayonnaise. Stir in lemon juice and salt and pepper to taste. Turn into a bowl, cover and keep in a cool place.

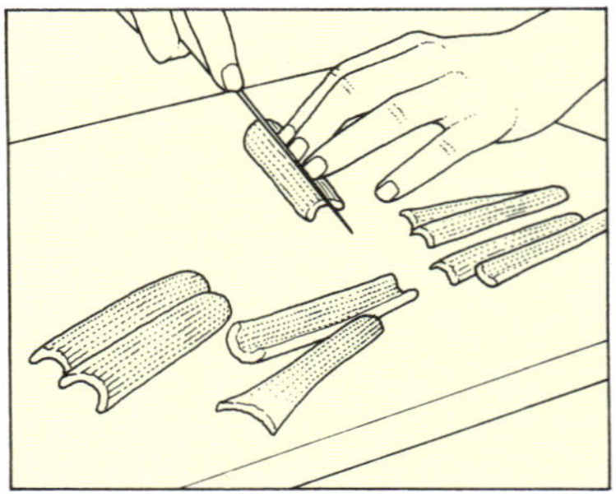

3 Meanwhile, prepare the vegetables. Cut the celery in half crossways, then cut into sticks lengthways. Cut the carrot and cucumber into thin sticks.

4 Lay the mushrooms down with the stalks uppermost, and, using a sharp knife, slice downwards into 'T' shapes.

5 To serve, arrange all the vegetables on one large or two small serving dishes. Serve with the dip.

Menu Suggestion
Serve with Chicken and Cucumber Mousse (page 32) and Almond and Cherry Flan (page 122).

CRUDITÉS
Crudités – French for raw vegetables – does not have to include all the vegetables suggested in the recipe on this page. The choice depends simply on personal taste and seasonal availability. Make sure, however, that they are all as crisp and fresh as possible.

If you want to make this starter ahead of time, the aïoli – garlic mayonnaise – will keep in a covered container for several days in the refrigerator. The vegetables can be prepared 1–2 hours ahead of time and kept in a bowl of iced water in the refrigerator.

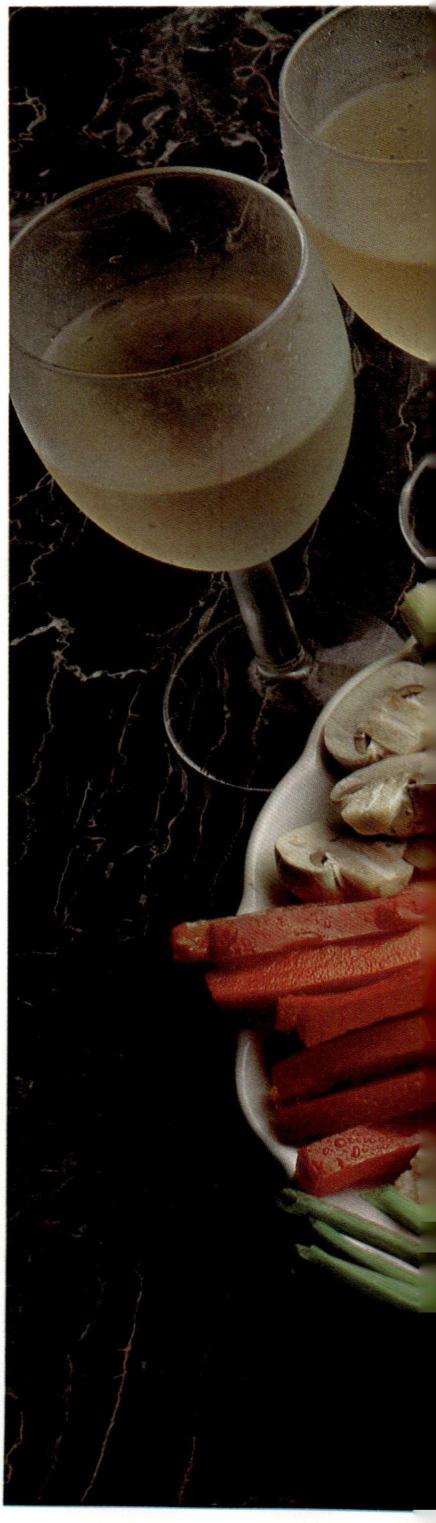

Main Courses

Summer main courses can be a problem if you are not well prepared. Think in advance and plan dishes that keep you out of the kitchen. Summer's too short to spend inside, and your family and guests won't appreciate elaborate food that involves your being out of their company for any length of time. Here's a selection of summer dishes that can be prepared ahead of time.

SMOKED CHICKEN AND AVOCADO SALAD

0.30* £ £ 506–760 cals

* plus 30 minutes–1 hour standing time

Serves 4–6

1 kg (2 lb) smoked chicken

135 ml (9 tbsp) olive oil

juice of 1 lemon

5 ml (1 tsp) bottled grated horse-radish

2.5 ml ($\frac{1}{2}$ tsp) green peppercorn mustard

2 ripe avocados

salt and freshly ground pepper

sprigs of fresh coriander and lemon slices, to garnish

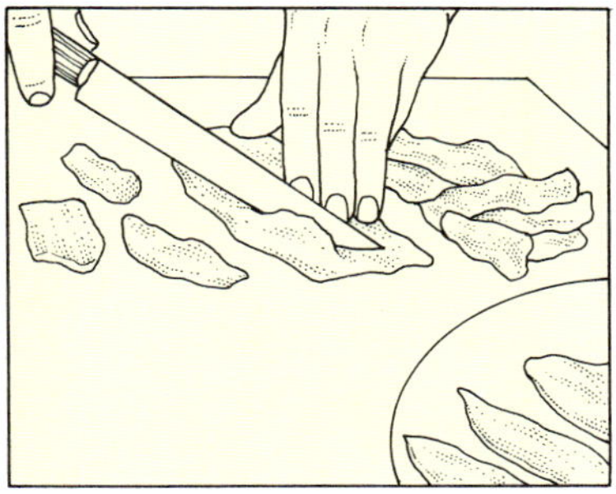

1 Remove all the meat from the chicken carcass, taking care to cut thin, even slices which will look attractive in the finished dish.

2 Make the dressing. In a large bowl, whisk together the oil, lemon juice, horseradish and mustard. Add chicken and coat in the dressing. Cover and leave for 30 minutes to 1 hour.

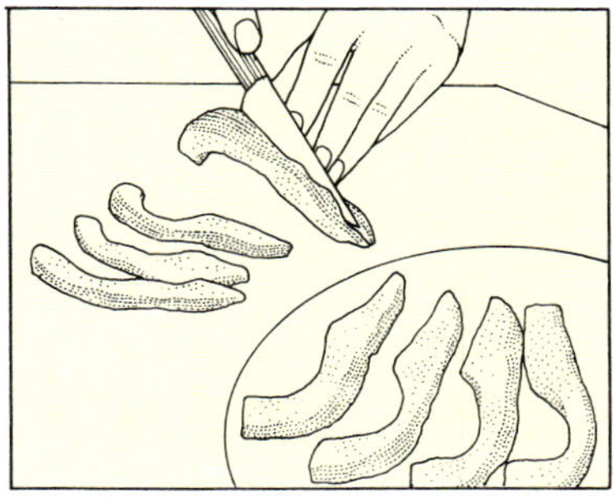

3 Halve the avocados and remove the stones. Peel off the skin, then cut the flesh lengthways into thin, even slices.

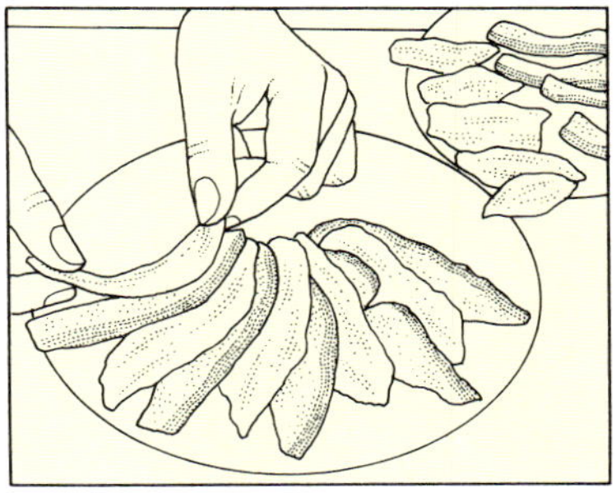

4 Arrange the chicken and avocado slices alternately on a flat, round plate, overlapping them in a 'Catherine-wheel' shape.

5 Chop any remaining odd pieces of chicken and avocado and toss them together. Pile this mixture into the centre of the plate.

6 Season dressing remaining in bowl. Brush over avocado slices to prevent discolouration.

7 Garnish the centre of the salad with sprigs of fresh coriander and thinly cut lemon slices, and serve immediately with the dressing.

Menu Suggestion
Serve with Hummus (page 10) and Frosted Mint Cheesecake (page 111).

PISSALADIÈRE

1.30 £ ✳ 323 cals

Serves 6

25 g (1 oz) butter or margarine
25 g (1 oz) lard
100 g (4 oz) plain flour
salt
30 ml (2 tbsp) water
450 g (1 lb) onions, skinned and finely sliced
2 garlic cloves, skinned and crushed
90 ml (6 tbsp) vegetable oil
225 g (8 oz) tomatoes, skinned
30 ml (2 tbsp) tomato purée
5 ml (1 tsp) fresh herbs (e.g. marjoram, thyme or sage)
freshly ground pepper
anchovy fillets and black olives

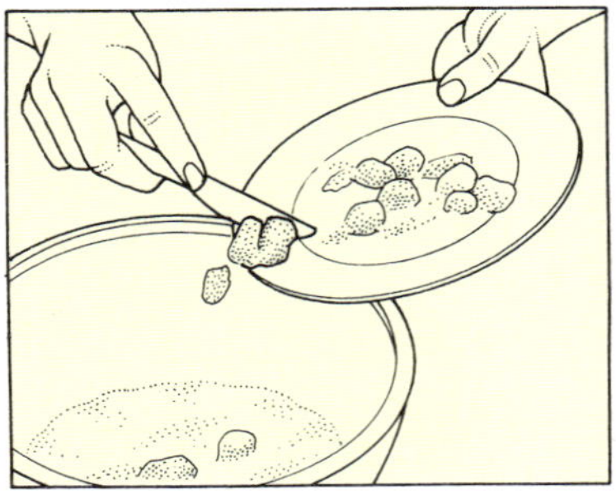

1 Make the pastry. Cut the butter or margarine and the lard into pieces and add these to the plain flour and a pinch of salt.

2 Mix until the mixture resembles fine breadcrumbs. Add water and mix until it forms a smooth dough. Wrap and chill in a refrigerator for 15 minutes.

3 When the dough is cool, roll out the pastry and use to line a 20.5-cm (8-inch) plain flan ring. Bake blind in the oven at 200°C (400°F) mark 6 for 20 minutes.

4 Meanwhile, make the filling. Fry onions and garlic in the oil in a large saucepan for 10 minutes until very soft but not brown.

5 Slice the tomatoes, add to the pan and continue cooking for 10 minutes until the liquid has evaporated. Stir in the tomato purée, herbs and seasoning.

6 Turn the mixture into the flan case. Brush with a little oil and cook in the oven at 200°C (400°F) mark 6 for 20 minutes.

7 To serve, garnish the pissaladière with a lattice of anchovy fillets and the black olives. Serve either hot or cold.

Menu Suggestion
Serve with Crudités with Aïoli (page 26), Fennel and Tomato Salad (page 84) and Iced Raspberry Mousse (page 115).

CHEF'S SALAD

0.15 £ 690 cals

Serves 4

225 g (8 oz) ham

225 g (8 oz) cold cooked chicken

225 g (8 oz) Emmenthal cheese

1 Iceberg or Webb lettuce

2 eggs, hard-boiled, shelled and quartered

6 small tomatoes, halved, or 2 large tomatoes, quartered

3 spring onions, washed, trimmed and finely chopped

150 ml ($\frac{1}{4}$ pint) basic vinaigrette (see page 143) or blue cheese dressing (see page 145), to serve

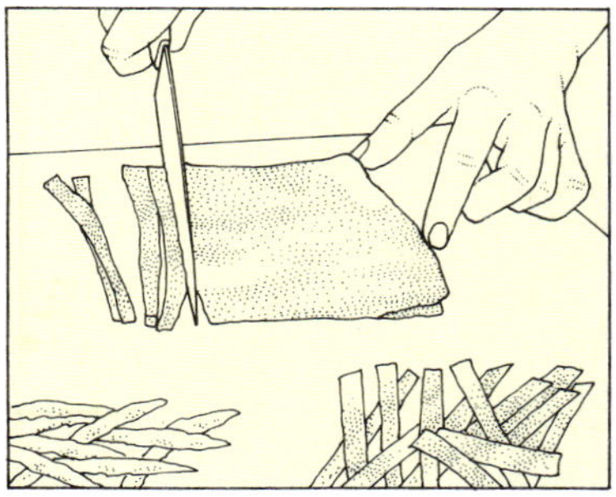

1 Using a sharp knife, cut the ham and the cold cooked chicken into fine strips and set aside.

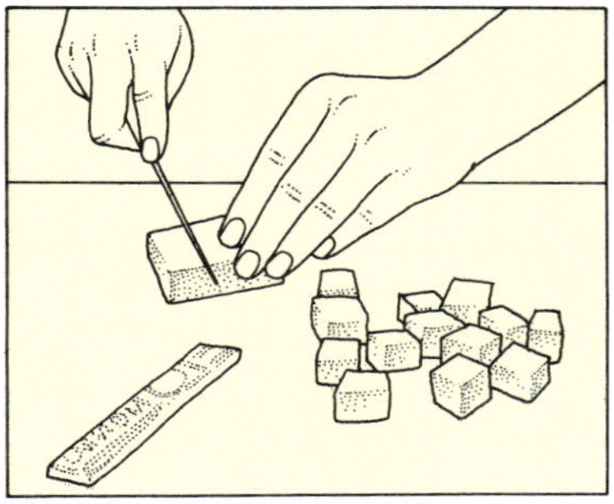

2 Remove any rind from the cheese. Using a small sharp knife, carefully cut the cheese into small dice. Wash the lettuce under cold running water and pat it dry with absorbent kitchen paper.

3 Finely shred the leaves, or leave them whole, and use to line an oval serving dish.

4 To serve. Arrange the meat and cheese alternately around the edge of the dish. Add egg and tomatoes, sprinkle over the finely chopped spring onions and serve the dressing separately.

Menu Suggestion
Serve with Chicken Liver Pâté with Green Peppercorns (page 21) and Hot Cherry Soufflé (page 125).

CHICKEN AND CUCUMBER MOUSSE

2.30* £ 263 cals

* plus 2–3 hours chilling

Serves 6

1.4-kg (3-lb) oven-ready chicken
slices of carrot and onion, for flavouring
15 ml (1 tbsp) chopped fresh tarragon or 5 ml (1 tsp) dried
salt and freshly ground pepper
10 ml (2 tsp) gelatine
30 ml (2 tbsp) water
small cucumber – about 275 g (10 oz) total weight
25 g (1 oz) butter or margarine
30 ml (2 tbsp) plain flour
30 ml (2 tbsp) lemon juice
150 ml (5 fl oz) whipping cream
1 egg white
tarragon sprigs, to garnish

1 Poach the chicken, flavouring vegetables, tarragon and seasoning in water to cover for about 45 minutes. Remove the chicken from the liquid and allow to cool.

2 Skin the chicken. Remove the flesh from the bones. Mince the chicken flesh in a mincer or food processor. Boil down the stock to 400 ml ($\frac{2}{3}$ pint); strain.

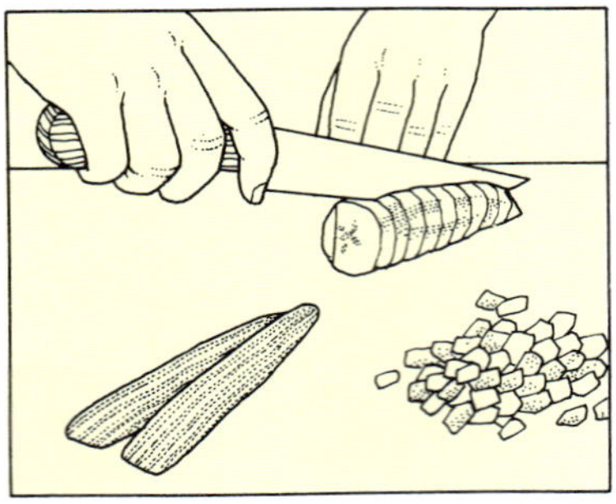

3 Soak gelatine in the water. Peel and finely dice about three-quarters of the cucumber, reserving the rest for garnish.

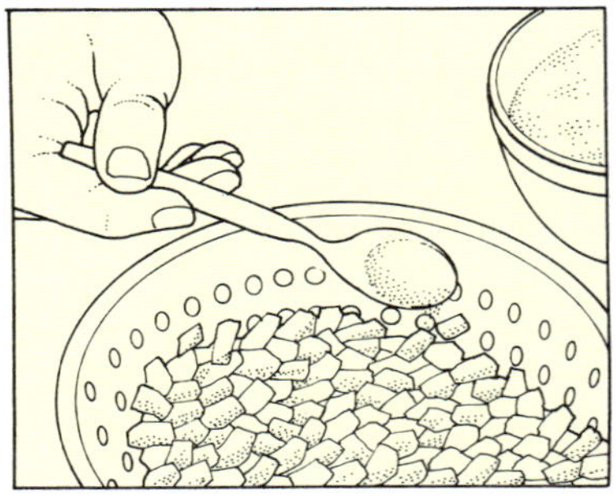

4 Sprinkle the diced cucumber with salt and leave for 30 minutes. Rinse and pat dry with absorbent kitchen paper.

5 Melt the butter in a saucepan, stir in the flour and cook gently for 1 minute, stirring. Remove from the heat and gradually stir in the strained stock. Bring to the boil and continue to cook, stirring, until the sauce thickens.

6 Stir in the gelatine until dissolved, beat in the chicken, cool. When cold, add the diced cucumber, lemon juice, 7.5 ml ($1\frac{1}{2}$ tsp) salt and plenty of freshly ground pepper.

7 Lightly whip the cream. Whisk the egg white until stiff. Fold the whipped cream and beaten egg white into the chicken mixture.

8 Spoon into a 1.7-litre (3-pint) soufflé dish, cover and refrigerate for 2–3 hours to set. Serve cold, garnished with cucumber slices and tarragon sprigs.

Menu Suggestion
Serve with Artichokes à la grecque (page 9) and Peach and Hazelnut Gateau (page 117).

COLD BEEF IN SOURED CREAM

0.30* £ £ 318 cals

* plus 2–3 hours chilling

Serves 6

1 large onion, skinned

350 g (12 oz) button mushrooms

700 g ($1\frac{1}{2}$ lb) lean rump steak in a thin slice

45 ml (3 tbsp) vegetable oil

salt and freshly ground pepper

7.5 ml ($1\frac{1}{2}$ tsp) Dijon mustard

7.5 ml ($1\frac{1}{2}$ tsp) chopped fresh thyme or 5 ml (1 tsp) dried

1 large green eating apple

284 ml (10 fl oz) soured cream

15 ml (1 tbsp) lemon juice

crisp lettuce and freshly toasted French bread, to serve

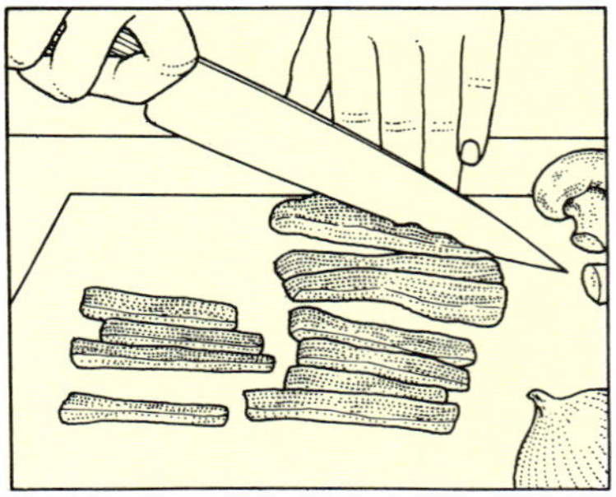

1 Using a sharp knife, finely chop the onion and finely slice the mushrooms. Slice the rump steak into thin strips.

2 Heat the oil in a large frying pan. Quickly brown the steak in a shallow layer, turning occasionally. Don't crowd the pan; cook the meat in two batches if necessary. The beef should remain pink in the centre.

3 Transfer the meat to a bowl using a slotted spoon. Season with salt and pepper.

4 Reheat the fat remaining in the pan. Fry the onion for 5 minutes until golden brown. Add the mushrooms, mustard and thyme. Cook over high heat for 1 minute. Add to beef; allow to cool; refrigerate for 2–3 hours.

5 Quarter and core the apple; slice thinly. Combine with the soured cream and lemon juice.

6 Line a shallow dish with lettuce. Combine the beef and apple mixtures and season. Pile into the centre of the lettuce. Serve with toasted French bread.

Menu Suggestion

Serve with Potato Salad (page 83) and Strawberry and Orange Mousse (page 119).

SMOKED FISH TIMBALE

0.40* £ 292 cals

* plus 2–3 hours chilling

Serves 6

350 g (12 oz) long grain rice

15 ml (1 tbsp) ground turmeric

7.5 ml ($1\frac{1}{2}$ tsp) salt

350 g (12 oz) smoked haddock or cod fillet

1 small bunch spring onions, washed

2 eggs, hard boiled and shelled

salt and freshly ground pepper

watercress sprigs and fresh prawns, to garnish

1 Cook the rice with the turmeric and salt in a saucepan of water for 10–15 minutes. Drain well and cool.

2 Poach the fish in a little water to just cover for 12–15 minutes. Drain. Flake the fish.

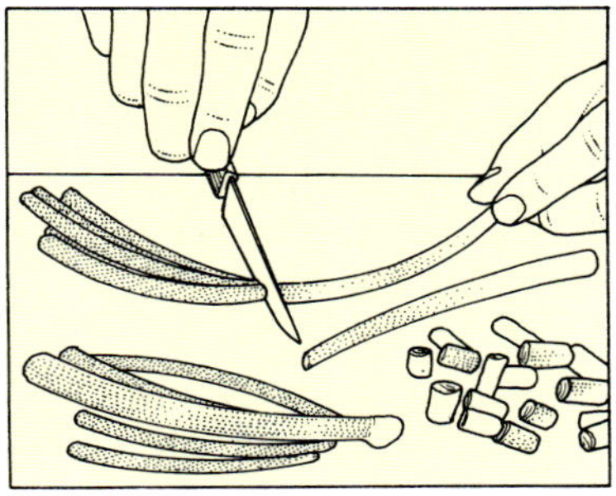

3 Trim the spring onions, then roughly chop them with the hard-boiled eggs, mix with the cold rice and fish, seasoning well.

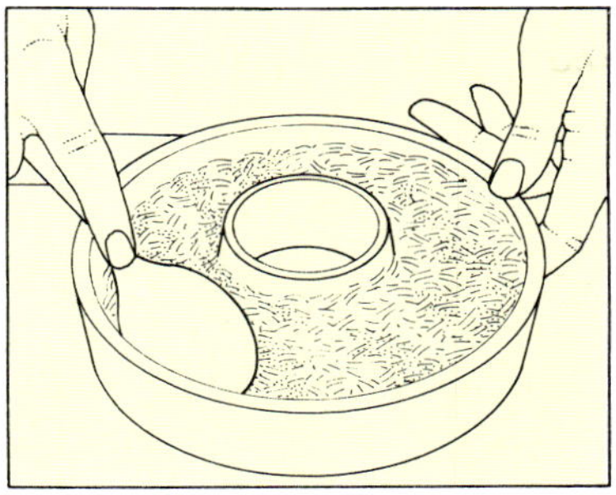

4 Spoon the mixture into an oiled 1.1-litre (2-pint) ring mould. Press down well, cover and chill for 2–3 hours.

5 To serve, unmould the fish ring on to a plate, and garnish with watercress sprigs and prawns.

Menu Suggestion
Serve with Waldorf Salad (page 78) and Mixed Berry Sorbet (page 121).

Jellied Tomato Ring

2.00* £ 340 cals

* plus 2–3 hours chilling

Serves 6

two 330-ml ($11\frac{1}{2}$-oz) cans tomato and vegetable juice
60 ml (4 tbsp) lemon juice
pinch of sugar
salt and freshly ground pepper
30 ml (2 tbsp) gelatine
90 ml (6 tbsp) water
100 g (4 oz) long grain rice
50 ml (2 fl oz) basic vinaigrette (see page 143)
30 ml (2 tbsp) whole grain mustard
450 g (1 lb) cold cooked chicken
6 spring onions, trimmed and chopped
50 g (2 oz) cucumber diced
142 ml (5 fl oz) soured cream
cucumber slices and sprigs of mint, to garnish

1 Prepare the tomato ring. Place the tomato and vegetable juice, sugar and seasonings in a measuring jug and make up to 1 litre (2 pints) with water.

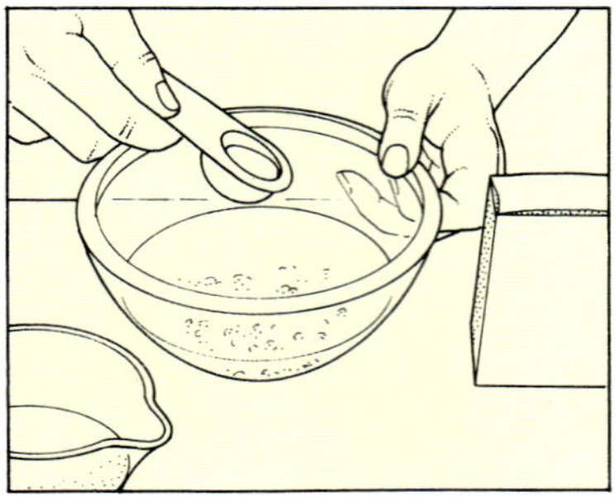

2 Soak the gelatine in a small bowl with the 90 ml (6 tbsp) water. Place the bowl over a pan of hot water and stir until dissolved. Remove from the heat and stir into the tomato juice mixture.

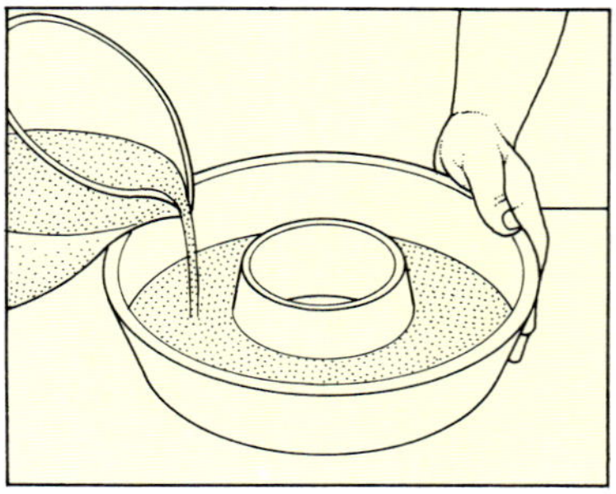

3 Pour the mixture into a 1-litre (2-pint) ring mould and leave in the refrigerator for about 1 hour until set.

4 Meanwhile, make the filling. Cook the rice in boiling salted water for 10–15 minutes until tender. When cooked, drain the rice, transfer to a bowl and pour over the dressing with the mustard. Stir then leave until cold. Cover and chill for 2–3 hours.

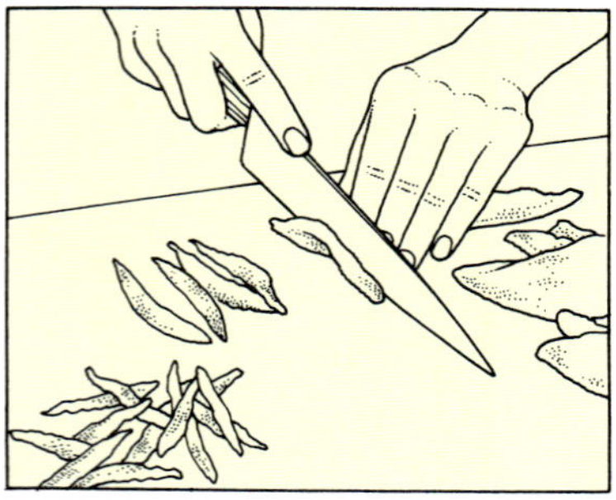

5 Cut the chicken into strips. Add to the rice with the spring onions, diced cucumber and soured cream. Season and toss gently.

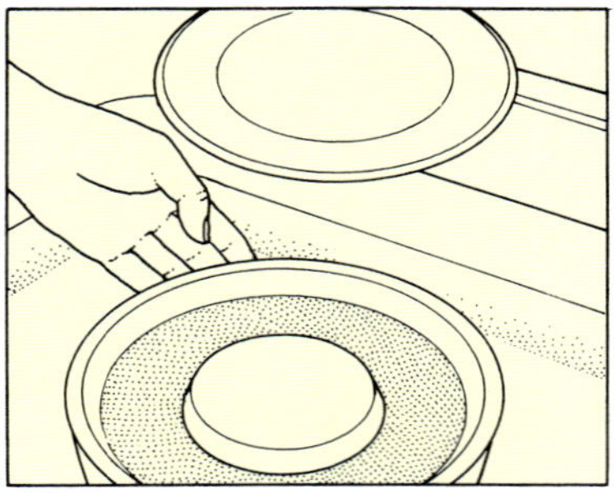

6 To serve, quickly dip the mould into hot water to loosen the jelly ring, then turn out on to a flat plate. Fill the centre with the chicken mixture and serve any remaining filling separately. Garnish with cucumber slices and sprigs of mint.

Menu Suggestion
Serve with Potted Prawn Pâté (page 24) and Hot Apricot Soufflé (page 124).

HINTS FOR SLIMMERS
For slimmers, this tomato ring makes a perfect main course dish if served with a different filling in the centre. For a more slimming filling, try finely chopped raw vegetables such as celery, cucumber and radish, with shredded lettuce and sprigs of watercress. A handful of nuts and raisins would add extra protein, and would go perfectly with the chicken and vegetables instead of the rice and vinaigrette dressing—although you could replace the basic vinaigrette used here with one of the commercially prepared low-calorie dressings. There is also a slimmers' dressing on page 143 at the back of this book; this would go perfectly well with the tomato ring.

COURGETTE QUICHE

2.00* £ ✳ 732 cals

* includes 45 minutes chilling and 15 minutes standing time

Serves 4

175 g (6 oz) plain flour
salt
125 g (4 oz) butter or margarine
125 g (4 oz) grated Cheddar cheese
1 egg yolk, beaten
350 g (12 oz) courgettes
3 eggs
150 ml (5 fl oz) double cream
10 ml (2 tsp) chopped fresh basil
finely grated rind of 1 lime (optional)
freshly ground pepper
a little egg white

1 Make the pastry. Sift the flour into a bowl with a pinch of salt. Add the butter in pieces and rub in thoroughly with the fingertips until the mixture resembles fine breadcrumbs.

2 Stir in the cheese, then the egg yolk. Gather the mixture together with your fingers to make a smooth ball of dough. Wrap and chill the dough in the refrigerator for about 30 minutes.

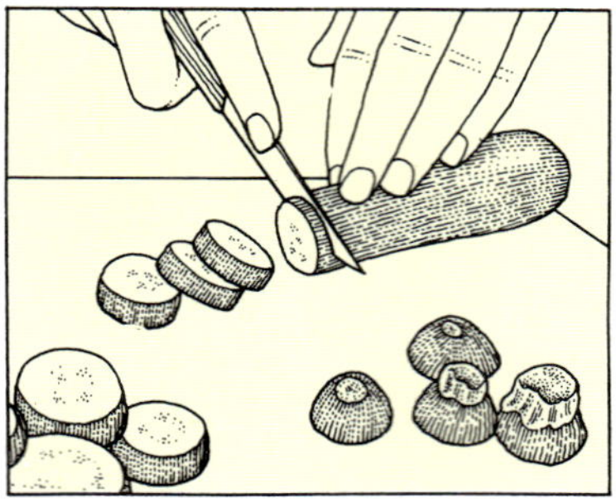

3 Meanwhile, prepare the filling. Trim the ends off the courgettes, then cut the courgettes into 2-cm ($\frac{3}{4}$-inch) chunks.

4 Plunge the courgette pieces into boiling salted water, bring back to the boil, then simmer for 3 minutes. Drain and set aside.

5 Put the eggs in a jug and beat lightly together with the cream. Stir in the basil, lime rind if using, and season to taste. Set aside.

6 Roll out the chilled dough on a floured surface and use to line a loose-bottomed 23-cm (9-inch) flan tin. Refrigerate for 15 minutes.

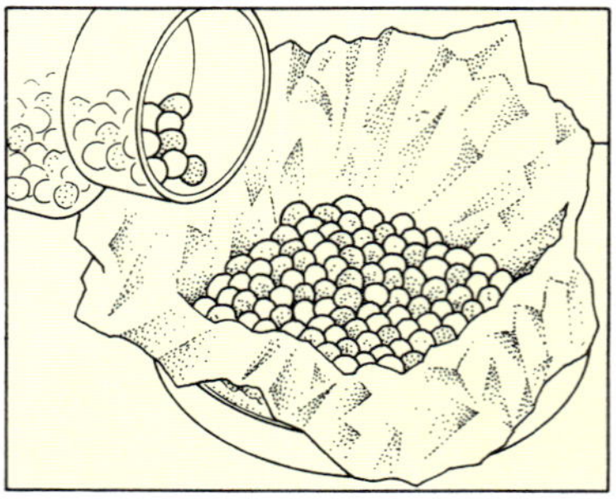

7 Prick the base of the dough with a fork, then line with foil and baking beans. Stand the tin on a preheated baking sheet and bake blind in the oven at 200°C (400°F) mark 6 for 10 minutes.

8 Remove the foil and beans and brush the inside of the pastry case with the egg white to seal. Return to the oven for 5 minutes.

9 Stand the courgette chunks upright in pastry case; slowly pour in egg and cream mixture. Return to oven for 20 minutes.

Menu Suggestion
Serve with Endive, Orange and Walnut Salad (page 90) and Iced Strawberry Meringues (page 126).

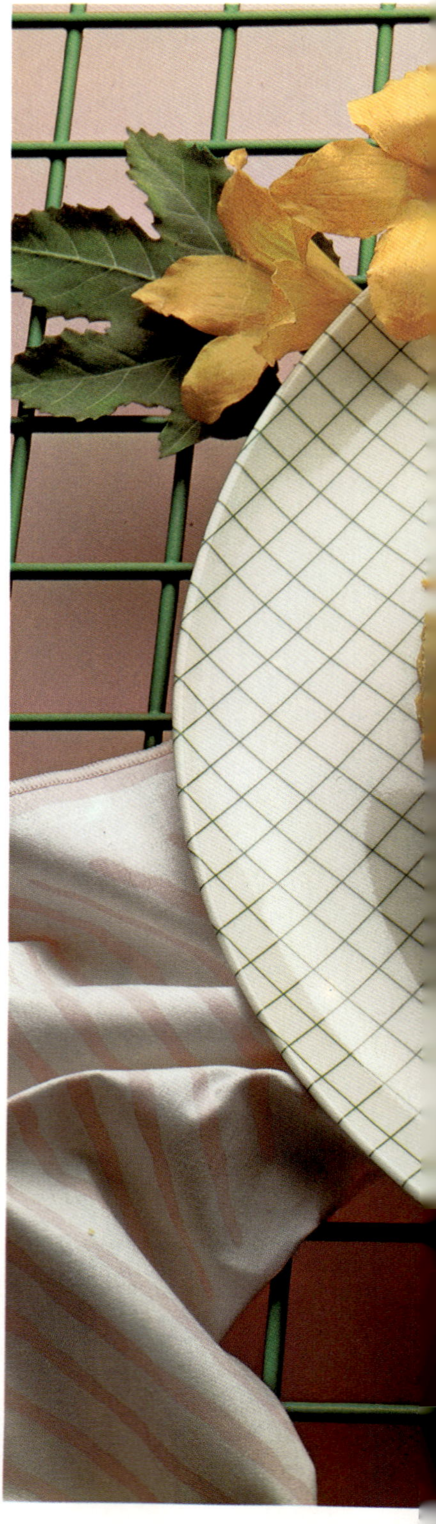

VITELLO TONNATO

1.10* £ £ 722–1083 cals

* plus 2 hours cooling and overnight chilling

Serves 4–6

1 kg (2 lb) boned leg of veal

150 ml (¼ pint) water

75 ml (5 tbsp) dry white wine

75 ml (5 tbsp) white wine vinegar

1 onion, skinned and quartered

1 small carrot, peeled

1 stick of celery, washed and trimmed

sprig of parsley

salt

4 black peppercorns

198-g (7-oz) can tuna, drained

4 anchovy fillets, drained

300 ml (½ pint) lemon mayonnaise (see page 145)

15 ml (1 tbsp) capers

freshly ground pepper

capers, lemon slices and black olives, to garnish

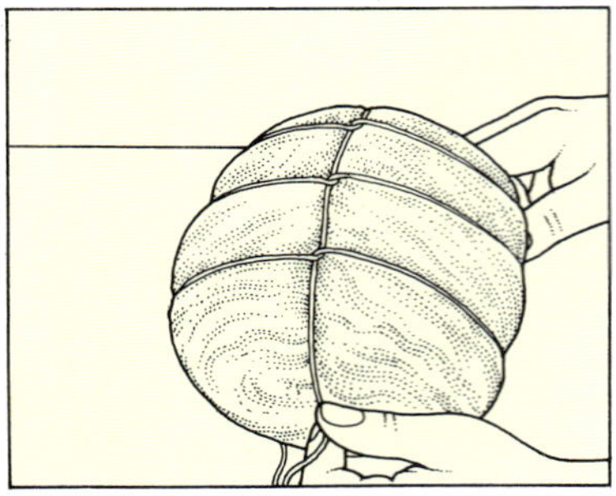

1 Tie the meat securely in a neat roll. Place in a saucepan and add the water, wine, vinegar, onion, carrot, celery, parsley and salt and peppercorns. Bring to the boil, then cover and simmer gently for 1 hour until meat is tender.

2 Remove the meat and leave to cool. Place the cooking liquid and vegetables in a blender or food processor and blend to form a smooth purée.

3 Make the tuna mayonnaise. Mash together the tuna and anchovies with a fork or purée in a blender or food processor.

4 Mix into the mayonnaise. Stir in the capers and pepper (do not add salt—the anchovies and cooking liquid should flavour it enough).

5 Thin the tuna mayonnaise sauce to the consistency of thick cream with the puréed cooking liquid.

6 When the meat is cold, cut into slices and arrange overlapping on a shallow serving dish. Cover with the sauce.

7 Cover and leave in the refrigerator overnight. Serve cold, garnished with capers, lemon slices and black olives.

Menu Suggestion
Serve with Mozzarella, Avocado and Tomato Salad (page 18) and Hot Apricot Soufflé (page 124).

TURKEY IN TUNA FISH MAYONNAISE

0.30* £ £ 788–1121 cals

* plus 2–3 hours chilling

Serves 4–6

6 turkey escalopes (total weight 450–700 g [1–1½ lb])

30 ml (2 tbsp) vegetable oil

25 g (1 oz) butter

198-g (7-oz) can tuna, drained

4 anchovy fillets, drained

300 ml (½ pint) lemon mayonnaise (see page 145)

142 ml (5 fl oz) soured cream

15 ml (1 tbsp) capers

freshly ground pepper

capers, lemon slices and black olives, to garnish

1 Beat out the turkey escalopes between two sheets of damp greaseproof paper or non-stick paper. Cut into thin slices.

2 Heat the oil and butter in a pan and cook the turkey strips for about 5 minutes until lightly browned. Remove from the pan and set aside.

3 Make the tuna mayonnaise. Mash together the tuna and anchovies with a fork or purée in a blender or food processor.

4 Mix into the mayonnaise with the soured cream. Stir in the capers and pepper.

5 When the meat is cold, toss into the tuna mayonnaise and turn into a serving dish. Serve cold, garnished with capers, lemon slices and black olives.

VITELLO TONNATO

A classic Italian dish of cold boned leg of veal coated in a tuna fish mayonnaise, this is the perfect recipe for a hot summer's day, particularly as it must be made the night before to allow the full flavour to develop. Serve outside if possible, with chilled Italian dry white wine—Frascati would go very well—and a simple tossed green salad.

OLIVES

Most of the olives we buy come from Spain, Italy and Greece. The olives in this recipe are black, which are simply fully-ripened green olives, preserved in brine. Green olives are mature, but unripe, when they are shaken off the trees onto huge nets on the ground; for black olives, they are left on the trees until they are fully ripe before harvesting.

Greek black olives can be small, with crinkly skins and a sharp, pungent flavour, or they can be succulent and fat, sometimes called 'jumbo' olives—these would be ideal for this recipe.

DRESSED CRAB

0.30 £ £

151–227 cals

Serves 2–3

shell and meat from 1 medium (900-g/2-lb) cooked crab (to remove the crabmeat and prepare the shell, see Dressing a Crab, pages 148–149)

salt and freshly ground pepper

15 ml (1 tbsp) lemon juice

30 ml (2 tbsp) fresh white breadcrumbs

1 egg, hard-boiled

chopped fresh parsley

lettuce or endive, to serve

1 Using two forks, flake all the white meat from the crab, removing any shell or membrane. Season, adding about 5 ml (1 tsp) lemon juice.

2 Pound brown meat and work in the breadcrumbs with the remaining lemon juice and seasoning. Adjust seasonings to taste.

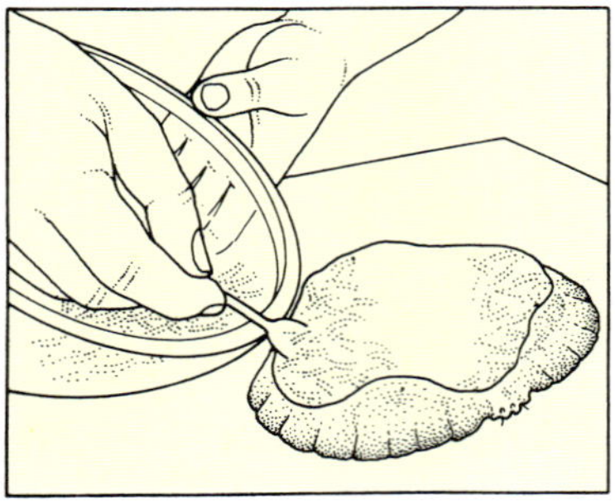

3 Using a small spoon, put the white meat in both ends of the crab's empty shell, making sure that it is well piled up into the shell. Keep the inside edges neat.

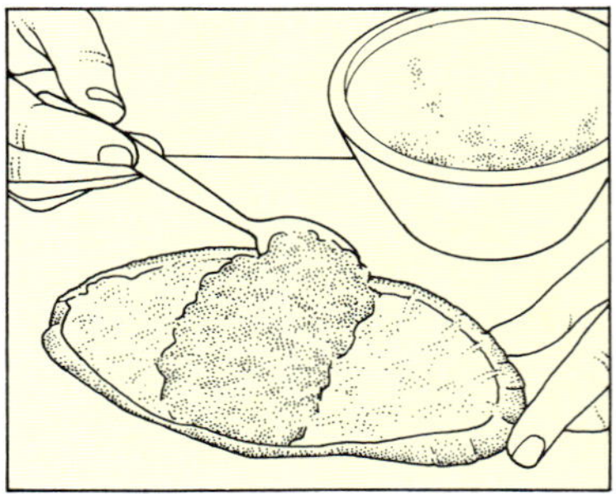

4 Then spoon the brown meat in a neat line down the centre, between the two sections of white crabmeat.

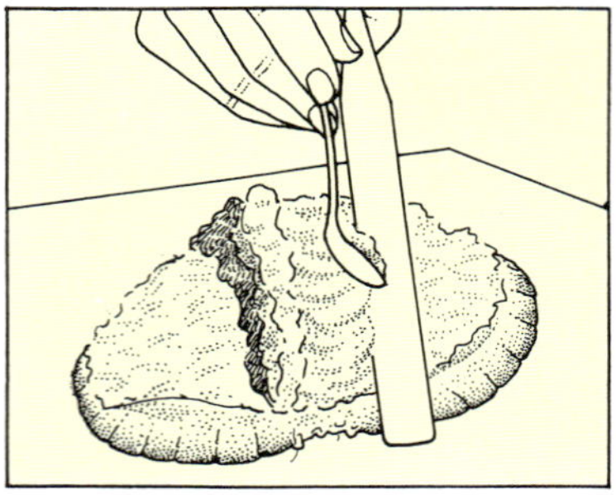

5 Hold a blunt knife between the white and brown crabmeat and carefully spoon lines of parsley, sieved egg yolk and chopped egg white across crab, moving knife as you go to keep a neat edge. Serve the stuffed shell on a bed of lettuce or endive, surrounded by the small legs.

Menu Suggestion
Serve with Potato Salad (page 83) and Fennel and Tomato Salad (page 84).

DEVILLED DUCKLING SALAD

2.15* £ £ 390 cals

* plus 2–3 hours chilling

Serves 6

two 1.4-kg (3-lb) oven-ready ducklings

salt

142 ml (5 fl oz) soured cream

90 ml (6 tbsp) mayonnaise (see page 145)

15 ml (1 tbsp) clear honey

15 ml (1 tbsp) mild curry paste

salt and freshly ground pepper

50 g (2 oz) cashew nuts

350 g (12 oz) fresh apricots, stoned and thickly sliced

endive leaves, to serve

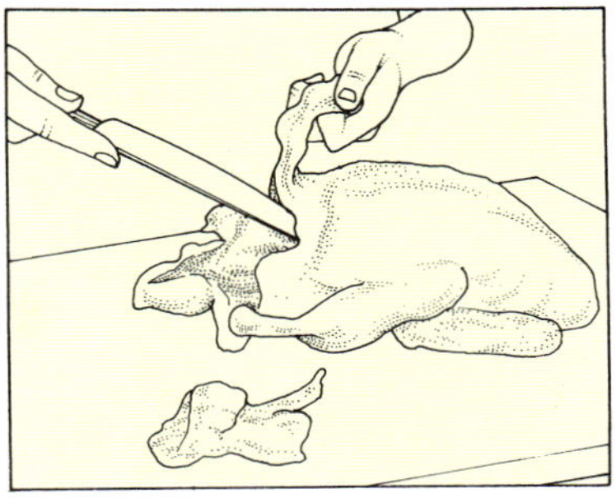

1 Cut away any surplus fat from the ducklings, then wipe them with a damp cloth. Pat dry.

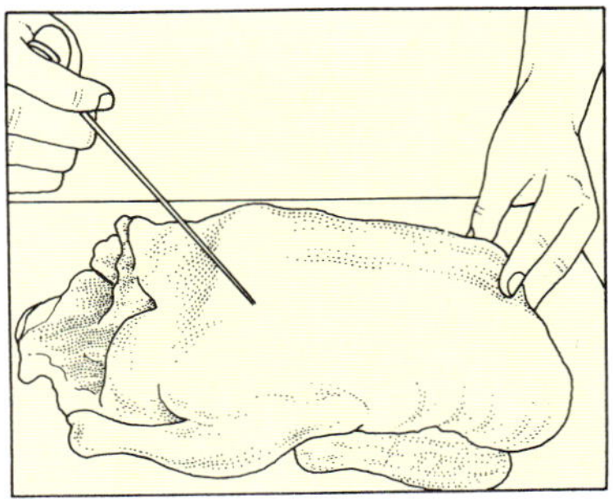

2 Prick the birds all over with a sharp fork or skewer and sprinkle generously with salt. Place the ducklings, breast-side down, side by side on a wire rack or trivet in a large roasting tin.

3 Roast in the oven at 180°C (350°F) mark 4 for about $1\frac{3}{4}$ hours, or until the birds are really tender, basting occasionally. Halfway through the cooking time, turn the birds over so they are standing breast-side up.

4 Meanwhile, prepare the dressing. In a large bowl, mix together the soured cream, mayonnaise, honey and curry paste. Season and stir in the cashew nuts and apricots.

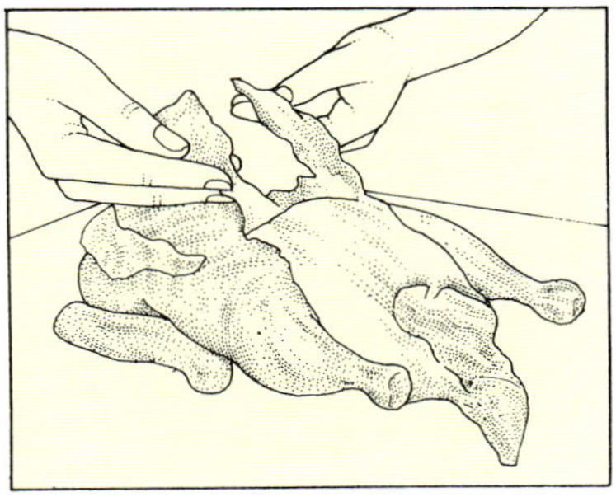

5 While the ducklings are still warm, strip off the crisp breast skin and reserve. Remove the meat from the bones.

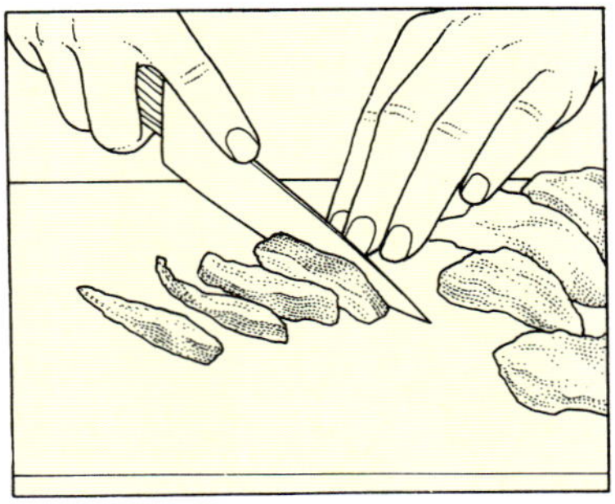

6 Coarsely shred the meat, discarding all the remaining skin, fat and bones. Fold the shredded duckling meat into the dressing, cover and chill well for 2–3 hours in the refrigerator.

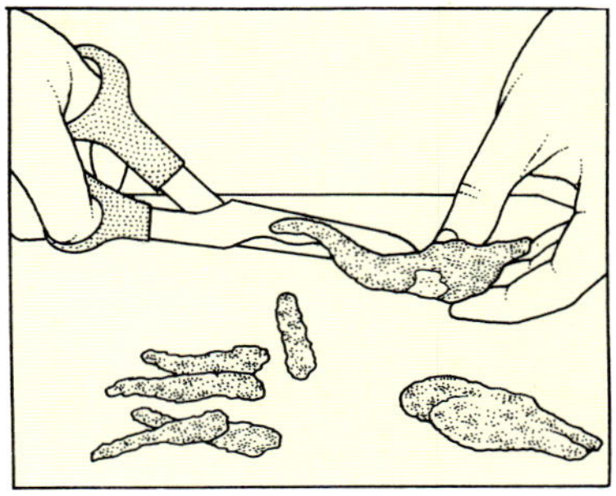

7 Using a pair of kitchen scissors, cut the reserved duckling skin into strips and quickly crisp it further under a hot grill.

8 To serve, spoon the duckling salad down the centre of a large flat platter, then arrange the crisp duck skin over the top. Serve on a bed of endive leaves.

Menu Suggestion
Serve with Tabbouleh (page 86) and Blackcurrant Sorbet (page 120).

DUCKLINGS

The Chinese were the first to eat ducklings – as long ago as 168 BC! The nobles of the Han dynasty used to breed domestic white ducks for the table – especially for banquets and royal feasts, and they also enjoyed wild duck in stews for more humble occasions. In those days duck meat was served completely unseasoned, and was recommended as a sacrificial offering to appease the gods. Duck soup was also recommended as a remedy for estranged husband and wives – a drop of duck soup was supposed to bring the couple back together again!

Henry the Eighth had a passion for duck, and was said to retire to bed at night on a supper of roast duckling – not the ideal food for a good night's sleep, but certainly rich enough to satisfy his notoriously large appetite!

LAMB CUTLETS EN CROÛTE

1.00* £ ✳ 890 cals

* freeze after cooking only if serving cold

Serves 6

25 g (1 oz) butter

1 onion, skinned and chopped

25 g (1 oz) fresh white breadcrumbs

1 egg, beaten

30 ml (2 tbsp) chopped fresh mint

salt and freshly ground pepper

squeeze of lemon juice

12 lamb cutlets, trimmed

450 g (1 lb) puff pastry or two 368-g (13-oz) packets frozen puff pastry, thawed

beaten egg, to glaze

sprig of fresh mint, to garnish

1 Make the stuffing. Melt the butter in a pan and fry the onion for about 5 minutes until soft but not brown. Remove from the heat. Stir in the breadcrumbs and bind with the beaten egg. Mix in the mint, salt, freshly ground pepper and lemon juice.

2 Grill or fry the cutlet for 3 minutes on both sides. They should be browned, but pink inside. Leave to cool.

3 Roll out each piece of pastry thinly and cut each one into six squares.

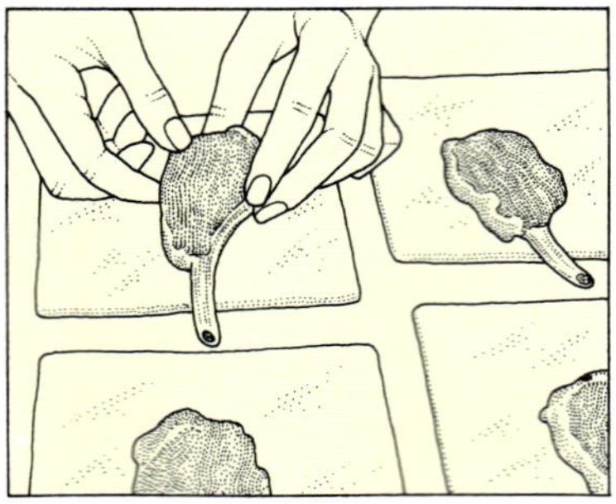

4 Place each of the lamb cutlets on a square of pastry so that the bone extends over the edge of the pastry.

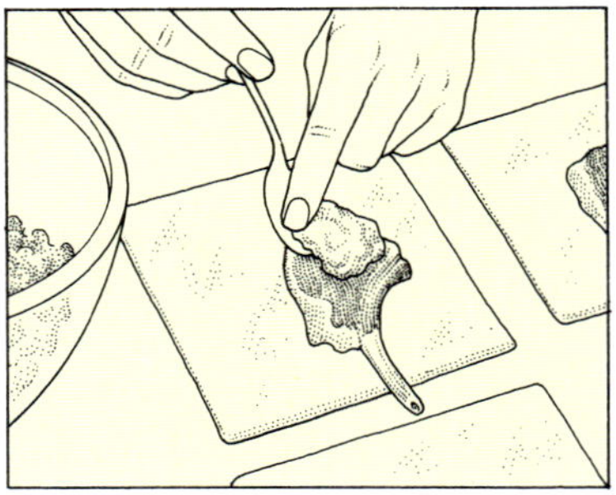

5 Press even amounts of stuffing on the eye of each cutlet. Dampen the pastry edges, wrap the pastry over the cutlets and seal.

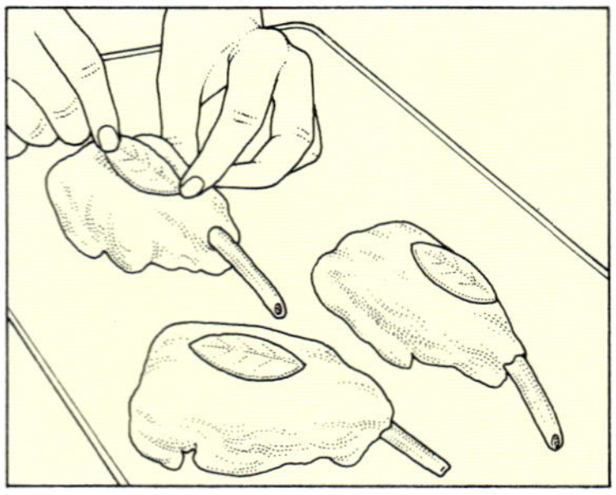

6 Place on a dampened baking tray, folded sides underneath. Use any pastry trimmings to decorate the cutlets. Brush with a little beaten egg.

7 Bake in the oven at 220°C (425°F) mark 7 for 15–20 minutes, then reduce the oven temperature to 190°C (375°F) mark 5 and bake for a further 15 minutes until the pastry is golden. Serve hot or cold, garnished with a sprig of fresh mint, if wished.

Menu Suggestion

Serve with Artichokes à la grecque (page 9), Tomatoes au Gratin (page 63) and Almond and Cherry Flan (page 122).

CHAMPAGNE

LAMB WITH CUCUMBER AND MINT STUFFING

1.30 £ £ ✳ 695 cals

Serves 4

- ½ cucumber, washed
- salt and freshly ground pepper
- 25 g (1 oz) butter or margarine
- 1 onion, skinned and chopped
- 30 ml (2 tbsp) chopped fresh mint
- 50 g (2 oz) fresh white breadcrumbs
- 1 egg yolk
- 1.4 kg (3 lb) loin of lamb, boned
- mint sprigs, to garnish
- soured cream dressing (see page 143), to serve (optional)

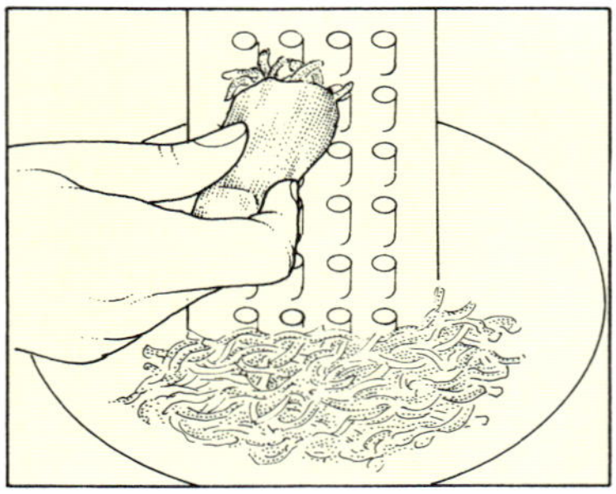

1 Coarsely grate the cucumber, sprinkle with salt and leave to stand for 30 minutes. Drain well. Melt the butter in a frying pan. Add onion and cook gently for about 5 minutes. Stir in the cucumber, mint, breadcrumbs, yolk and seasoning; cool for 30 minutes.

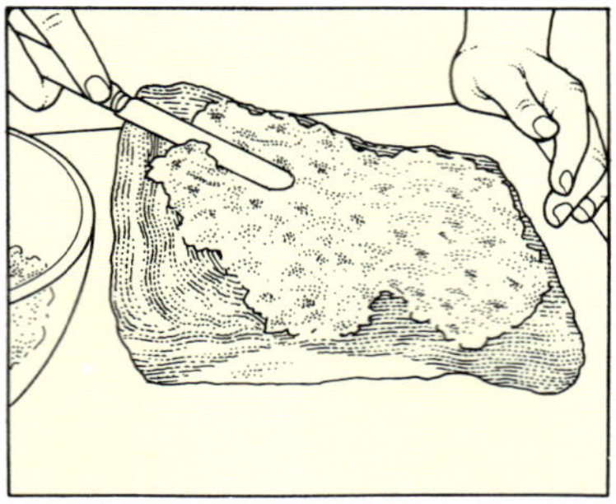

2 Lay the lamb out flat, fat side down, and spread the cold stuffing over the lamb.

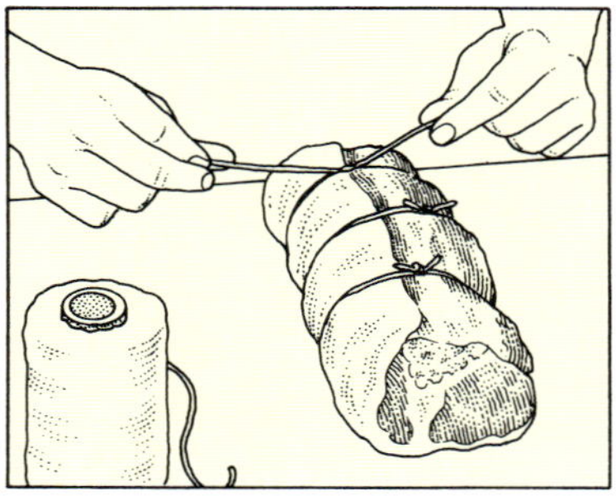

3 Roll up the meat and tie with fine string at regular intervals. Place the joint in a roasting tin and cook in the oven at 180°C (350°F) mark 4 for about 1 hour.

4 To serve, remove the string and carve into thick slices. Garnish with mint sprigs and serve with soured cream dressing if liked. Eat hot or cold.

Menu Suggestion
Serve with Asparagus Maltaise (page 22), New Potatoes with Tarragon Cream (page 65) and Hot Apricot Soufflé (page 124).

CORONATION CHICKEN

1.10	£	640 cals

Serves 8

2.3 kg (5 lb) cold cooked chicken
15 ml (1 tbsp) vegetable oil
1 small onion, skinned and chopped
15 ml (1 tbsp) mild curry paste
15 ml (1 tbsp) tomato purée
100 ml (4 fl oz) red wine
1 bay leaf
juice of ½ lemon
4 canned apricot halves, finely chopped
300 ml (½ pint) mayonnaise (see page 145)
100 ml (4 fl oz) whipping cream
salt and freshly ground pepper
watercress sprigs, to garnish

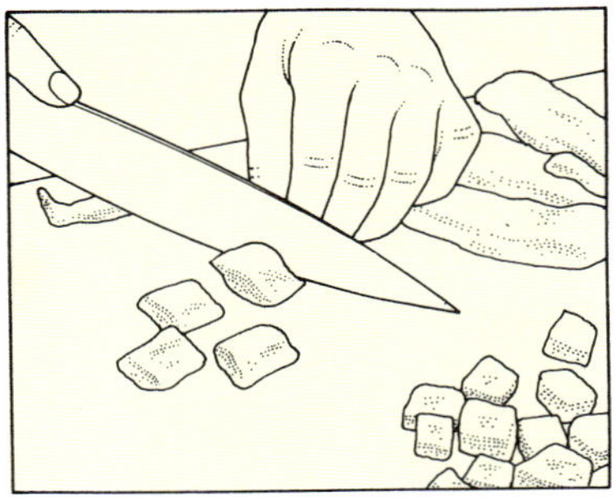

1 Remove the skin from the chicken. Then remove all the meat and dice, making sure to discard all the bones.

2 Make the curry sauce. Heat the oil in a small pan. Add the onion and cook for about 3 minutes, or until softened. Add the curry paste, tomato purée, wine, bay leaf and lemon juice. Simmer, uncovered, for about 10 minutes until well reduced. Strain and leave to cool for 30 minutes.

3 Press the chopped apricots through a sieve or use a blender or food processor to produce a purée. Beat the cooled curry sauce into the mayonnaise with the apricot purée. Lightly whip the cream and fold into the mixture. Season; add extra lemon juice, if necessary.

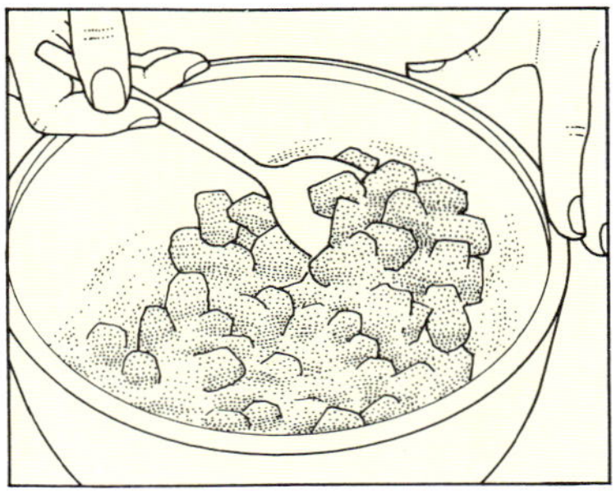

4 Toss the chicken pieces in the sauce and transfer to a serving dish. To serve, garnish with fresh watercress sprigs.

Menu Suggestion
Serve with Three Bean Salad (page 75) and Frosted Mint Cheesecake (page 111).

CORONATION CHICKEN
This delicious recipe – diced cold chicken tossed in a curried apricot mayonnaise – was created in 1953 by the Cordon Bleu School in London, in honour of the coronation of Queen Elizabeth II.

If you prefer, you can garnish the dish with sliced cucumber.

CEVICHE

0.30* £ ✳* 307 cals

24 hours refrigeration; freeze after step 4. Defrost in refrigerator overnight, then continue from step 5

Serves 4

500 g (1 lb) haddock fillets

5 ml (1 tsp) coriander seeds

5 ml (1 tsp) black peppercorns

juice of 6 limes

5 ml (1 tsp) salt

30 ml (2 tbsp) olive oil

bunch of spring onions, washed, trimmed and sliced

4 tomatoes, skinned and chopped

dash of Tabasco, or to taste

30 ml (2 tbsp) chopped fresh coriander

1 avocado, to finish

lime slices and fresh coriander, to garnish

1 Skin the haddock fillets. Put the fillets skin-side down on a board and grip the tail end of the skin with fingers dipped in salt. Using a sharp knife, work away from you with a sawing action.

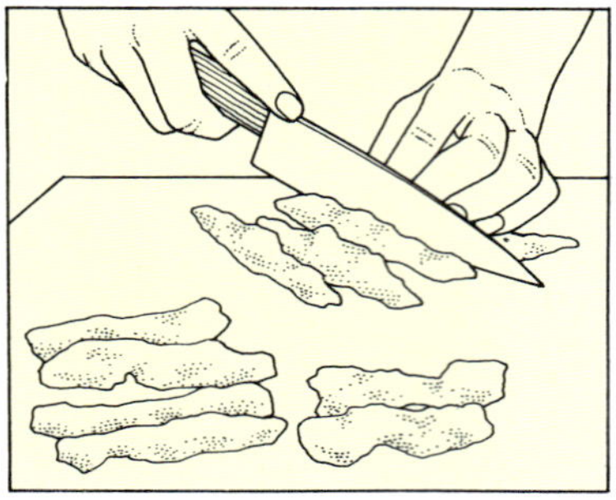

2 Wash the fillets, then pat them dry with absorbent kitchen paper. Cut the fish fillets diagonally into thin, even strips and place in a bowl.

3 Crush the coriander seeds and peppercorns to a fine powder in a mortar and pestle. Mix with the lime juice and salt, then pour over the fish. Cover and chill in the refrigerator for 24 hours, turning the fish occasionally.

4 The next day, heat the oil in a pan, add the spring onions and fry gently for 5 minutes. Add the tomatoes and Tabasco to taste and toss together over brisk heat for 1–2 minutes. Remove from the heat and leave to cool for 20–30 minutes.

5 To serve. Drain the fish from the marinade, discarding the marinade. Combine the fish with the spring onion and tomatoes and the chopped coriander. Taste and adjust seasoning, if necessary.

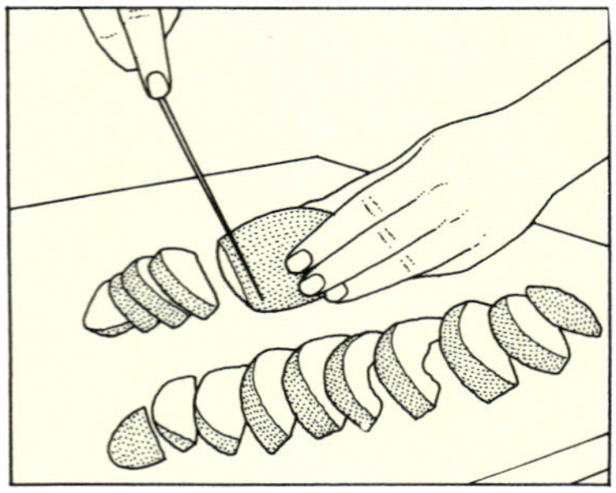

6 Halve the avocado, peel and remove the stone. Slice the flesh crossways. Arrange the slices around the inside of a serving bowl and pile the ceviche in the centre. Garnish with lime slices and coriander leaves. Serve chilled.

Menu Suggestion
Serve with Fresh Spinach Salad with Hot Bacon Dressing (page 88) and Blackcurrant Sorbet (page 120).

CYPRUS STUFFED PEPPERS

1.45*	£	392 cals

* plus overnight chilling

Serves 4

8 peppers
75 ml (5 tbsp) olive oil
2 onions, skinned and chopped
4 garlic cloves, skinned and crushed
350 g (12 oz) tomatoes, skinned, seeded and chopped
15 ml (1 tbsp) tomato purée
5 ml (1 tsp) sugar
salt and freshly ground pepper
45 ml (3 tbsp) chopped fresh coriander
225 g (8 oz) Italian risotto rice
2.5 ml ($\frac{1}{2}$ tsp) ground cinnamon
150 ml ($\frac{1}{4}$ pint) water
hot garlic bread, to serve

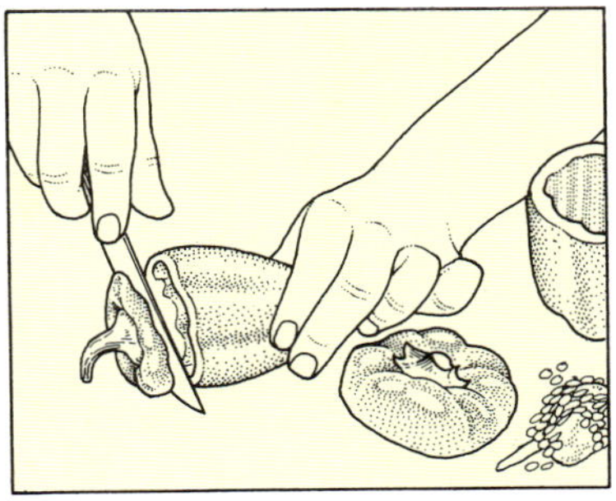

1 Cut a slice off the top of each pepper and reserve. Remove the cores, seeds and membranes and discard. Wash peppers, pat dry.

2 Heat 60 ml (4 tbsp) of the oil in a large frying pan, add the peppers and fry gently for 10 minutes, turning them frequently so that they soften and colour on all sides. Remove from the pan with a slotted spoon and drain on absorbent kitchen paper.

3 Make the stuffing. Drain off all but 30 ml (2 tbsp) oil from the pan, then add the onion and garlic and fry very gently for about 15 minutes.

4 Add the tomatoes and fry gently to soften, stirring constantly. Increase the heat and cook rapidly to drive off the liquid – the mixture should be thick and pulpy.

5 Lower the heat, add the tomato purée, sugar and salt and pepper to taste and simmer gently for 5 minutes. Then remove the pan from the heat and stir in the chopped fresh coriander and the risotto rice. Spoon the stuffing into the peppers, dividing it equally between them.

6 Stand the peppers close together in a heavy-based pan or casserole into which they just fit. Sprinkle with the cinnamon, then the remaining 15 ml (1 tbsp) oil. Put the reserved 'lids' on top.

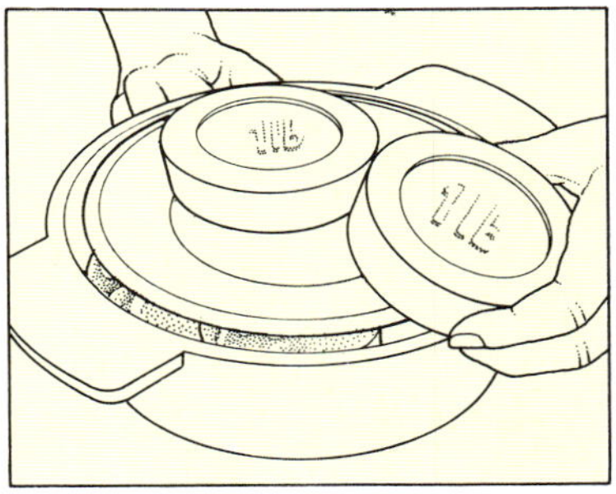

7 Pour the water into the base of the pan, then bring to the boil. Lower the heat, cover with a plate or saucer which just fits inside the rim of the pan, then place heavy weights on top.

8 Simmer gently for 1 hour, then remove from the heat and leave to cool. Chill in the refrigerator overnight, still with the weights on top. Serve the peppers chilled, with hot garlic bread.

Menu Suggestion
Serve with Feta, Avocado and Tomato Salad and Frosted Mint Cheesecake (page 111).

BUYING PEPPERS

When buying peppers for this recipe, look for squat ones which are of a uniform shape and size so that they will stand upright for serving. For a pretty effect, make sure to buy as many different colours as possible.

Sometimes peppers are sold under the name 'capsicum', and the red ones are also called 'pimientoes', but they are all from the same family. The difference between the different colours is in their botanical variety and degree of ripeness: green peppers become red when they are fully ripe, yellow and purple peppers were white before they became ripe! If you like peppers to taste sweet, then choose red or purple ones.

SALMAGUNDY

3.30* | £ £ | 560 cals

* plus 2–3 hours cooling

Serves 8

2.3 kg (5 lb) oven-ready duckling
salt
2 kg (4 lb) oven-ready chicken
25 g (1 oz) butter, melted
freshly ground pepper
450 g (1 lb) carrots, peeled
450 g (1 lb) potatoes, peeled
450 g (1 lb) peas, cooked
300 ml ($\frac{1}{2}$ pint) basic vinaigrette (see page 143)
1 cucumber, peeled and sliced
225 g (8 oz) tomatoes, thinly sliced
4 sticks celery, washed, trimmed and thinly sliced
slices of stuffed olives and radishes, to garnish
4 eggs, hard-boiled (optional)
mayonnaise (optional)

1 Prick the duck all over with a sharp fork and sprinkle liberally with salt. Place breast-side down on a rack or trivet in a roasting tin. Roast in the top of the oven at 200°C (400°F) mark 6, basting occasionally, for 2 hours.

2 Brush the chicken with melted butter and sprinkle with salt and pepper. Place in a shallow roasting tin and roast below the duck on the lowest shelf of the oven for about 1$\frac{1}{2}$ hours. Cool both, for 2–3 hours.

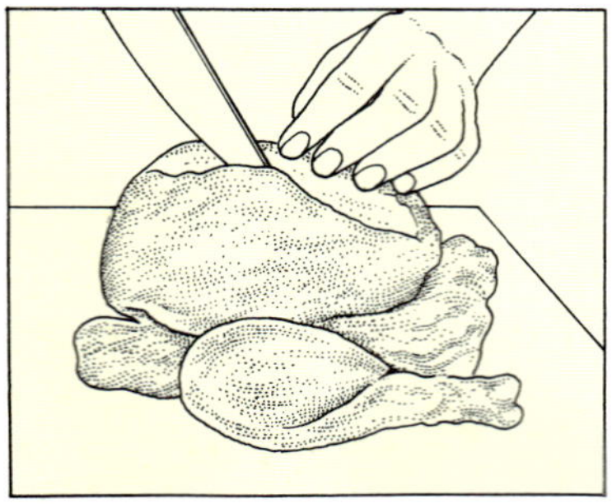

3 Using a sharp knife, make a slit along each side of the breastbone of both the chicken and duck. Remove and discard the skin.

4 Carefully remove all the flesh from the carcasses of both birds. Discard the carcasses and cut the flesh of the birds into thin strips, measuring about 5 cm (2 inches) in length.

5 Cut the carrots into 0.5-cm ($\frac{1}{4}$-inch) wide long strips and cook in boiling salted water for 8–10 minutes, or until tender. Drain. Cook the potatoes in boiling salted water for 15 minutes until tender, drain and dice finely.

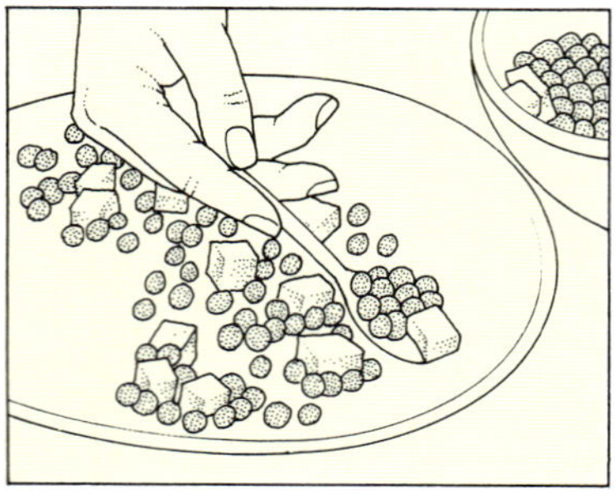

6 Choose a large oval platter for making up the salmagundy. Place potato dice and peas in the bottom of the dish to give a flat base. Arrange carrot strips or a layer of cucumber on top, following the oval pattern.

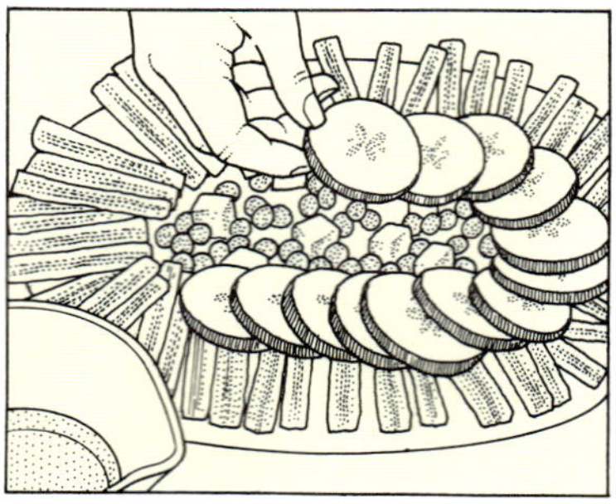

7 Pour over a little dressing. Next, arrange a layer of cucumber or carrot, slightly inside the first layer so that it may be easily seen.

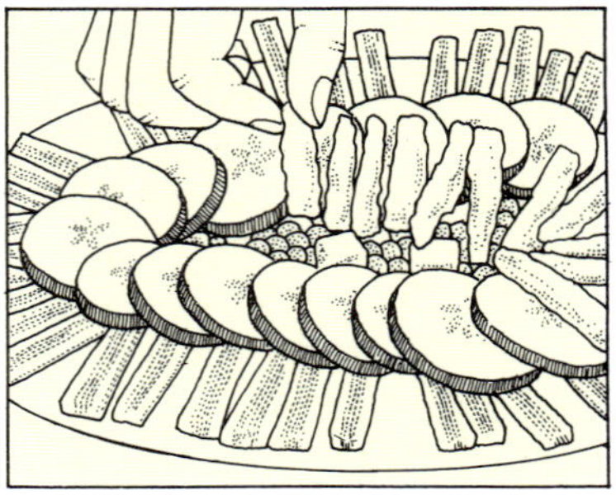

8 Top with more layers of chicken meat, peas, tomato slices, celery, duck meat, etc. Make each layer smaller than the previous one so that the lower layers may all be seen. Sprinkle each one with dressing.

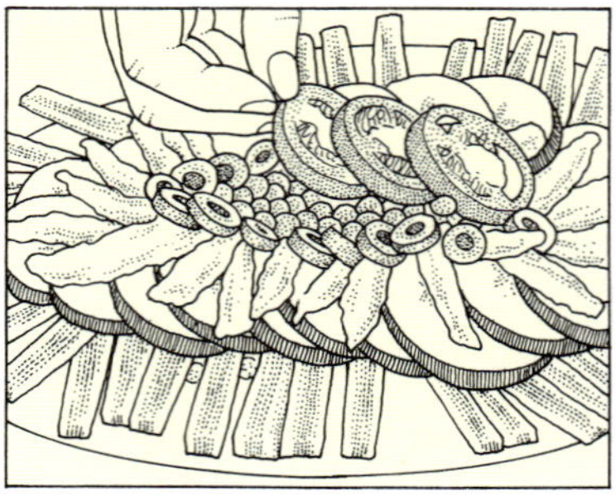

9 Add the tomatoes and continue layering until all the ingredients are used. If using the eggs, halve them and top each half with a little mayonnaise, if used. Garnish with a few radish slices and stuffed olives. Arrange around edge of dish.

Menu Suggestion
Serve with Potted Prawn Pâté (page 24) and Hot Apricot Soufflé (page 124).

PAN BAGNA WITH AVOCADO

0.30 £ 316–421 cals

Serves 6–8

2 ripe avocados
15 ml (1 tbsp) lemon juice
15 ml (1 tbsp) vegetable oil
garlic salt and black pepper
two 35-cm (14-inch) French loaves
225 g (8 oz) tomatoes, sliced
1 small green pepper, cored, seeded and sliced into thin rings
63-g ($2\frac{1}{2}$-oz) can anchovies, drained
few capers and black olives, stoned

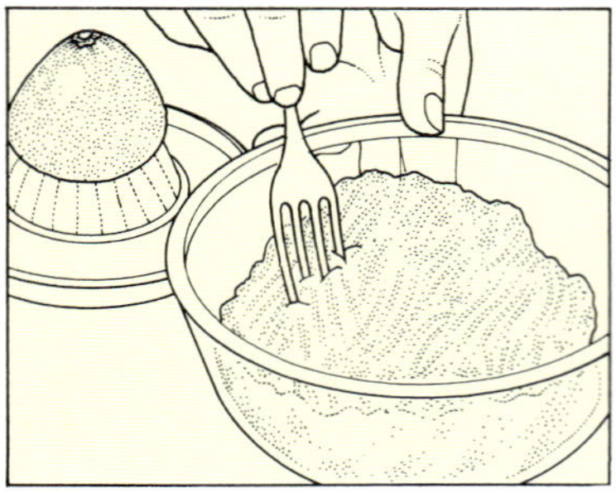

1 Halve avocados and remove stones. Mash flesh with lemon juice, oil and seasoning. Cut anchovies in thin strips.

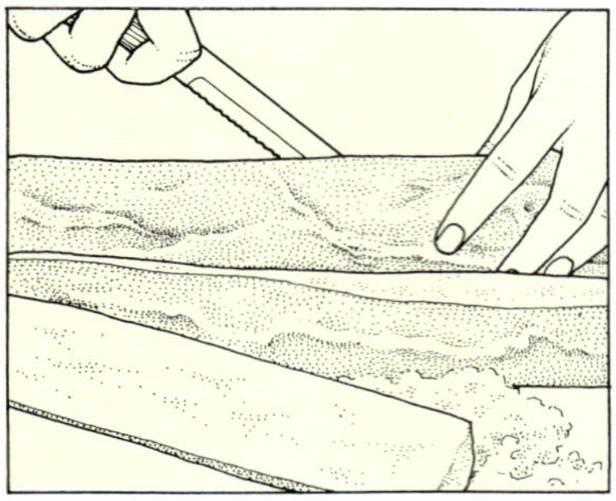

2 Halve loaves lengthwise; discard some of crumbs. Spread bases with avocado. Top with tomatoes and pepper. Lattice with anchovies, capers and olives. Close up and serve, in chunks.

Menu Suggestion
Serve with Three Bean Salad (page 75).

PAN BAGNA WITH MUSHROOMS

0.30 £ 317–422 cals

Serves 6–8

225 g (8 oz) button mushrooms
60 ml (4 tbsp) olive oil
25 g (1 oz) butter
1 garlic clove, skinned and crushed
salt and freshly ground pepper
two 35-cm (14-inch) French loaves
225 g (8 oz) tomatoes, sliced
4 sticks of celery, washed and sliced
63-g ($2\frac{1}{2}$-oz) can anchovies, drained and cut into thin strips
few capers
black olives, stoned or green stuffed olives

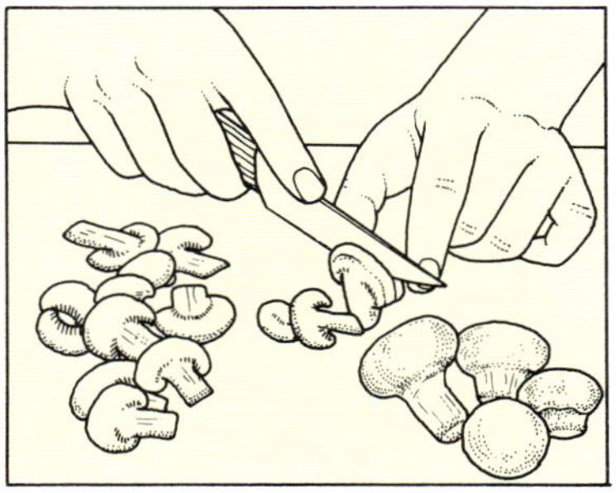

1 Wipe and slice the mushrooms. Heat 30 ml (2 tbsp) oil and butter in a pan, add the mushrooms and garlic and cook gently for 5 minutes until soft. Season with salt and pepper.

2 Halve loaves lengthwise; discarding some of the crumbs. Sprinkle the halves with the remaining oil.

3 Spoon the mushrooms on the bases. Top with the tomatoes, celery, anchovies, capers and olives. Close up and serve, in hunks.

PAN BAGNA

Provençal *Pan Bagna* is the ideal picnic food with which you can ring many changes. French bread or a small, round country bread should traditionally be used (in the Nice area a loaf is specially baked for this purpose) and the filling very moist. Translated, *Pan Bagna* literally means 'wet bread'. Often the bread is sprinkled with olive oil. Other filling ingredients could include hard-boiled eggs, tuna fish, French beans, broad beans or globe artichokes.

PREPARING AVOCADOS

To prepare avocados, use a stainless steel knife, cut the avocados in half lengthways, through to the stone. Hold the pear in both hands and gently twist. Open the halves and remove the stone. If necessary, the peel can either be removed with a potato peeler or lightly score the skin once or twice and peel back the skin. Always brush the exposed flesh immediately with lemon juice to prevent discoloration.

Pâté de Campagne with Black Olives

2.20* £ 475 cals

* plus 2–3 hours chilling and 30 minutes standing time; prepare a day ahead

Serves 8

275 g (10 oz) streaky bacon
75 g (3 oz) black olives
450 g (1 lb) belly pork
275 g (10 oz) pie veal
175 g (6 oz) lamb's liver
2 onions, skinned
1 garlic clove, skinned and crushed
7.5 ml (1½ tsp) salt
freshly ground pepper
5 ml (1 tsp) dried rubbed sage
30 ml (2 tbsp) olive oil
15 ml (1 tbsp) lemon juice
30 ml (2 tbsp) brandy
bay leaves or parsley and black olives, to garnish

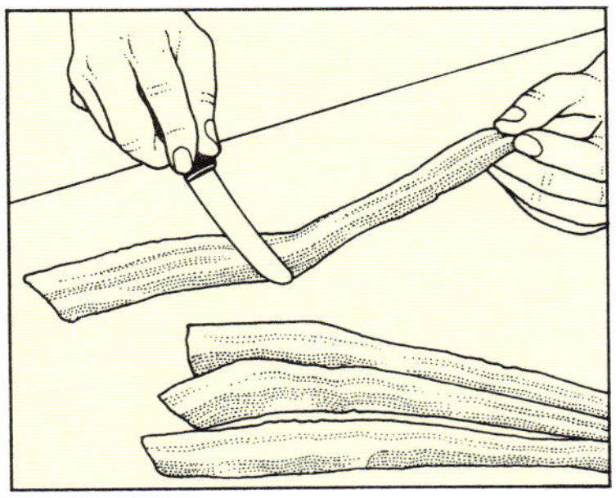

1 Using a sharp knife, cut the rind off the streaky bacon. Stretch the rashers with the back of the knife.

2 Halve, stone and roughly chop the olives. Then pass the belly pork, veal, liver and onions twice through the finest blades of a mincer or food processor. Add the remaining ingredients, except the bacon: mix well.

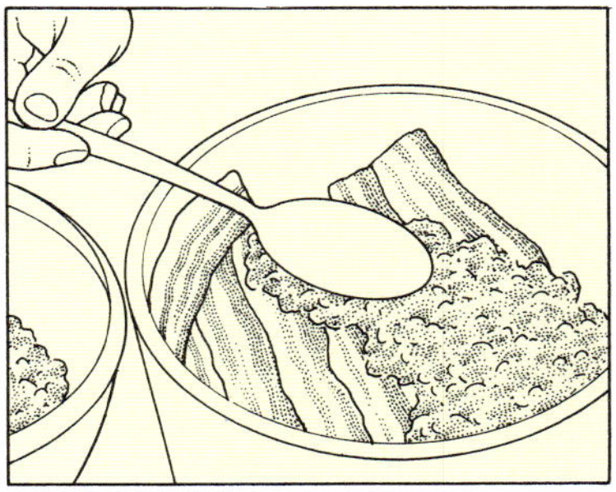

3 Layer the bacon and minced ingredients in a 1.1-litre (2-pint) terrine, topping with the streaky bacon rashers.

4 Cover tightly with foil and lid, if any, and place in a roasting tin, half filled with boiling water. Cook in the oven at 170°C (325°F) mark 3 for about 2 hours until the pâté is firm.

5 Remove the lid and foil. Pour off juices and reserve in the refrigerator. Weight down the pâté and refrigerate overnight.

6 Skim the fat off the jellied juices. Gently warm the juices. Garnish with herbs and black olives, then spoon over the juices. Refrigerate for 2–3 hours to set. Leave to stand at room temperature for 30 minutes.

Menu Suggestion
Serve with Potato Salad (page 83) and Fennel and Tomato Salad (page 84).

SALADE NIÇOISE

1.00* £ 574 cals

* includes 30 minutes standing time

Serves 4

198-g (7-oz) can tuna fish, drained

225 g (8 oz) tomatoes, quartered

50 g (2 oz) black olives, stoned

½ small cucumber, thinly sliced

225 g (8 oz) cooked French beans

2 hard-boiled eggs, shelled and quartered

15 ml (1 tbsp) chopped fresh parsley

15 ml (1 tbsp) chopped fresh basil

150 ml (¼ pint) garlic vinaigrette (see page 143)

8 anchovy fillets, halved and drained

French bread, to serve

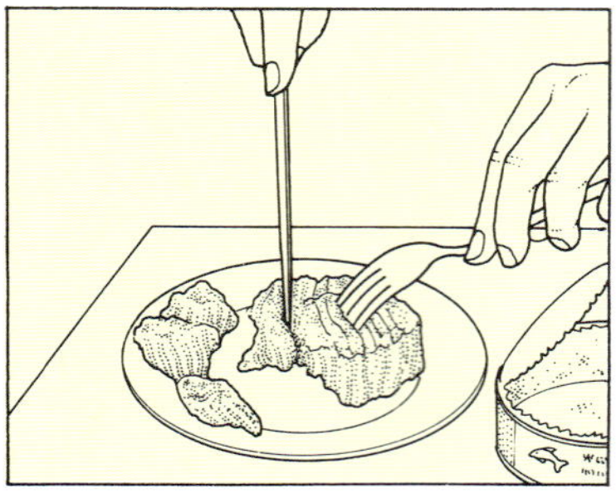

1 Flake the canned tuna into fairly large chunks. Arrange the tuna chunks in a salad bowl with the tomatoes, olives, cucumber slices, beans and eggs.

2 Add the parsley and basil to the garlic vinaigrette, mix well and pour dressing over salad.

3 Arrange the anchovy fillets in a lattice pattern over the salad and allow to stand for 30 minutes before serving. Serve with crusty French bread.

Menu Suggestion
Serve with Chicken Liver Pâté (page 21) and Coeurs à la Crème (page 112).

Greek Salad

0.25 £ 511 cals

Serves 4

2 large tomatoes
1 green pepper
½ medium cucumber
50 g (2 oz) Greek black olives
225 g (8 oz) Feta cheese
120 ml (8 tbsp) olive oil
30–45 ml (2–3 tbsp) lemon juice
salt and freshly ground pepper
large pinch dried oregano
pitta bread, to serve

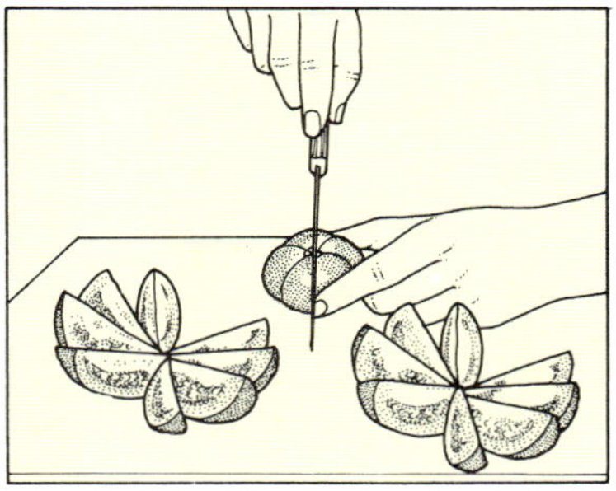

1 Using a sharp knife, cut each tomato in half. Then cut each of the halves into four equal-sized wedges.

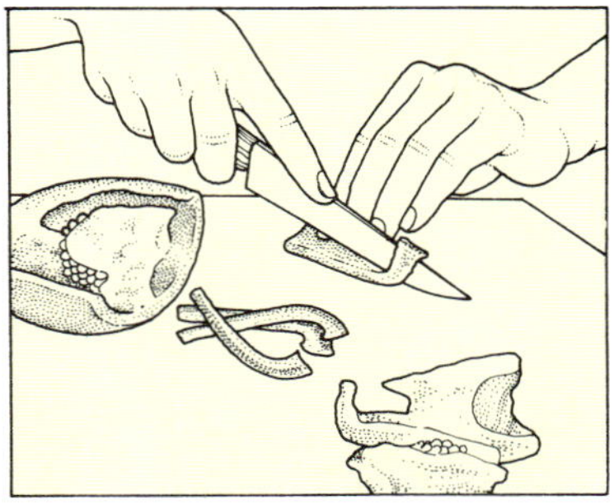

2 Halve, seed and slice the green pepper thinly; then cut the cucumber half into thick slices.

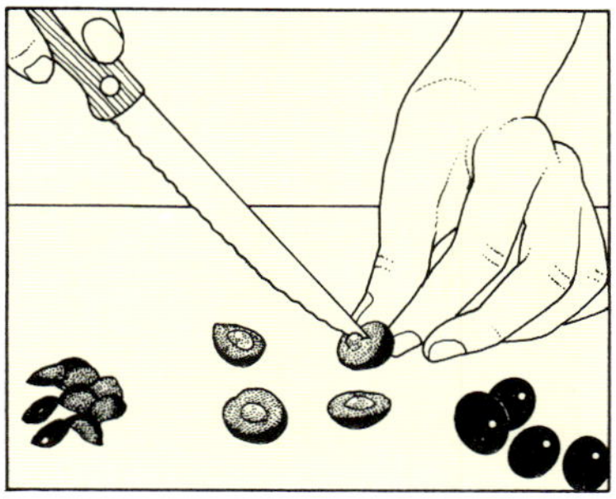

3 Stone the black olives. Arrange the tomato wedges, sliced pepper and cucumber and the olives in a salad bowl.

4 Dice the cheese and add to the bowl, reserving a few dice for garnish. Pour over the olive oil, followed by the lemon juice and season well.

5 Toss the salad well together. Crumble over the remaining cheese cubes, sprinkle with oregano and serve with pitta bread.

Menu Suggestion
Serve with Hummus (page 10) or Taramasalata (page 12) and Almond and Cherry Flan (page 122).

Vegetables

You're absolutely spoilt for choice with summer vegetables. Freshly picked from the garden are best, but local farms and markets also have good-quality produce at keen prices.
Enjoy them at their best: cook them for the minimum amount of time—you simply can't go wrong.

Tomatoes au Gratin

0.55 £ £ 347 cals

Serves 6

900 g (2 lb) tomatoes

50 g (2 oz) butter or margarine, softened

2–3 garlic cloves, skinned and chopped

5 ml (1 tsp) sugar

20 ml (4 tsp) chopped fresh basil or 10 ml (2 tsp) dried

salt and freshly ground pepper

300 ml (10 fl oz) double cream

50 g (2 oz) dried breadcrumbs

25 g (1 oz) freshly grated Parmesan cheese

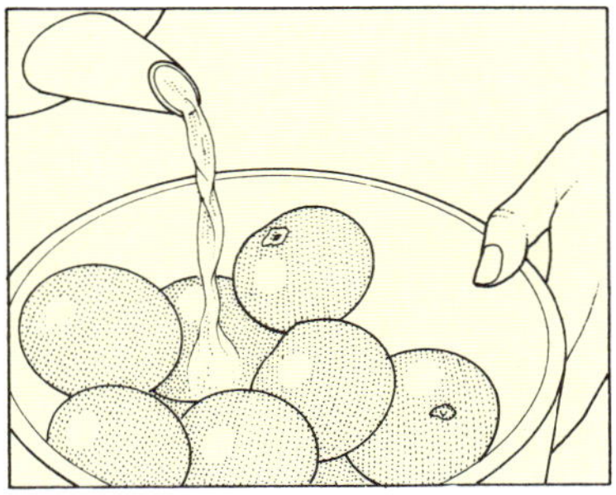

1 Skin the tomatoes: put them in a large bowl, pour over boiling water and leave for 10 seconds. Drain, then plunge the tomatoes into a bowl of cold water.

2 Remove from the bowl one at a time and peel off the skin with your fingers. Then slice the tomatoes thinly.

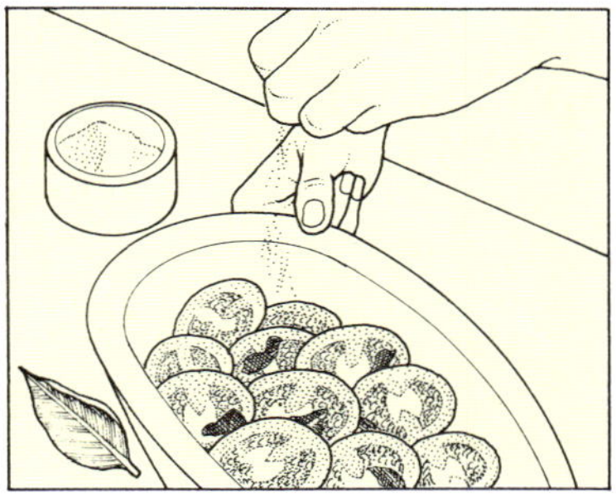

3 Brush the inside of an ovenproof dish liberally with some of the butter. Arrange a layer of tomato slices in the bottom of the dish then sprinkle with a little of the garlic, sugar and basil, then salt and pepper to taste. Pour over a thin layer of cream.

4 Repeat these layers until all the ingredients are used up. Mix the breadcrumbs and Parmesan together, then sprinkle over the top of the tomatoes and cream. Dot with the remaining butter.

5 Bake in the oven at 180°C (350°F) mark 4 for 40 minutes until the topping is golden brown. Serve hot.

Menu Suggestion

Serve with Lamb Cutlets en Croûte (page 46) or Turkey and Ham Parcels (page 93).

TOMATOES AU GRATIN

A recipe with a South of France flavour—both tomatoes and basil grow prolifically in Provence, where this dish originated. Tomatoes come in many different varieties, but for this dish try to buy the large continental type which are sweet, juicy and full of flavour. English tomatoes are beautifully firm for garnishes and salads, but not for a dish like this one where flavour is more important than perfect looks.

Basil and tomatoes have an affinity with one another that is quite unique – no other herb tastes quite so good with tomatoes. If cut basil is difficult to buy, then buy a plant or some seed from a nursery.

FRENCH BEANS IN SOURED CREAM WITH PAPRIKA

0.25	£	141 cals

Serves 4

700 g ($1\frac{1}{2}$ lb) French beans
25 g (1 oz) butter or margarine
1 small onion, skinned and chopped
5 ml (1 tsp) paprika
salt and freshly ground pepper
150 ml ($\frac{1}{4}$ pint) chicken stock
142 ml (5 fl oz) soured cream

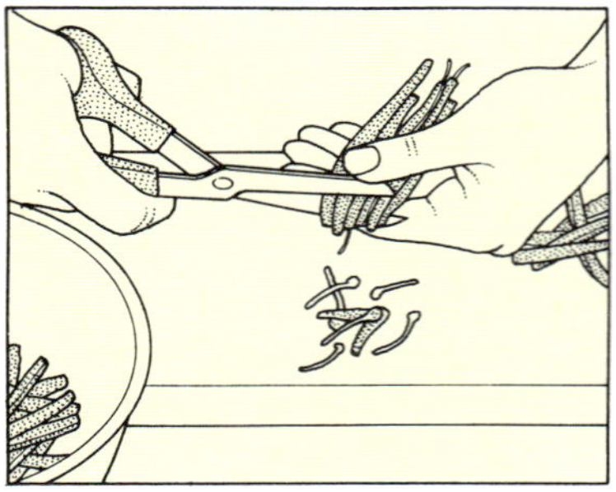

1 Using kitchen scissors, top and tail the French beans and cut them into 2.5-cm (1-inch) lengths. Melt the butter in a pan, add the onion and cook gently for 5 minutes until soft and golden, but do not brown.

2 Stir in 2.5 ml ($\frac{1}{2}$ tsp) paprika, beans, seasoning and stock. Bring to the boil, cover and simmer for 5–10 minutes until the French beans are tender.

3 Stir the cream into the pan and reheat without boiling. Turn into a heated serving dish and dust the top with the remaining paprika.

Menu Suggestion
Serve with Chilli Chicken (page 94).

New Potatoes with Tarragon Cream

0.15 £ 204 cals

Serves 4

- **15 g ($\frac{1}{2}$ oz) butter or margarine**
- **4 spring onions, washed, trimmed and chopped**
- **142 ml (5 fl oz) soured cream**
- **salt and freshly ground pepper**
- **3 sprigs of fresh tarragon**
- **700 g ($1\frac{1}{2}$ lb) cooked new potatoes, drained and kept hot**

1 Melt the butter in a pan, add the onions and cook for 5 minutes until soft. Stir in the cream, seasoning, and two tarragon sprigs and heat without boiling.

2 Add the cooked potatoes to the creamy onion and tarragon mixture in the pan. Reheat gently, do not boil.

3 Turn the potatoes and the sauce into a warm serving dish and serve garnished with a sprig of fresh tarragon.

Menu Suggestion
Serve with Salmon Trout with Prawns (page 57).

Spinach Timbale

1.20 £ £ 257 cals

Serves 6

25 g (1 oz) butter or margarine
1 onion, skinned and finely chopped
900 g (2 lb) fresh spinach, washed, trimmed and roughly chopped
150 ml ($\frac{1}{4}$ pint) milk
150 ml (5 fl oz) single cream
4 eggs
50 g (2 oz) Gruyère cheese, grated
50 g (2 oz) fresh white breadcrumbs
pinch of grated nutmeg
salt and freshly ground pepper
thin tomato strips and fresh coriander, to garnish
tomato sauce, (right)

1 Melt the butter in a saucepan, stir in the onion and cook gently for about 5 minutes until soft. Stir in the spinach and cook for a further 5 minutes until soft, stirring occasionally. Stir in the milk and cream and heat gently.

2 Beat the eggs in a bowl and stir in the spinach mixture, cheese, breadcrumbs, nutmeg and salt and pepper.

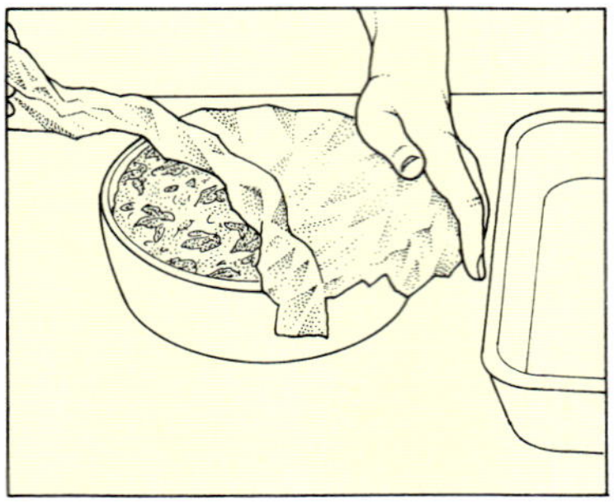

3 Turn the mixture into a greased 1.1-litre (2-pint) ring mould, cover with foil and place the dish in a roasting tin, half filled with hot water. Bake in the oven at 180°C (350°F) mark 4 for $1\frac{1}{4}$ hours until firm to the touch and a knife, inserted in the centre, comes out clean. Meanwhile, prepare the tomato sauce.

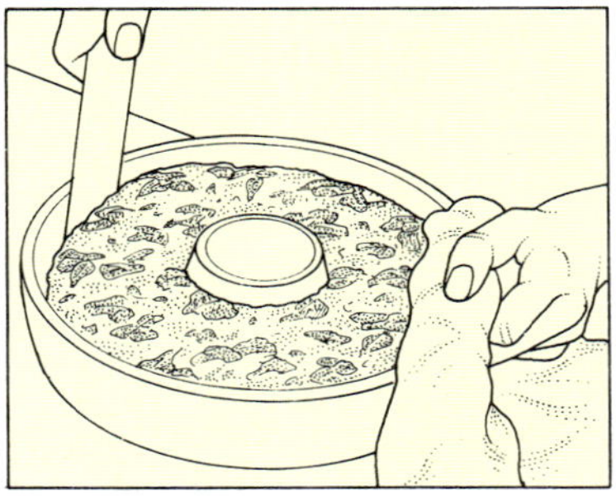

4 Remove the dish from the water and leave for 5 minutes. Loosen the timbale from the sides of the dish with a knife.

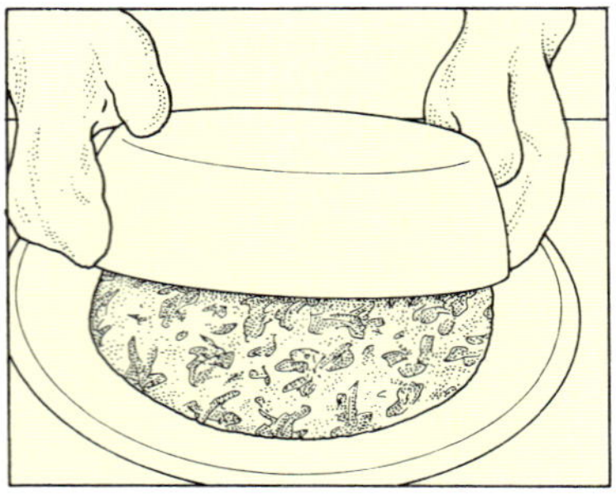

5 Turn the timbale out on to a warmed flat serving dish. Garnish with thin tomato strips and coriander. If liked, serve with a tomato sauce.

Menu Suggestion
Serve with Lamb with Cucumber and Mint Stuffing (page 48).

TIMBALES
The French word *timbale* is used to describe a container, usually silver or gold, which has a handle on either side and is designed for holding drinks. The word has also taken on a broader meaning in culinary terms, however, and is now generally used to describe a dish which is baked and then turned out of its cooking dish – as in this recipe.

Tomato Sauce

Makes about 300 ml ($\frac{1}{2}$ pint)

1 small onion, skinned and chopped
1 small carrot, peeled and chopped
25 g (1 oz) butter
25 ml ($1\frac{1}{2}$ tbsp) flour
450 g (1 lb) tomatoes, quartered, or a 397-g (14-oz) can tomatoes, drained
300 ml ($\frac{1}{2}$ pint) chicken stock
1 bay leaf
1 clove
2.5 ml ($\frac{1}{2}$ tsp) sugar
10 ml (2 tsp) tomato purée
15–60 ml (1–4 tbsp) dry white wine (optional)
salt and freshly ground pepper

1 Lightly fry the onion and carrot in the butter for 5 minutes. Stir in the flour and add the tomatoes, stock, bay leaf, clove, sugar, tomato purée, wine, if used, and salt and pepper.

2 Bring to the boil, cover and simmer for 30–45 minutes, or until the vegetables are cooked. Sieve, reheat and adjust seasoning, if necessary.

VARIATION

NEAPOLITAN TOMATO SAUCE

450 g (1 lb) tomatoes, skinned or a 397-g (14-oz) can tomatoes, drained
1 garlic clove, skinned and crushed
50 ml (2 fl oz) olive oil
2.5 ml ($\frac{1}{2}$ tsp) sugar
3 basil leaves, torn, or 10 ml (2 tsp) chopped fresh parsley, or 5 ml (1 tsp) oregano
salt and freshly ground pepper

Place all the ingredients in a saucepan and simmer, uncovered, stirring occasionally for about 10 minutes until the oil has separated from the tomatoes.

RATATOUILLE

2.05*	£	✳	252 cals

* includes 30 minutes standing time

Serves 6

450 g (1 lb) aubergines
salt
450 g (1 lb) courgettes
3 red or green peppers
120 ml (8 tbsp) olive oil
450 g (1 lb) onions, skinned and chopped
1 garlic clove, skinned and crushed
450 g (1 lb) tomatoes, skinned, seeded and chopped, or one 397-g (14-oz) can tomatoes, drained
30 ml (2 tbsp) tomato purée
bouquet garni
freshly ground pepper

1 Cut the aubergines into thin slices. Sprinkle liberally with salt and set aside to drain in a sieve or colander for 30 minutes. Rinse under cold running water and pat dry with absorbent kitchen paper.

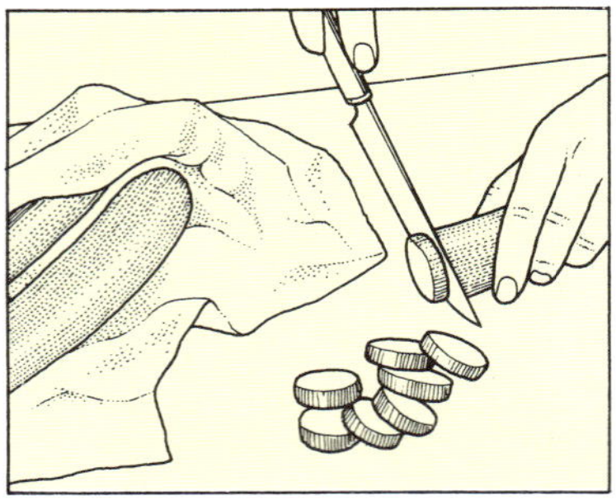

2 Meanwhile, wash the courgettes and pat dry with absorbent kitchen paper. Top and tail them and then cut into thin slices.

3 Wash the peppers; pat dry with absorbent kitchen paper. Slice off the stems and remove the seeds. Cut into thin rings.

4 Heat the oil in a large saucepan. Add the onions and garlic and cook gently for about 10 minutes until soft and golden.

5 Add the tomatoes and purée and cook for a few more minutes, then add the aubergines, courgettes, peppers, bouquet garni and salt and pepper. Cover and simmer gently for 1 hour. The vegetables should be soft and well mixed but retain their shape and most of the cooking liquid should have evaporated.

6 To reduce the liquid, remove the lid and cook gently for another 20 minutes. Check the seasoning and serve hot or cold.

Menu Suggestion
Serve with Bass on the Barbecue (page 103).

SUMMER VEGETABLE FRICASSÉE

0.30 £ £ 114–171 cals

Serves 4–6

4 courgettes, washed and trimmed
225 g (8 oz) French beans, topped and tailed and cut into 5-cm (2-inch) lengths
salt and freshly ground pepper
45 ml (3 tbsp) olive oil
1 onion, skinned and sliced
2 garlic cloves, skinned and crushed
5 ml (1 tsp) crushed coriander seeds
3 peppers (red, yellow, green), cored, seeded and sliced
150 ml ($\frac{1}{4}$ pint) dry white wine
10 ml (2 tsp) tomato purée
2.5 ml ($\frac{1}{2}$ tsp) sugar

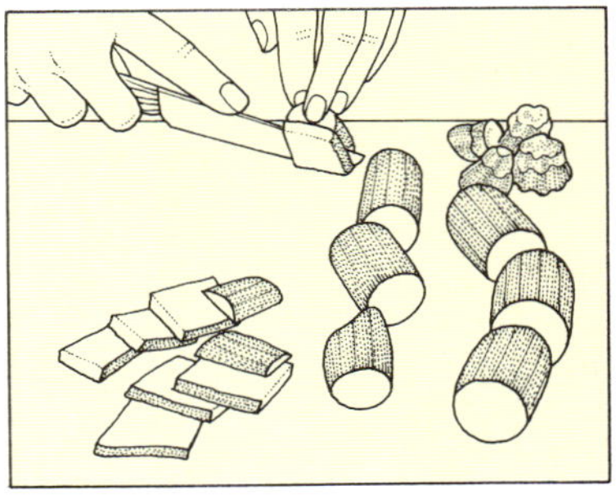

1 Cut the courgettes crossways into thirds, then cut them lengthways into slices about 0.5 cm ($\frac{1}{4}$ inch) thick.

2 Blanch the courgettes and beans in boiling salted water for 5 minutes only. Drain and set aside until required.

3 Heat the oil in a flameproof casserole, add the onion, garlic and coriander seeds and fry gently for 5 minutes until onion is soft.

4 Add the pepper slices and fry gently for a further 5 minutes, stirring constantly. Stir in the wine, tomato purée and sugar, with salt and pepper to taste. Bring to the boil, then simmer for a few minutes, stirring all the time until the liquid begins to reduce.

5 Add the courgettes and beans to the pan and stir gently to combine with the sauce. Heat through, taking care not to over-cook the vegetables. Taste and adjust seasoning. Serve hot, straight from the casserole.

Menu Suggestion
Serve with Spicy Lamb Kebabs (page 99).

PETITS POIS WITH PARMA HAM

0.25 | 206 cals

Serves 4

50 g (2 oz) Parma ham
50 g (2 oz) butter or margarine
900 g (2 lb) fresh young peas, shelled
12 spring onions, washed, trimmed and sliced
1 firm-hearted lettuce, washed and shredded
5 ml (1 tsp) sugar
salt and freshly ground pepper
150 ml ($\frac{1}{4}$ pint) chicken stock
sprig of mint, to garnish

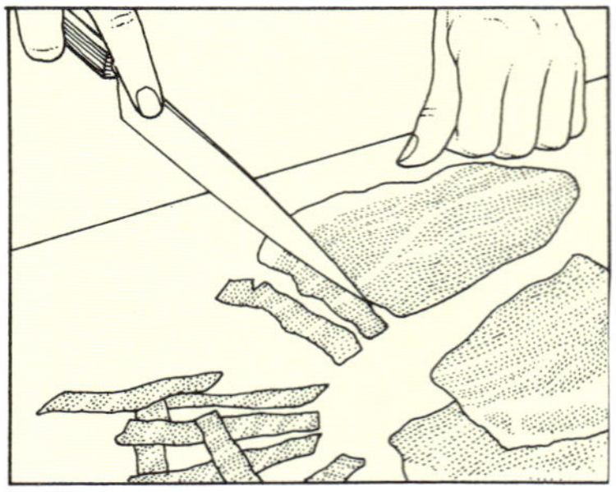

1 Using a sharp knife, cut the ham into small strips. Then melt the butter in a large pan, add the peas, ham and the next 6 ingredients.

2 Bring to the boil, cover and simmer gently for 15–20 minutes. Serve in a warm serving dish with the cooking liquid. Garnish with a sprig of mint.

Menu Suggestion
Serve with Lamb with Cucumber and Mint Stuffing (page 48).

PETITS POIS

These are small, sweet, tender young peas, much used in continental Europe. The term literally means 'little peas' in French. This recipe, with Parma ham, is claimed by the Italians. The ham can be omitted if liked, or other varieties of ham used. Without the addition of ham it is known as *petits pois à la française*, a traditional, well-known French dish.

This recipe can only be made in spring and summer, when all the vegetables are fresh and young. Fresh young peas should be eaten with their cooking liquid so that their full flavour is appreciated.

It is essential to cook peas as soon as possible after they are picked, as the sugar in them begins to 'die' and turn to starch the moment they leave the parent plant. When you are picking or buying fresh peas, the pods should be crisp, young and well-filled.

If fresh peas are unavailable, good quality frozen varieties are available, and make a good substitute. Ordinary frozen peas, however, cannot be substituted for *petits pois*.

SAUTÉED CUCUMBER WITH HERBS

0.45 £ 101–151 cals

Serves 4–6

1 cucumber

salt

50 g (2 oz) butter or margarine

2 shallots or 1 small onion, skinned and finely chopped

15 ml (1 tbsp) fresh chopped rosemary or 10 ml (2 tsp) dried

2.5 ml ($\frac{1}{2}$ tsp) sugar

freshly ground pepper

60 ml (4 tbsp) soured cream

fresh rosemary sprigs, to garnish

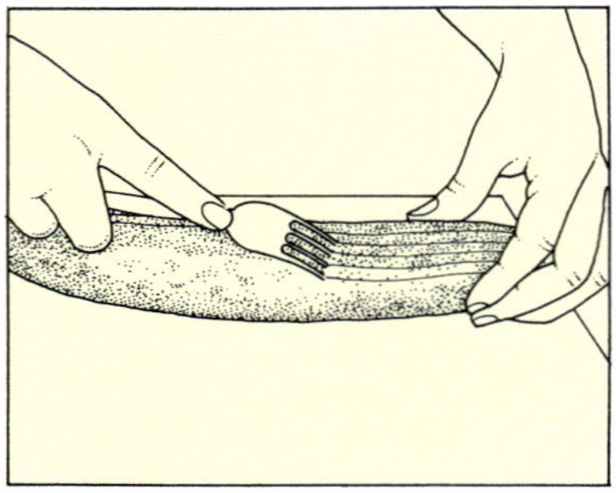

1 Using a sharp fork, run the prongs down the length of the cucumber to score. (This will give an attractive effect.)

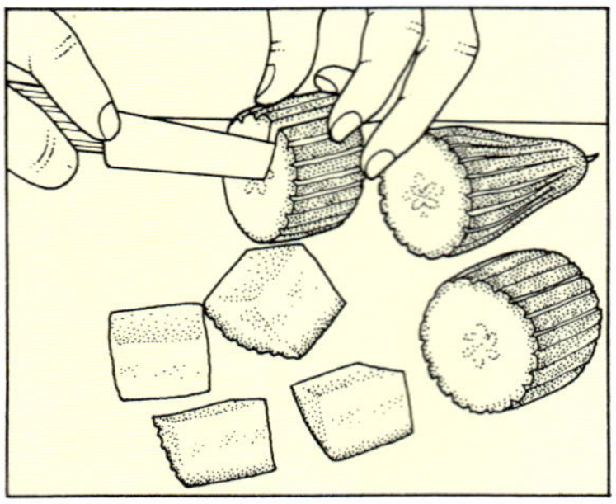

2 Using a sharp knife, cut the cucumber into 5-cm (2-inch) lengths, then cut each piece lengthways into quarters.

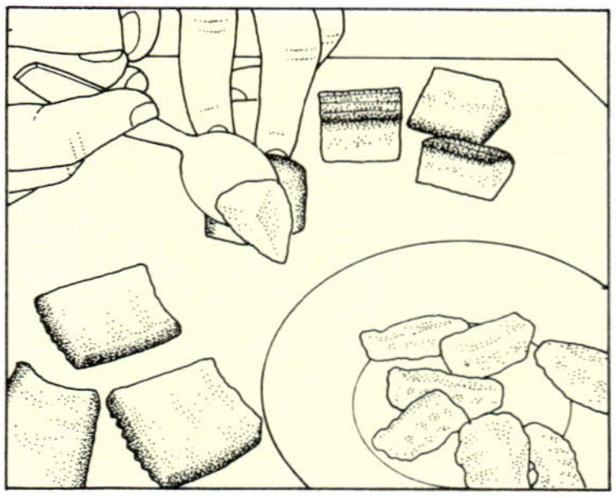

3 Remove the seeds from the cucumber, then put the cucumber in a colander and sprinkle with the salt. Cover with a plate and leave to drain for 30 minutes, pressing the plate down occasionally to press out the liquid from the cucumber. Rinse and pat dry with absorbent kitchen paper.

4 Melt the butter in a large, heavy-based frying pan. Add the shallots and fry gently for 5 minutes until they are soft and lightly coloured.

5 Add the cucumber pieces to the pan, together with the rosemary, sugar and pepper to taste. Cook for 5 minutes only, stirring frequently to ensure even cooking.

6 Remove the pan from the heat and stir in the soured cream. Taste and adjust seasoning. Garnish with rosemary sprigs and serve immediately.

Menu Suggestion

Serve with Bass on the Barbecue (page 103).

SAUTÉED COURGETTES WITH CHIVES

0.15 £ 105 cals

Serves 4

450 g (1 lb) courgettes
25 g (1 oz) butter
15 ml (1 tbsp) vegetable oil
grated rind and juice of $\frac{1}{2}$ lemon
salt and freshly ground pepper
15 ml (1 tbsp) fresh chives

1 Wash the courgettes and pat dry with absorbent kitchen paper. Top and tail them and thinly slice.

2 Heat the butter and oil in a pan, add the courgettes and cook over medium heat, uncovered, for 5–8 minutes. When tender but still slightly crisp, add the lemon rind and juice and seasoning to taste.

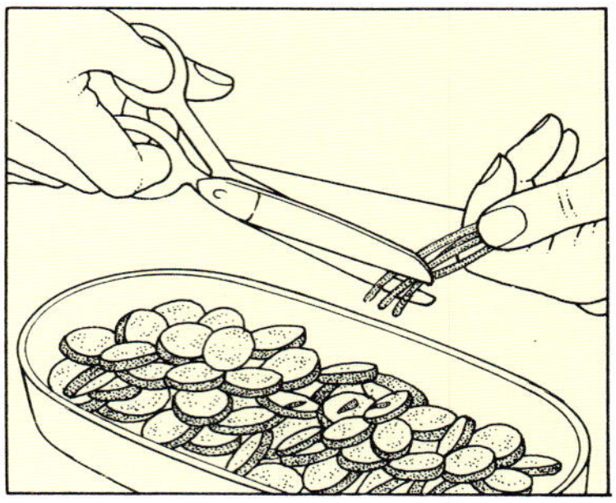

3 Turn into a heated serving dish. Snip fresh chives over the courgettes and serve immediately, while still hot.

Menu Suggestion
Serve with Barbecued Spare Ribs (page 95).

Side Salads

Side salads are an important part of summer eating. Hot weather and eating outside call for light meals – and hot vegetable dishes are not usually popular. A simple main course accompanied by one or two interesting and unusual side salads is all that is needed to make the perfect summer meal. Here we've used unusual ingredients including endive, radicchio, cracked wheat and pulses to add interest.

THREE BEAN SALAD

1.15* £ 223–334 cals

* plus 30 minutes cooling; 2–3 hours chilling

Serves 4–6

75 g (3 oz) dried red kidney beans, soaked overnight

75 g (3 oz) dried black-eyed beans, soaked overnight

75 g (3 oz) dried pinto or borlotti beans, soaked overnight

100 ml (4 fl oz) basic sauce vinaigrette (see page 143)

15 ml (1 tbsp) chopped fresh coriander

1 small onion, skinned and sliced into rings

salt and freshly ground pepper

sprig of fresh coriander, to garnish

1 Drain the beans and place in a saucepan of water. Bring to the boil and boil rapidly for 10 minutes (this is important), then boil gently for $1\frac{1}{2}$ hours until tender.

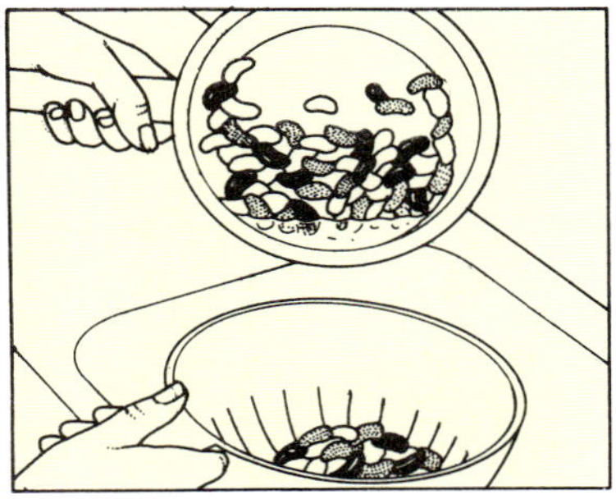

2 Using a colander or a metal sieve, drain the cooked beans thoroughly and place them in a large salad bowl.

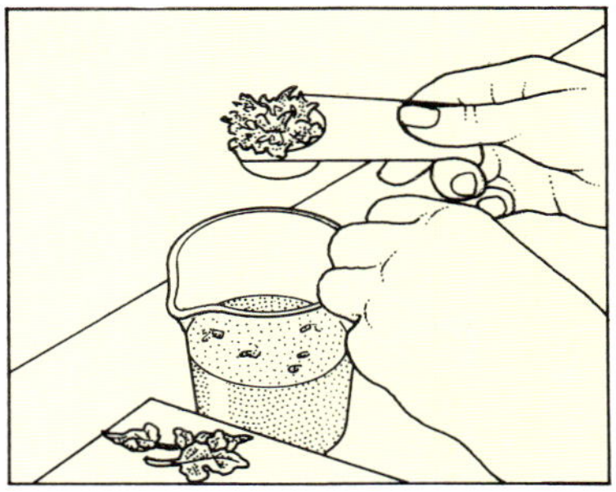

3 Combine the vinaigrette and coriander, and pour over the beans while they are still warm.

4 Toss thoroughly and leave to cool for 30 minutes. Mix the onion into the beans, season well and chill for 2–3 hours before serving. To serve, garnish with fresh coriander.

Menu Suggestion
Serve with Barbecued Sausages with Spicy Tomato Dip (page 105).

COOKING BEANS

If you don't have time to soak the beans overnight and you want to cook them quickly, then there is a short cut: the hot-soak method. Put the beans in a pan, cover with cold water and bring to the boil. Boil rapidly for 2 minutes, then remove from the heat, cover with a tight-fitting lid and leave to soak for 1 hour. Drain, then continue with the recipe as when using beans which have been soaked in cold water overnight. *Always* boil red kidney beans for a full 10 minutes before you cook them – this is to destroy the poisonous enzyme they contain.

CAESAR SALAD

0.45 £ 438 cals

Serves 4

1 large garlic clove, skinned and crushed
150 ml ($\frac{1}{4}$ pint) olive oil
75 g (3 oz) stale white bread
1 lettuce
salt and freshly ground pepper
1 egg
30 ml (2 tbsp) lemon juice
25 g (1 oz) grated Parmesan cheese
8 anchovy fillets, chopped and drained
croûtons, to serve

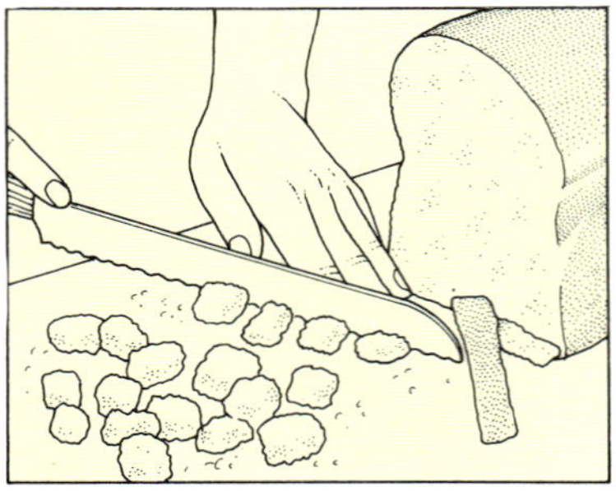

1 Add the garlic to the oil and leave to stand for 30 minutes. Cut the stale white bread into 0.5-cm ($\frac{1}{4}$-inch) dice.

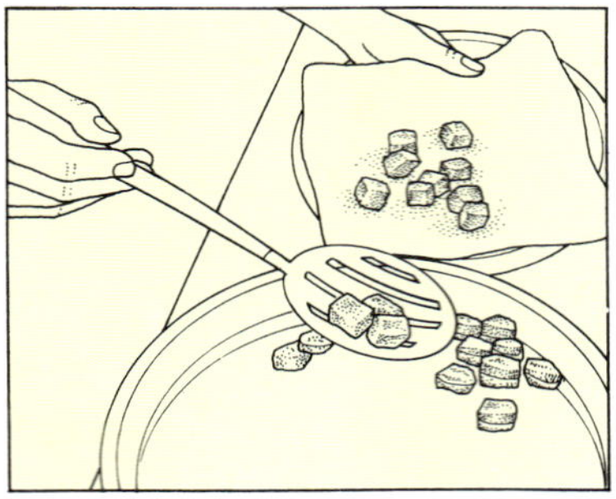

2 Heat a little of the garlic oil in a frying pan and fry the bread until golden brown on all sides. Lift from the pan and drain.

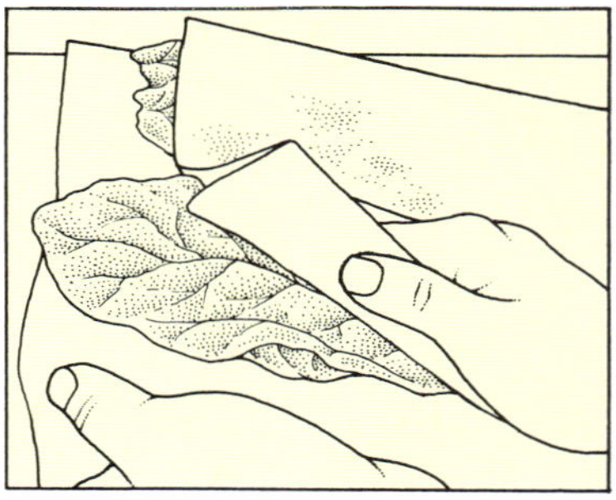

3 Carefully wash the lettuce under cold running water. Drain well and pat dry with absorbent kitchen paper.

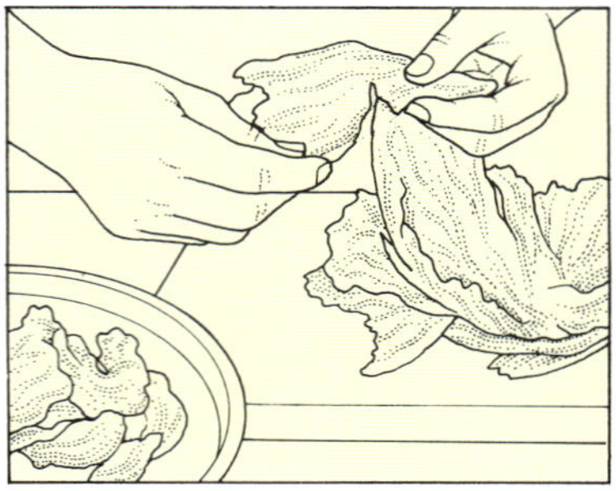

4 Tear into bite-sized pieces and place in a salad bowl. Pour over the remaining garlic oil and toss until the leaves are completely coated. Season well.

5 Add the lemon juice, cheese, anchovies and croûtons and toss well. Boil the egg for 1 minute only, add to the salad and give the salad a final toss. Serve immediately.

Menu Suggestion
Serve with Jellied Tomato Ring (page 36).

WALDORF SALAD

0.40 £ 402 cals

Serves 4

450 g (1 lb) eating apples
juice of 1 lemon
5 ml (1 tsp) sugar
150 ml ($\frac{1}{4}$ pint) mayonnaise (see page 145)
$\frac{1}{2}$ head celery, washed, trimmed and sliced
50 g (2 oz) walnuts, chopped
1 lettuce
few walnut halves, to garnish (optional)

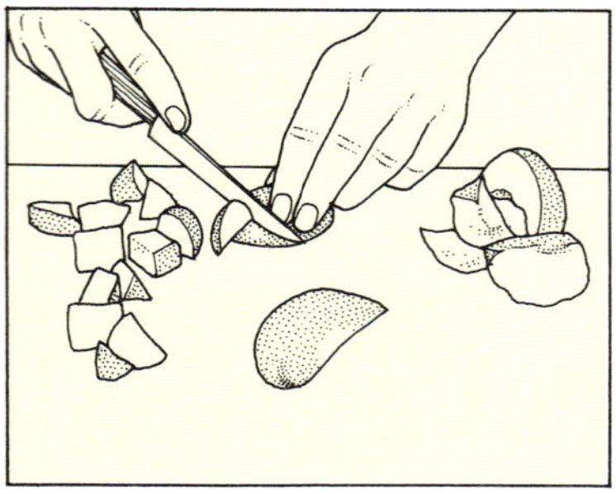

1 Core the apples, slice one and dice the rest. Dip the slices in lemon juice to prevent discoloration of the fruit.

2 Toss the diced apples in 30 ml (2 tbsp) lemon juice, the sugar and 15 ml (1 tbsp) mayonnaise and leave to stand for about 30 minutes.

3 Just before serving, add the sliced celery, chopped walnuts and the remaining mayonnaise, and toss together.

4 Serve in a bowl lined with lettuce leaves and garnish with the apple slices and a few walnut halves, if liked.

Menu Suggestion
Serve with Smoked Fish Timbale (page 35).

PASTA, PRAWN AND APPLE SALAD

0.30* £ 176 cals

* plus 2–3 hours chilling

Serves 6

175 g (6 oz) pasta shells

150 ml ($\frac{1}{4}$ pint) unsweetened apple juice

5 ml (1 tsp) chopped fresh mint

5 ml (1 tsp) white wine vinegar

salt and freshly ground pepper

225 g (8 oz) peeled prawns

225 g (8 oz) crisp eating apples

lettuce leaves

paprika, to garnish

1 Cook the pasta in boiling salted water for 10–15 minutes until tender. Drain well, rinse in cold running water and drain again.

2 Meanwhile, make the dressing. Whisk together the apple juice, mint, vinegar and seasoning.

3 Dry the prawns with absorbent kitchen paper. Quarter, core and roughly chop the apples. Stir the prawns, apple and cooked pasta into the dressing until well mixed. Cover tightly with cling film and refrigerate for 2–3 hours.

4 Wash the lettuce leaves, dry and shred finely. Place a little lettuce in six individual serving dishes. Spoon the prawn salad on top and dust with paprika.

Menu Suggestion
Serve with Courgette Quiche (page 38).

INDONESIAN FRUIT AND VEGETABLE SALAD

0.55* £ 260 cals

* including 30 minutes standing time

Serves 4

1 small fresh pineapple
¼ cucumber
175 g (6 oz) young carrots, peeled
1 crisp green eating apple
100 g (4 oz) beansprouts
30 ml (2 tbsp) crunchy peanut butter
20 ml (4 tsp) soy sauce
60 ml (4 tbsp) olive oil
juice of ½ lemon
salt and freshly ground pepper

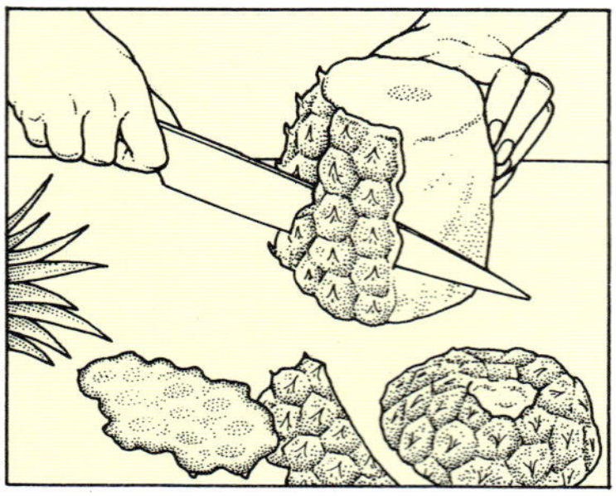

1 Cut the top and bottom off the pineapple. Stand the fruit upright on a board. Using a large, sharp knife, slice downwards in sections to remove the skin and 'eyes' of the fruit.

2 Slice off the pineapple flesh, leaving the core. Then discard the core.

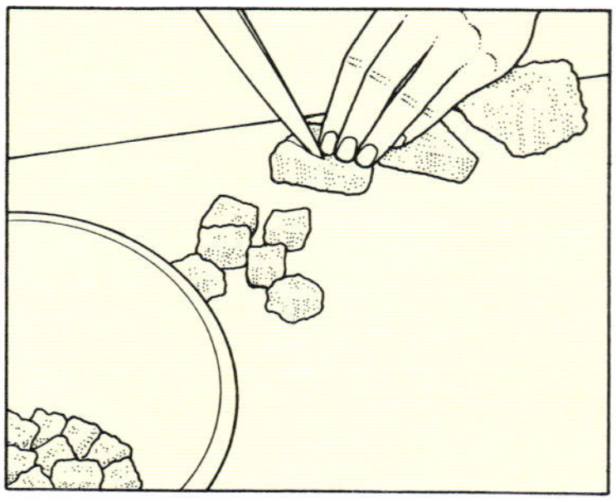

3 Cut the pineapple flesh into small cubes, then cut the cucumber and carrots lengthways into thin matchstick shapes. Quarter and core the apple (but do not peel), then chop roughly. Then combine all the fruit and vegetables together in a bowl with the beansprouts.

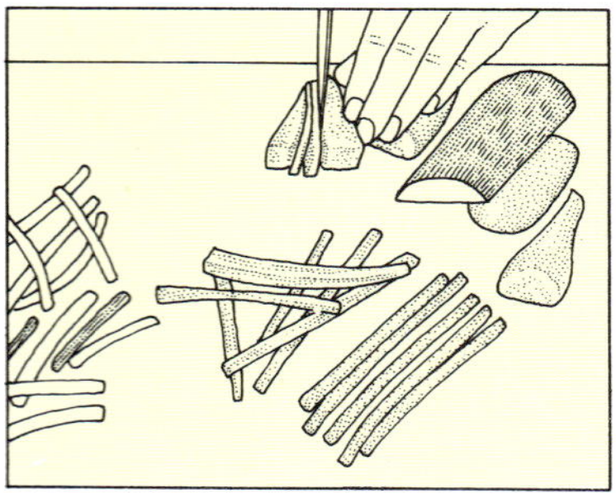

4 Make the dressing. Put the peanut butter in a bowl, then gradually whisk in the remaining ingredients with a fork. Season.

5 Pour the dressing over the salad and toss well to mix. Cover and leave to stand for 30 minutes before serving.

Menu Suggestion
Serve with Chicken and Beef Satay (page 104).

CUCUMBER RAITA

0.10* £ 30 cals

* plus 30 minutes standing time

Serves 4

1 cucumber
salt
142 g (5 oz) natural yogurt
pinch of chilli powder
pinch of ground cumin
freshly ground pepper
cucumber slice dusted with paprika, to garnish

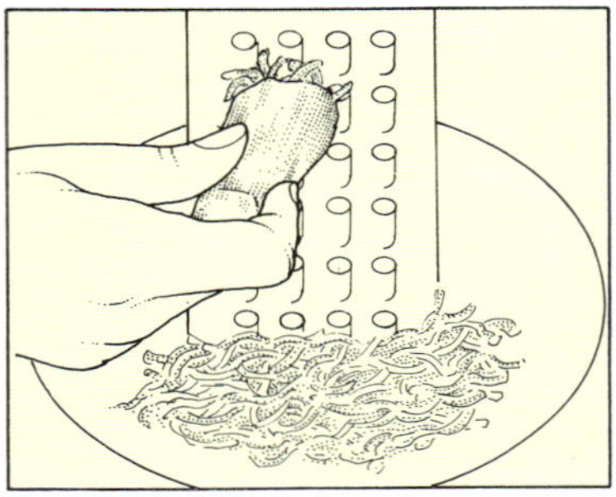

1 Coarsely grate the cucumber on to a plate, sprinkle with salt and leave to stand for 30 minutes.

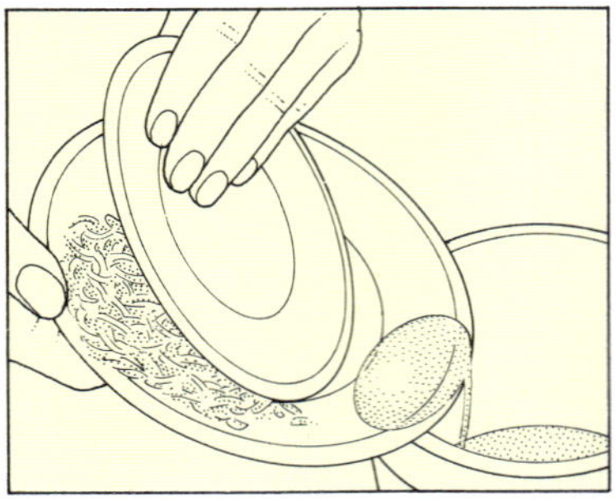

2 Drain well. Then put the yogurt in a small bowl and stir in the chilli powder, ground cumin and cucumber. Season well with salt and pepper and chill in the refrigerator.

3 Serve the cucumber slice and poppadoms, if liked.

Menu Suggestion
Serve with Spicy Lamb Kebabs (page 99) or Seekh Kebab (page 100).

ONION AND TOMATO RAITA

0.10	£	60–90 cals

Serves 4–6

2 firm tomatoes
1 onion, skinned
568 ml (20 oz) natural yogurt, well chilled
15 ml (1 tbsp) finely chopped fresh mint
2.5 ml ($\frac{1}{2}$ tsp) chilli powder
pinch of ground cumin
salt and freshly ground pepper
15 ml (1 tbsp) chopped coriander leaves and poppadoms, to garnish (optional)

1 Cut the tomatoes into quarters, remove the pulp and finely chop the flesh. Finely chop the onion.

2 Put the yogurt in a bowl and stir in the tomato and onion with the mint, chilli powder and cumin. Season well with salt and pepper.

3 Serve garnished with chopped coriander leaves and poppadoms, if liked.

POPPADOMS
Poppadoms are an ideal accompaniment to serve with raita. These round, thin, crisp wafers are difficult to make at home, but ready made, dried varieties can be bought from Indian stores and supermarkets.

Poppadoms are made from rice flour and come either plain or flavoured with chillies or made from various pulse flours and flavoured with chillies and black peppercorns.

Finish off the cooking, at home, by either shallow-frying in oil or grilled, as preferred.

FENNEL AND TOMATO SALAD

0.25 £ 160 cals

Serves 6

90 ml (6 tbsp) vegetable oil or half vegetable, half walnut oil
45 ml (3 tbsp) lemon juice
salt and freshly ground pepper
12 black olives, halved and stoned
450 g (1 lb) Florence fennel
450 g (1 lb) ripe tomatoes

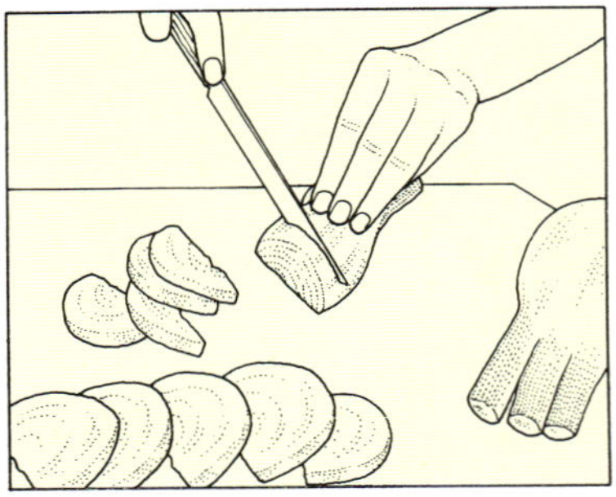

1 In a medium mixing bowl, whisk the oil(s), lemon juice and seasoning together. Add the olives to the dressing.

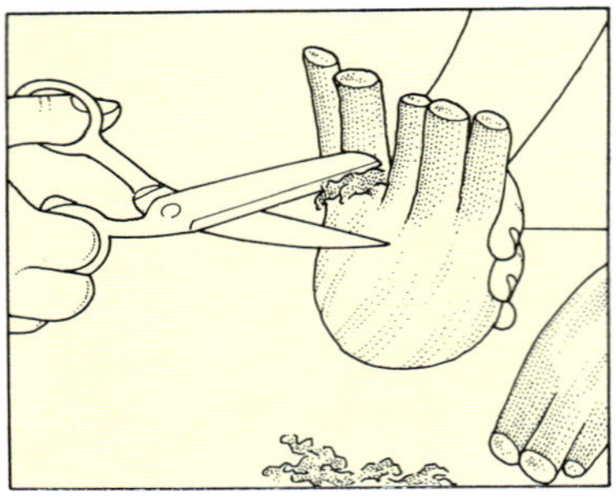

2 Snip off the feathery ends of the fennel and refrigerate them in a polythene bag until required.

3 Halve each blub of fennel lengthways, then slice thinly crossways, discarding the roots. Blanch in boiling salted water for 2–3 minutes, then drain. While it is still warm, stir into the dressing.

4 Leave to cool, cover tightly with cling film and refrigerate until required. Meanwhile, skin and slice the tomatoes and refrigerate covered.

5 Just before serving, arrange the tomatoes and fennel mixture on individual serving plates and snip the fennel tops over them.

Menu Suggestion
Serve with Dressed Crab (page 42).

FENNEL AND TOMATO SALAD

All the ingredients used in this recipe are summery and Mediterranean in flavour – walnut oil, lemon juice, black olives, fennel and tomatoes – and only the freshest, best-quality ingredients should be used if the salad is to taste good.

Florence fennel is a bulbous-looking vegetable with an aniseed – or some say, liquorice – flavour. Do not confuse it with the herb fennel, although they are closely related and have similar flavours. Florence fennel is an unusual vegetable, which can be used raw in salads as here, or it can be cooked in the same way as celery (to which it is also related). In salads, fennel marries well with raw fruits, especially oranges and grapes; it also has a special affinity with walnuts, hence the suggestion in this recipe to use walnut oil in the dressing. Walnut oil comes from France, it is expensive, but well worth the cost for its unique, nutty flavour and thick texture – a little goes a long way. Look for it in good continental delicatessens and specialist kitchen shops and refrigerate it once opened.

TABOULEH

0.40* £ 181–241 cals

* includes 30 minutes soaking

Serves 6–8

225 g (8 oz) burghul (cracked wheat)

4 spring onions, washed and trimmed

1 large bunch fresh parsley, total weight about 125 g (4 oz)

3 large sprigs fresh mint

60 ml (4 tbsp) olive oil

rind and juice of $1\frac{1}{2}$ lemons

salt and freshly ground pepper

few vine or Cos lettuce leaves

lemon wedges and fresh mint sprigs, to garnish

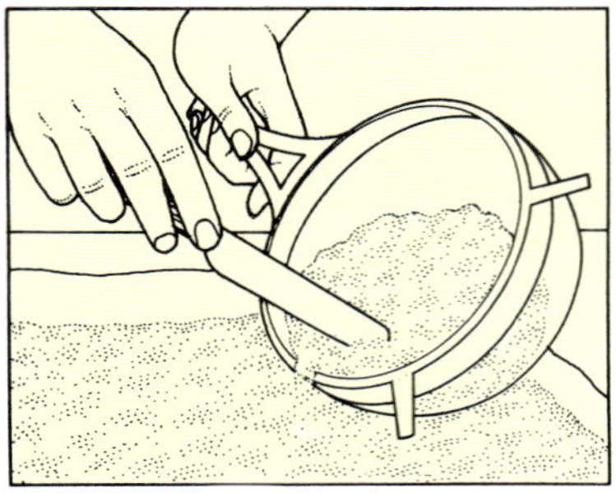

1 Put the burghul in a bowl and add cold water to cover by about 2.5 cm (1 inch). Soak for 30 minutes. Drain well in a sieve, then spread it out on a tea towel and leave to dry.

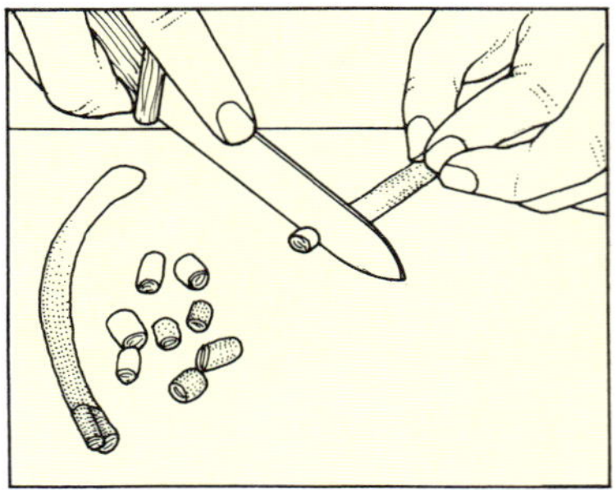

2 Meanwhile, finely chop the spring onions. Then, using a blender or food processor, chop the parsley and mint.

3 Mix the burghul, onion, parsley and mint together in a bowl, add the olive oil, lemon rind and juice and season well to taste.

4 To serve, place the salad on a serving dish lined with lettuce or vine leaves. Garnish with a few lemon slices.

Menu Suggestion
Serve with Spicy Lamb Kebabs (page 99).

MIDDLE EASTERN SALADS

This strange-sounding salad is Lebanese in origin, and there are numerous different versions. All are based on burghul or cracked wheat and all contain masses of parsley and mint, with a dressing of olive oil and lemon juice, although the proportion of these ingredients varies from one cook – and one occasion – to another. Some versions even contain crushed tomatoes, though this is not traditional.

If you can buy or grow the frondy, continental-type parsley for this salad, then so much the better – this is the type that would be used in the Middle East. Curly-leaved English parsley can be used, but it does have a different flavour.

Burghul is available at health food shops – it is whole wheat grain which has been boiled and baked then cracked. It does not need cooking, simply soaking in cold water for 30 minutes until the grains swell.

TABOULEH WITH SALAD VEGETABLES AND YOGURT DRESSING

0.40*	£	108 cals

* includes 30 minutes soaking

Serves 8

225 g (8 oz) burghul (cracked wheat)
3 spring onions, washed and trimmed
½ small cucumber
3 tomatoes
1 green pepper
1 large bunch fresh parsley, total weight about 125 g (4 oz)
3 large sprigs fresh mint
60 ml (4 tbsp) natural yogurt
rind and juice of 1½ lemons
salt and freshly ground pepper
1 Cos lettuce

1 Prepare the burghul as in step 1 opposite. Leave to dry out on a clean tea towel.

2 Meanwhile, finely chop the spring onions, tomatoes and cucumber. Core and finely chop the green pepper. Using a blender or food processor, chop the parsley and lemon.

3 Mix the burghul, vegetables, parsley and mint together in a bowl, add the yogurt, lemon rind and juice and season well to taste.

4 Separate the lettuce leaves and wash under cold running water, drain and pat dry on absorbent kitchen paper. Arrange the lettuce leaves around the edge of a serving dish and pile the salad in the centre.

Menu Suggestion
Serve with Chilli Chicken (page 94).

Fresh Spinach Salad with Hot Bacon Dressing

0.20 £ 305 cals

Serves 4

225 g (8 oz) fresh young spinach, washed and trimmed

2 large slices of white bread

45 ml (3 tbsp) vegetable oil

1 garlic clove, skinned and crushed

8 rashers streaky bacon, rinded and chopped

15 ml (1 tbsp) white wine vinegar

salt and freshly ground pepper

1 Shred any large spinach leaves into small strips and place in a salad bowl. Set aside until required.

2 Make the croûtons. Remove the crusts from the bread and cut the bread into 1-cm ($\frac{1}{2}$-inch) cubes. Put the oil in a frying pan and fry the bread cubes until golden brown.

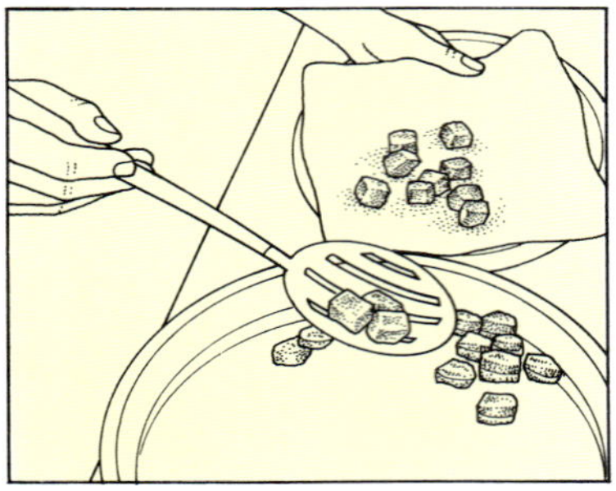

3 Stir the crushed garlic into the bread croûtons, then drain them on absorbent kitchen paper.

4 Add the bacon to the pan and fry for about 5 minutes until crisp and golden brown. Pour the fried bacon and any fat over the spinach leaves.

5 Add the vinegar to the pan, stir well to deglaze, then pour over the salad. Add seasoning, toss quickly, scatter the croûtons on top and serve at once.

Menu Suggestion
Serve with Turkey and Ham Parcels (page 93) or Seekh Kebab Burgers (page 101).

RAW SPINACH
Raw spinach makes a perfect summer salad ingredient – it requires very little preparation and no cooking, therefore very little time needs to be spent in the kitchen. Raw spinach is also excellent from a nutritional point of view: rich in calcium and iron and a good source of vitamins A and C as well as dietary fibre.

This unusual salad, which combines raw and cooked ingredients together in a hot dressing of oil and wine vinegar, is an American idea. Another popular American spinach salad has the same ingredients as this one – but it is served with a creamy blue cheese dressing.

ENDIVE, ORANGE AND WALNUT SALAD

0.30 £ 160 cals

Serves 8

2 endives

6 oranges

25 g (1 oz) walnut pieces

15 ml (1 tbsp) caster sugar

142 ml (5 fl oz) soured cream

60 ml (4 tbsp) vegetable oil

30 ml (2 tbsp) lemon juice

salt and freshly ground pepper

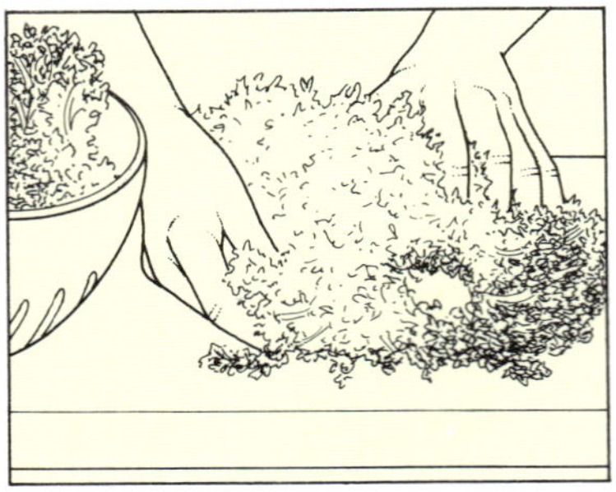

1 Pull the endives apart, wash and dry thoroughly. Tear into pieces and place in a salad bowl. Grate the rind of one orange into a bowl and squeeze in the juice.

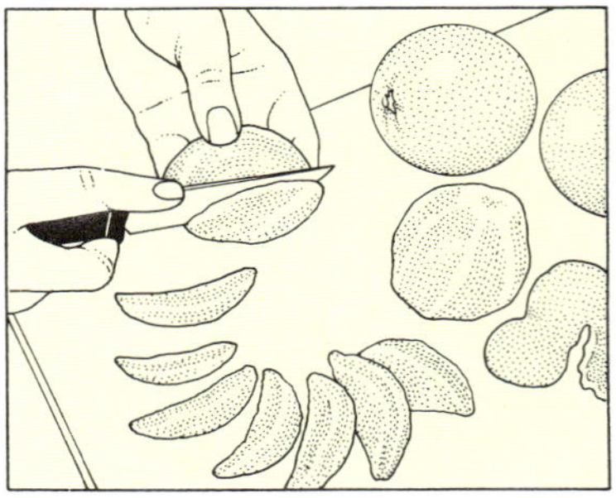

2 Remove peel and white pith from remaining oranges. Segment oranges and add segments to endive. Add the walnuts.

3 Just before serving, combine the sugar, soured cream, reserved orange juice and rind. Beat in the oil gradually and stir in the lemon juice. Season well. Spoon dressing over endives, oranges and walnuts and toss together lightly.

Menu Suggestion
Serve with Courgette Quiche (page 38) or Pan Bagna (page 56).

ENDIVE AND CHICORY

There is always confusion over endive – because in the UK it is called endive, yet in France and the US it is called chicory!

The endive used in this recipe is the large, rather wild-looking salad vegetable; it has crinkly or frondy leaves, which vary in colour from dark green on the outside to pale green, almost yellow, in the very centre.

The flavour of curly endive is rather bitter – like chicory. For this reason it is most successfully used with other ingredients in a mixed salad, and its unusual looks also add interest. The combination of bitter endive with a sweet-tasting fruit such as orange is a good one, as this helps to take the edge off the endive. Adding a little sugar to the dressing ingredients – as in this recipe – also helps.

Like lettuce and most leafy salad vegetables, curly endive does not keep well – its curly fronds quickly go limp and sad-looking. Some greengrocers sell a half endive, or even a quarter, so check before buying because whole heads can be expensive. Store, loosely wrapped in a polythene bag or in a rigid polythene container, in the salad drawer of the refrigerator. Curly endive has too high a water content to freeze successfully.

Barbecues

The distinctive, smoky taste of freshly barbecued food is essentially a summery one. Cooking food over coals isn't difficult and summer barbecue parties are becoming increasingly popular. Wine, chilled beer or a fruit cup make ideal accompaniments. The following dishes, which also include desserts, can also be successfully cooked on a conventional grill.

TURKEY AND HAM PARCELS

2.35* | 242 cals

* includes 2 hours chilling time

Serves 8

700 g (1½ lb) turkey escalopes
8 thin slices of cooked ham
100 g (4 oz) Cotswold cheese
30 ml (2 tbsp) creamed horseradish
salt and freshly ground pepper
20 ml (4 tsp) plain flour
egg, beaten
90 ml (6 tbsp) dried breadcrumbs
vegetable oil
lime slices, to garnish

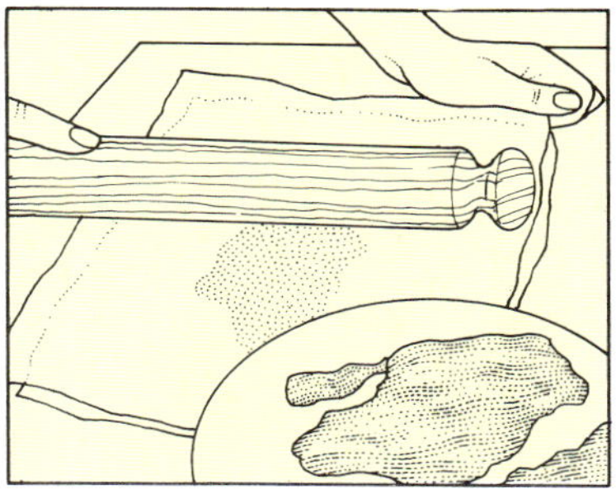

1 Cut the escalopes into sixteen even-sized pieces. Using a rolling pin or meat mallet, bat out thinly between sheets of greaseproof paper.

2 Halve each of the eight slices of ham and cut the cheese into sixteen pieces. Then wrap a piece of cheese, a little creamed horseradish and seasoning in each of the slices of ham.

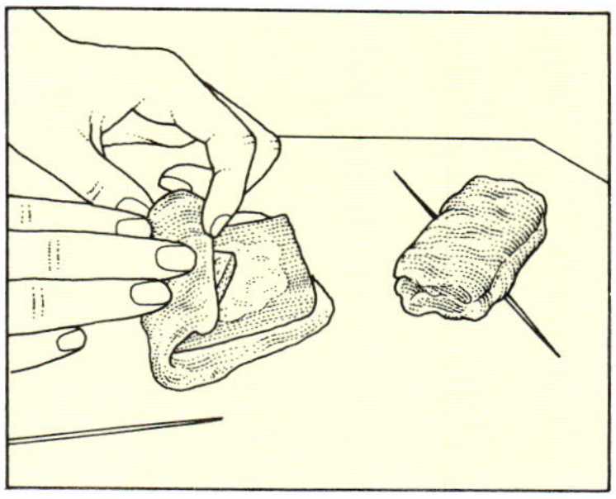

3 Enclose each ham roll in a slice of the turkey meat, securing firmly with wooden cocktail sticks pierced through the centre.

4 Coat the turkey parcels in flour, beaten egg and dried breadcrumbs. Then chill in the refrigerator for at least 2 hours.

5 Brush the turkey and ham parcels with plenty of oil and barbecue or grill them for about 8 minutes on each side. Serve hot, garnished with lime slices.

Menu Suggestion
Serve with Tabbouleh (page 86), Waldorf Salad (page 78) and Peach and Hazelnut Gateau (page 117).

COTSWOLD CHEESE

The Cotswold cheese specified for the filling of Turkey and Ham Parcels may sound unusual; but it is in fact a variety of Double Gloucester – an English semi-hard cheese which is now widely available in supermarkets and delicatessens. Cotswold is Double Gloucester flavoured with chopped onions and chives; it has a rich, golden colour, a velvety texture and a slightly sharp, tangy flavour. Like Cheddar, all Double Gloucester cheeses are excellent in cooking for their melting qualities.

CHILLI CHICKEN

0.35* £ ✱* 70 cals

* plus at least 4 hours marinating; freeze in marinade, before cooking

Serves 4

8 chicken drumsticks
150 ml ($\frac{1}{4}$ pint) vegetable oil
4 garlic cloves, skinned and roughly chopped
$\frac{1}{2}$ onion, skinned and chopped
45 ml (3 tbsp) natural yogurt
15 ml (1 tbsp) tomato purée
5 ml (1 tsp) ground turmeric
2.5 ml ($\frac{1}{2}$ tsp) chilli powder
2.5 ml ($\frac{1}{2}$ tsp) salt

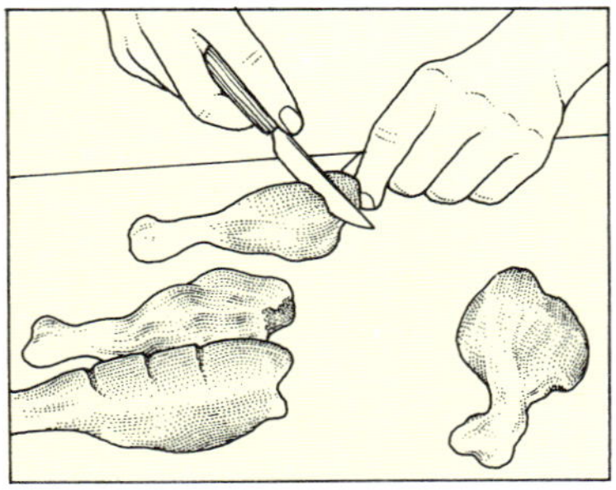

1 Skin the drumsticks, then slash the flesh with a sharp, pointed knife. Make the marinade. Blend the remaining ingredients in a blender or food processor to a smooth purée.

2 Put the drumsticks in a single layer in a shallow container, then pour over the marinade. Cover and leave for at least 4 hours, preferably overnight. Turn drumsticks occasionally and baste with the marinade.

3 Put the drumsticks on the barbecue and grill for 20 minutes, turning them frequently and basting them with the marinade until nicely charred on all sides. Serve hot or cold.

Menu Suggestion
Serve with Gazpacho (page 20), Caesar Salad (page 76) and Frosted Mint Cheesecake (page 111).

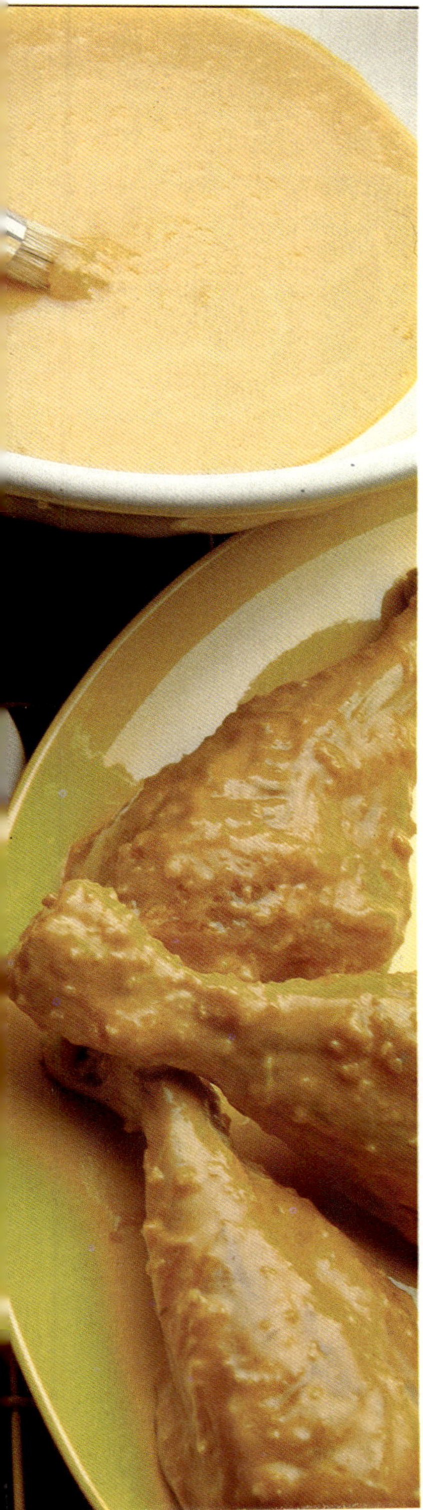

BARBECUED SPARE RIBS

1.35 | £ | 309 cals

Serves 4

- 1.8 kg (4 lb) American pork spare ribs
- 1 onion, skinned and sliced
- 350 ml (12 fl oz) tomato juice
- 45 ml (3 tbsp) cider vinegar
- 30 ml (2 tbsp) clear honey
- 10 ml (2 tsp) salt
- 5 ml (1 tsp) paprika
- 3.75 ml ($\frac{3}{4}$ tsp) chilli powder

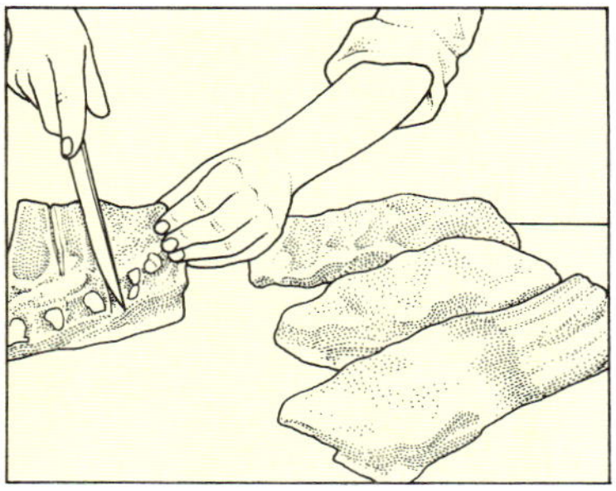

1 Divide the spare ribs into portions of two or three ribs each. Put them all in a large flameproof casserole or saucepan, add the onion and cover with cold water.

2 Bring to the boil, reduce the heat, cover and simmer for 1 hour or until almost tender. Drain and cover until required. Make the sauce. Mix all the remaining ingredients in a bowl together.

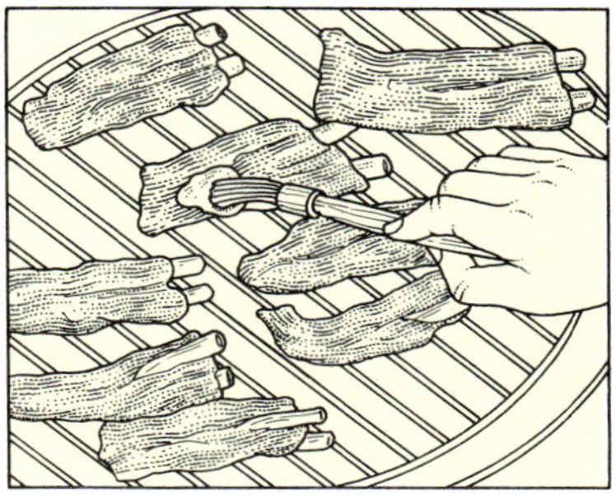

3 Put the spare ribs on the barbecue and brush with sauce. Cook for 20 minutes until tender; brush with sauce and turn occasionally. Heat remaining sauce to serve separately.

Menu Suggestion
Serve with Chilled Pea and Mint Soup (page 15) and Early Summer Pudding (page 115).

BARBECUED AUBERGINE DIP

0.40* £ 199 cals

* plus 2–3 hours chilling

Serves 4

2 large aubergines, wiped

3 garlic cloves, skinned

salt

about 150 ml ($\frac{1}{4}$ pint) tahini (paste of finely ground sesame seeds)

juice of about 3 lemons

coriander leaves, black olives and lemon wedges, to garnish

hot pitta bread, to serve

1 Place the aubergines on the barbecue and grill for about 20 minutes until the skin blisters and chars and the flesh feels soft. Turn the aubergines constantly.

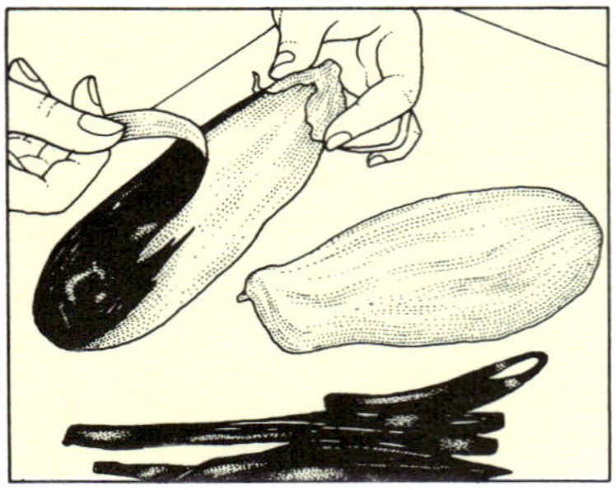

2 Remove from the heat and leave until cool enough to handle. Then carefully peel off the skins and discard them.

3 Put the aubergine flesh in a blender or food processor and blend to form smooth purée. Alternatively, push it through a sieve

4 Crush the garlic with salt, then add to the aubergine flesh. Add half the tahini paste and the juice of $1\frac{1}{2}$ lemons and work again until evenly incorporated.

5 Taste the dip and add a little more tahini paste and lemon juice. Continue adding tahini and lemon gradually until the flavour is to your liking. Add more salt if liked.

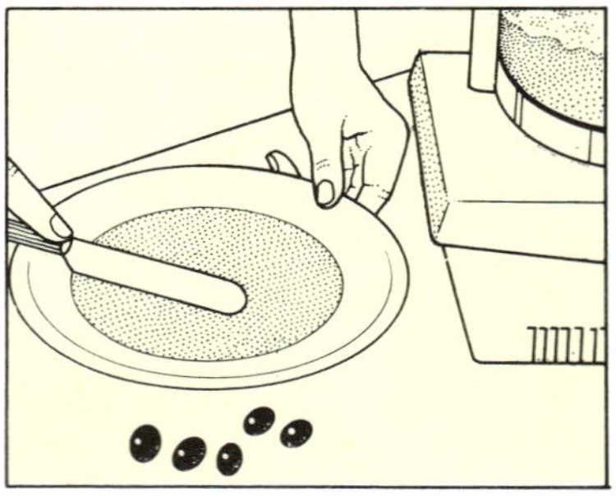

6 Turn the dip into a shallow serving bowl and smooth the surface. Garnish with coriander and olives and refrigerate for 2–3 hours until serving time. Serve with hot pitta bread cooked on the barbecue.

Menu Suggestion
Serve with Barbecued Spare Ribs (page 95) and Strawberrry and Orange Mousse (page 119).

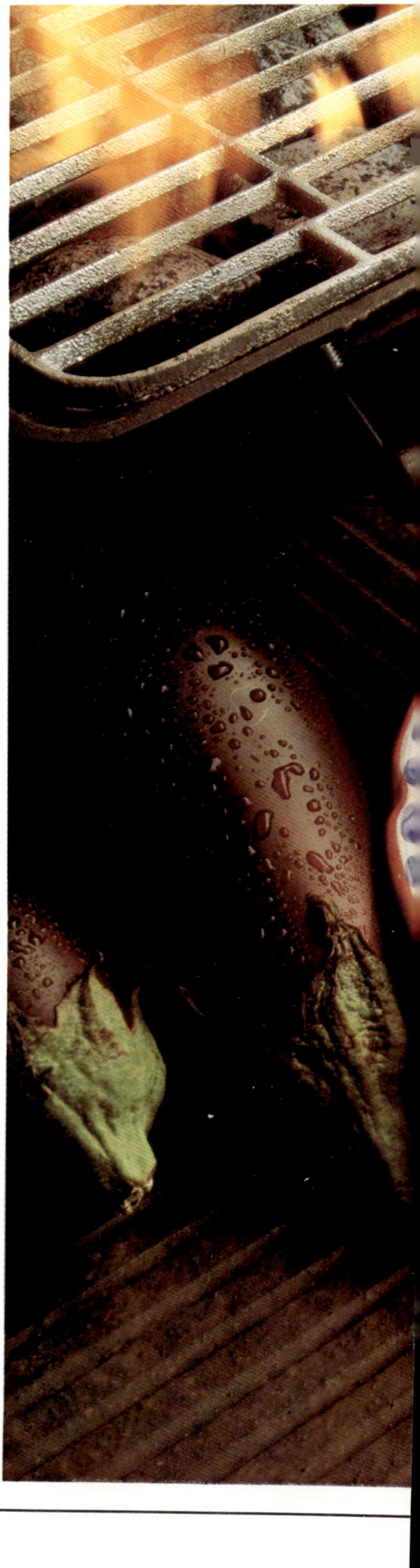

AUBERGINE DIP
A recipe from the Middle East, where it is called *baba ghanoush* or *papa ghanooye*, this Barbecued Aubergine Dip has a wonderfully smoky flavour and creamy texture. In the Middle East it is served as part of the *mezze* at the beginning of a meal, but you can serve it on its own as a starter—with hot pitta bread.

Although cooking the aubergines on the barbecue gives the dip its smoky flavour, this is not absolutely essential – the tahini paste made from finely ground sesame seeds is fairly strong. If you find it more convenient, grill the aubergines until their skins char and blister, taking care to watch them all the time they are under the grill and turning them frequently so they do not burn.

SPICY LAMB KEBABS

0.45* | 516 cals

* plus 2–3 hours marinating

Makes 8

700 g ($1\frac{1}{2}$ lb) boned leg of lamb
450 g (1 lb) courgettes
8 tomatoes, halved
1 large corn on the cob
8 shallots
salt
142 g (5 oz) natural yogurt
1 garlic clove, skinned and crushed
2 bay leaves, crumbled
15 ml (1 tbsp) lemon juice
15 ml (1 tbsp) vegetable oil
5 ml (1 tsp) ground allspice
15 ml (1 tbsp) coriander seeds
freshly ground pepper
lemon wedges, to garnish

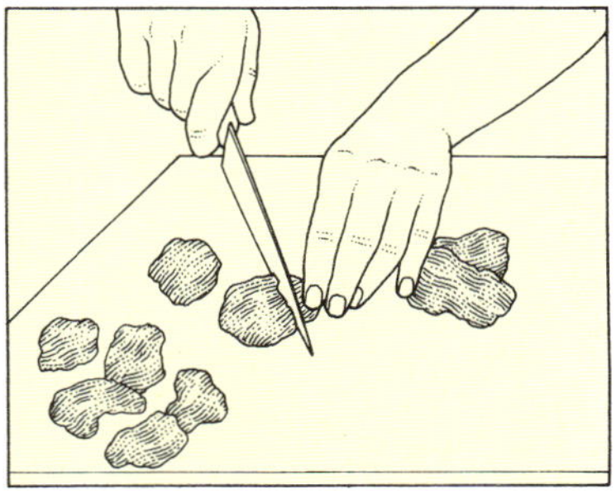

1 Using a sharp knife, cut the lamb into 2.5-cm (1-inch) cubes, making sure to trim off any excess fat from the meat.

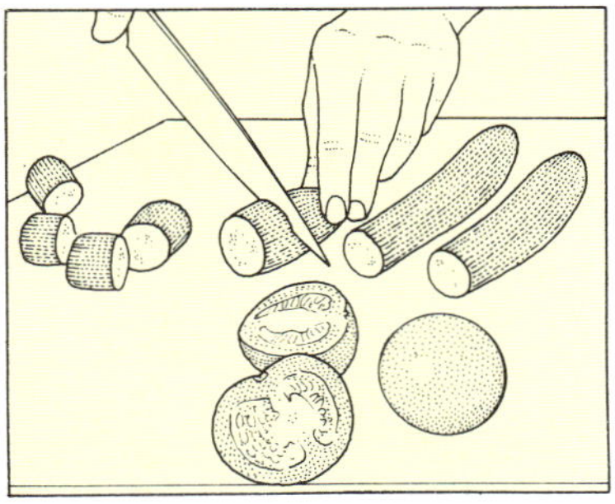

2 Cut the courgettes into 0.5-cm ($\frac{1}{4}$-inch) slices, discarding the tops and tails. Halve the tomatoes.

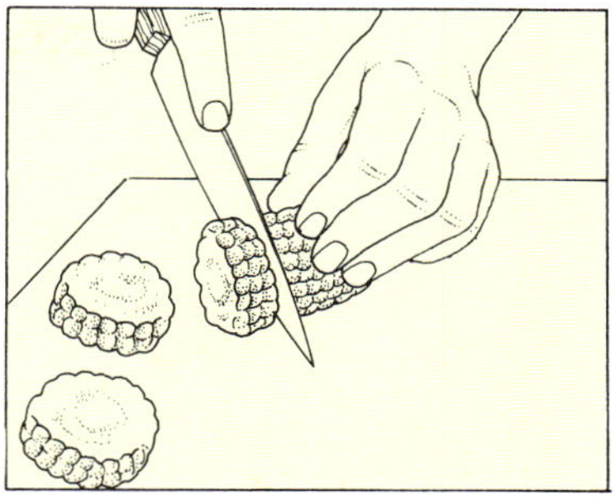

3 Cut the corn into eight slices. Blanch in boiling salted water, drain well and set aside.

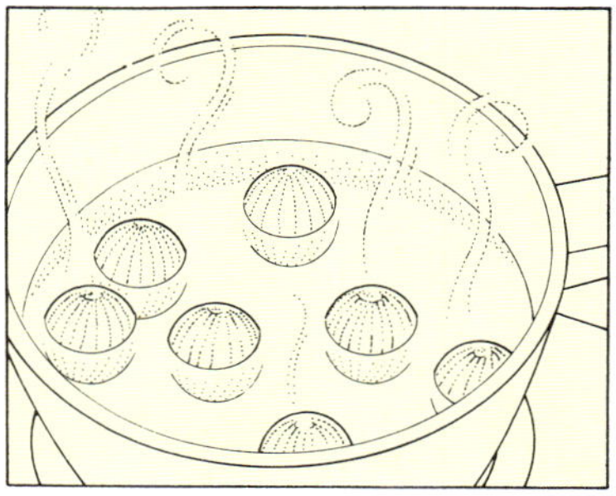

4 Blanch the shallots in boiling, salted water, skin and set aside. Make the marinade. Pour the yogurt into a shallow dish and stir in garlic, bay leaves, lemon juice, oil, allspice, coriander seeds and seasoning.

5 Thread the lamb cubes on to eight skewers with courgettes, tomatoes, corn and shallots. Place in dish, spoon over marinade, cover and leave for 2–3 hours, turning once to ensure even coating.

6 Cook the kebabs for about 15–20 minutes, turning and brushing with the marinade occasionally. To serve, spoon remaining marinade over the kebabs and garnish.

Menu Suggestion
Serve with Barbecued Aubergine Dip (page 96) and Barbecued Bananas (page 106).

SEEKH KEBAB

0.25* £ 199 cals

* plus at least 1 hour chilling time

Serves 4

450 g (1 lb) raw lean lamb, finely minced

1 large onion, skinned and grated

2 garlic cloves, skinned and crushed

1 green chilli, seeded and finely chopped

5 ml (1 tsp) ground cumin

2.5 ml ($\frac{1}{2}$ tsp) salt

2.5 ml ($\frac{1}{2}$ tsp) freshly ground pepper

grated rind and juice of 1 lemon or lime

vegetable oil

lime wedges, to garnish

hot pitta bread, to serve

1 Thoroughly blend all ingredients except oil in a bowl. Lightly cover and chill for at least an hour. Lightly grease four flat skewers with oil.

2 Divide the meat mixture into sixteen pieces and shape into thin strips about 10 cm (4 inches) long. Roll up the meat, or form it into tight balls.

3 Place four meat rolls on each skewer and brush each of the rolls lightly with vegetable oil.

4 Barbecue or cook under a grill for about 10 minutes, turning frequently for even browning. Serve garnished with lime wedges. These are excellent eaten in the pocket of pitta bread.

Menu Suggestion
Serve with Cucumber Raita (page 82), Tabouleh (page 86) and Blackcurrant Sorbet (page 120).

SEEKH KEBAB BURGERS

0.25* £ 383 cals

* plus at least 1 hour chilling

Serves 4

seekh kebab mixture (see opposite)

50 g (2 oz) basmati or long-grain rice

30 ml (2 tbsp) chopped fresh coriander leaves

salt and freshly ground pepper

vegetable oil

4 pitta bread, to serve

Cos lettuce to garnish

1 Prepare the kebab mixture as in step 2 of the recipe opposite and chill for at least 1 hour. Meanwhile prepare the filling. Cook the rice as directed on the packet. Drain well then stir in the coriander and seasonings.

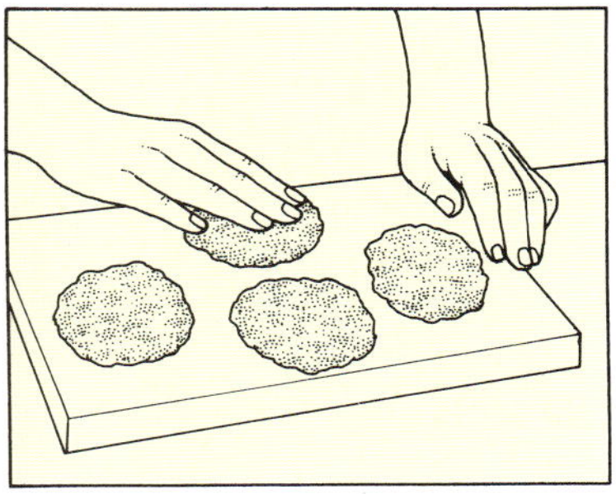

2 Divide the meat mixture into eight portions. Put four portions on a board and pat them out into flat, round burger shapes.

3 Divide the filling mixture into four; place equally on top of each burger. Flatten the remaining portions of beef mixture, then place on top of the filling.

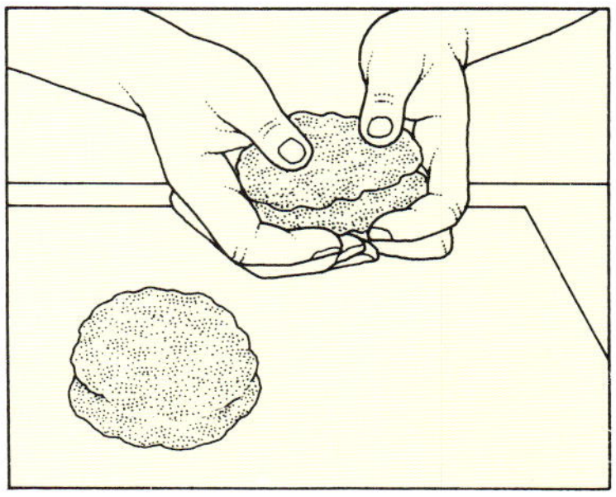

4 With your hands, mould the beef mixture around the filling and press it well to enclose it completely.

5 Place the burgers on the barbecue and brush each lightly with vegetable oil. Grill for about 10 minutes, turning them once during this time to ensure even cooking.

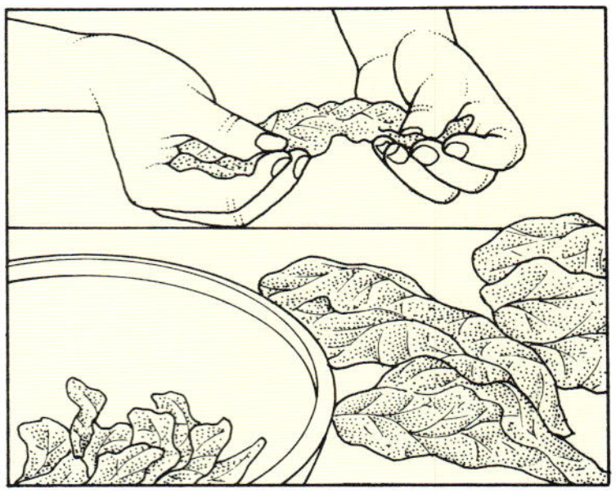

6 Meanwhile, separate the lettuce leaves and wash under cold running water; drain and pat dry on absorbent kitchen paper. Finely shred the lettuce with a knife.

7 Serve the burgers hot, in a pocket of pitta bread lined with shredded lettuce.

Menu Suggestion
Serve with Potted Shrimps (page 25), Ratatouille (page 68) and Fruit Kebabs with Yogurt and Honey Dip (page 108).

BASS ON THE BARBECUE

1.00* ££ ✳* 478 cals

* plus 2–3 hours chilling time; freeze before cooking

Serves 4

100 g (4 oz) unsalted butter
20 ml (4 tsp) dried dillweed
finely grated rind and juice of 1 lemon
salt and freshly ground pepper
1.5-kg (3-lb) sea bass, cleaned
75 ml (3 fl oz) dry white wine
lemon slices and dill sprigs, to garnish

1 Work the butter with the dill-weed, lemon rind and salt and pepper to taste. Form into a roll, wrap in foil and chill in the refrigerator for 2–3 hours until firm.

2 Cut a sheet of foil large enough to enclose the fish. Place the fish in the centre of the foil.

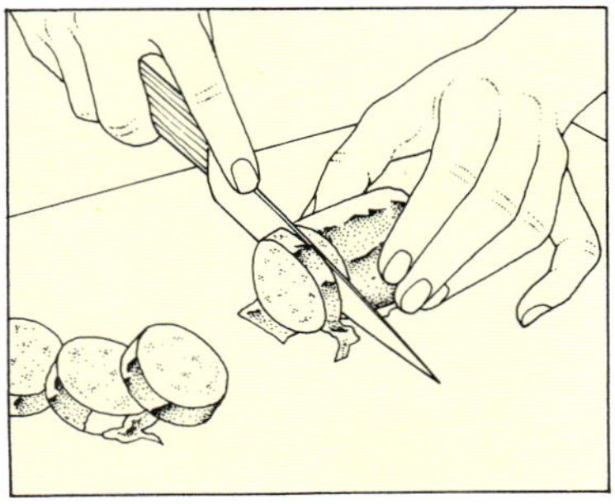

3 Using a sharp knife, cut the flavoured butter into slices. Peel off and discard foil after cutting.

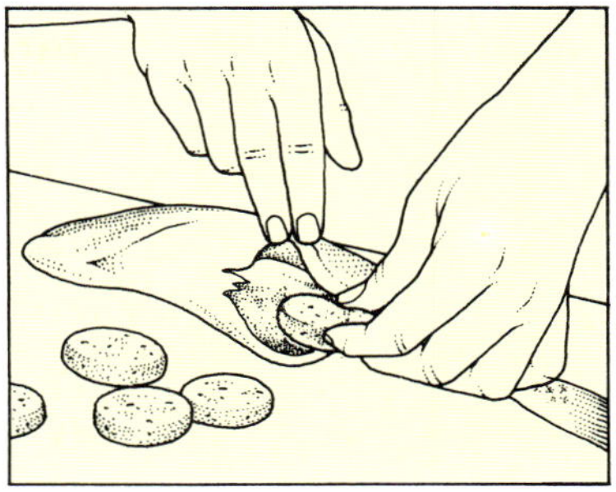

4 Place the butter slices inside the belly of the fish. Sprinkle the outside of the fish with salt and pepper, then slowly pour over the wine and lemon juice.

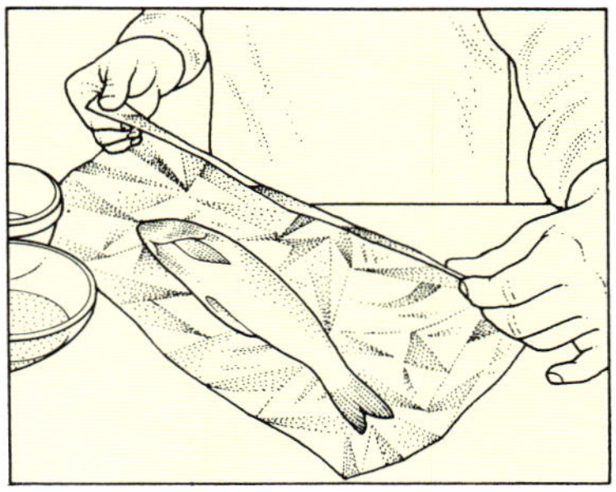

5 Fold the foil over the fish to form a loose package so that the wine and juices do not leak out. Place the foil package on the barbecue and grill for 45 minutes. Serve hot, straight from the foil, garnished with a few lemon slices and fresh dill sprigs.

Menu Suggestion
Serve with Chicken Liver Pâté (page 21), Potato Salad (page 83) and Late Summer Pudding (page 114).

Chicken and Beef Satay with Peanut Sauce

0.35* £ £ ✳ 594 cals

* plus 4 hours marinating

Serves 4

2 boneless chicken breast fillets, about 350 g (12 oz) total weight
350 g (12 oz) flash-fry steak
5 ml (1 tsp) coriander seeds
5 ml (1 tsp) cumin seeds
1 onion, skinned and chopped
60 ml (4 tbsp) tamarind liquid (see box, opposite)
30 ml (2 tbsp) soy sauce
2 garlic cloves, skinned and crushed
30 ml (2 tbsp) vegetable oil
5 ml (1 tsp) ground turmeric
5 ml (1 tsp) 5-spice powder
salt
100 g (4 oz) crunchy peanut butter
100 g (4 oz) creamed coconut, crumbled
300 ml (½ pint) boiling water
20 ml (4 tsp) lemon juice
15 ml (1 tbsp) soft brown sugar
2.5–5 ml (½–1 tsp) chilli powder

1 Prepare the satay. Using a sharp knife, cut the chicken and the flash-fry steak into small chunks. Set aside.

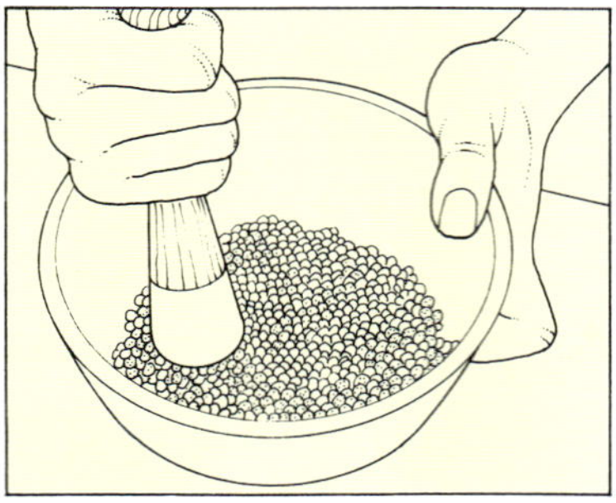

2 Heat a small frying pan, add the coriander and cumin and fry over dry heat for 1–2 minutes, stirring constantly. Remove from the heat and pound to a fine powder in a mortar and pestle.

3 Put the pounded spices in a blender or food processor with the onion, tamarind liquid, 15 ml (1 tbsp) soy sauce, garlic, vegetable oil, turmeric, 5-spice powder and a pinch of salt. Work for a few seconds, then pour over the meat. Cover and leave to marinate for 4 hours, turning the meat occasionally during this time.

4 Thread the meat on oiled wooden sticks, keeping the chicken and beef separate if liked. Place on the barbecue and grill for 10–15 minutes, turning frequently and basting with any remaining marinade.

5 Meanwhile, make the peanut sauce. Put the peanut butter, coconut, water, lemon juice, 15 ml (1 tbsp) soy sauce, sugar and chilli powder in a pan and bring slowly to the boil, stirring constantly. Lower the heat and simmer gently for about 5 minutes until the coconut has dissolved and the sauce thickens. Taste and adjust seasoning according to taste.

6 Serve the satay sticks hot on a platter, with a small bowl of peanut sauce for dipping.

Menu Suggestion
Serve with Crudités with Aïoli (page 26), Indonesian Fruit and Vegetable Salad (page 80) and Iced Strawberry Meringues (page 126).

SATAY

Satay is a Malaysian dish, which is usually served as a starter on wooden sticks, with the sauce for dipping. Although metal kebab skewers can be used, wooden ones are more authentic; they are available from oriental specialist shops. Remember to soak them in cold water for 2 hours before using – this helps prevent them setting alight on the barbecue!

Tamarind pulp and 5-spice powder are also available at oriental shops. Make tamarind liquid by soaking a 2.5-cm (1-inch) piece of tamarind pulp in about 100 ml (3 fl oz) hot water for a few minutes, then squeezing the pulp to extract as much liquid as possible. Discard the pulp.

In Malaysia, the traditional accompaniments to satay are wedges of unpeeled cucumber, spring onions and cubes of rice cake, which is made by boiling glutinous rice, then pressing it until it can be cut like a cake. Although not authentic, cubes of bean curd (available at health food shops as well as oriental stores) may be served instead of rice cake.

BARBECUED BANANAS

0.30 £ 223 cals

Serves 4

4 large bananas
60 ml (4 tbsp) dark rum
50 g (2 oz) demerara sugar
grated rind and juice of 1 large orange
2.5 ml ($\frac{1}{2}$ tsp) ground cinnamon
25 g (1 oz) butter or margarine
orange slices, to decorate
pouring cream or vanilla ice cream, to serve

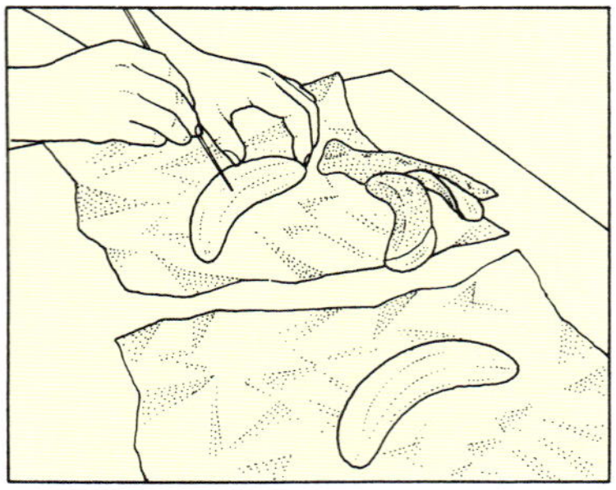

1 Cut four large rectangles of foil. Peel the bananas, then place one on each piece of foil. Prick them in several places with a fine skewer.

2 Mix together the rum, sugar, orange juice and cinnamon. Pour slowly over the bananas, dividing it equally between them. Dot with the butter.

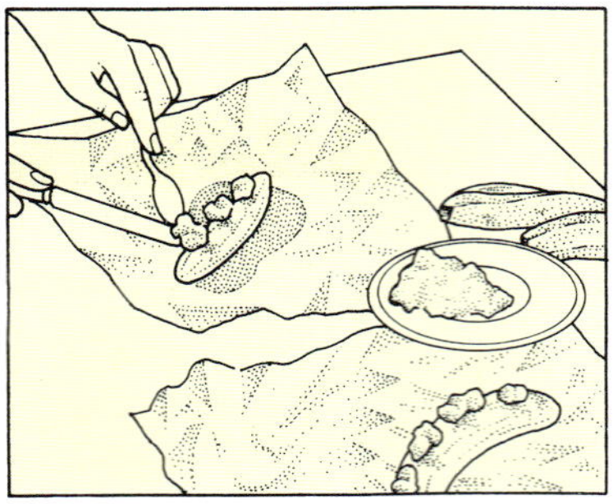

3 Bring the two long sides of the foil up over one banana, then fold the join over several times to seal thoroughly.

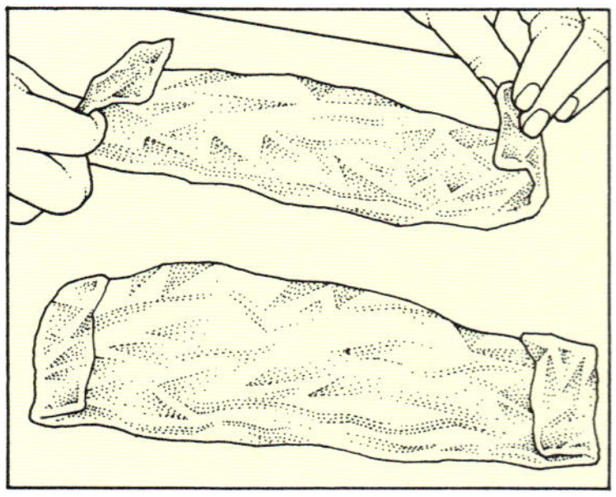

4 Fold up the ends of the foil so that the banana is enclosed completely and the juices cannot run out during cooking. Repeat with the remaining three bananas.

5 Place the parcels on the barbecue and grill for 15 minutes, turning them once during this time.

6 To serve, open the parcels carefully and transfer the bananas to individual serving dishes. Pour over the juices which have collected in the foil and decorate with orange rind and orange slices.

Menu Suggestion
Serve with Mozzarella, Avocado and Tomato Salad (page 18) and Spicy Lamb Kebabs (page 99).

BANANAS
There is an Indian legend that bananas were the 'forbidden fruit'. True or not, today they must be one of the most popular fruits in the world. Easy to eat and available at all times of year, they are also highly nutritious, rich in vitamins A, B and C.

The beauty of this recipe for Barbecued Bananas is that they can be parcelled up well in advance of a barbecue party, so that all you have to do when you want to serve them is pop them on the grid.

Fruit Kebabs with Yogurt and Honey Dip

1.15* £ £ 298 cals

* includes 30 minutes marinating

Serves 4

1 small pineapple
3 large firm peaches
2 large firm bananas
3 crisp eating apples
1 small bunch large black grapes, seeded
finely grated rind and juice of 1 large orange
60 ml (4 tbsp) brandy, or orange-flavoured liqueur
50 g (2 oz) unsalted butter, melted
200 ml (7 fl oz) natural yogurt
45 ml (3 tbsp) clear honey
few fresh mint sprigs

YOGURT AND HONEY
The combination of natural yogurt and honey is popular all over Greece, Turkey and the Middle East. Served on its own or with fresh fruit as in this sweet kebab recipe, it is most refreshing in hot climates.

When choosing natural yogurt, check the label on the carton carefully: there are many different varieties now available. All are suitable for this dip, choose according to your own personal taste.

Yogurt labelled 'live' means that it contains live bacteria, and that a special culture (or starter) has been used. Bulgarian and Greek 'live' yogurts are noted for being thick and creamy, although they can be tangy in flavour. Yogurt labelled simply 'natural', is always unsweetened; sometimes it is made with whole milk, sometimes it is low-fat—check the small print carefully. Natural set yogurt is very thick, as its name suggests; it is also sometimes called 'thick set' or 'dairy yogurt'. All the thick-set yogurts are made with whole milk.

1 Prepare the fruit. Cut the top and bottom off the pineapple. Stand the fruit upright on a board. Using a large, sharp knife, slice downwards in sections to remove the skin and 'eyes'. Slice off the flesh, leaving the core. Then cut the flesh into small cubes.

2 Skin and halve the peaches and remove the stones. Cut the flesh into chunks.

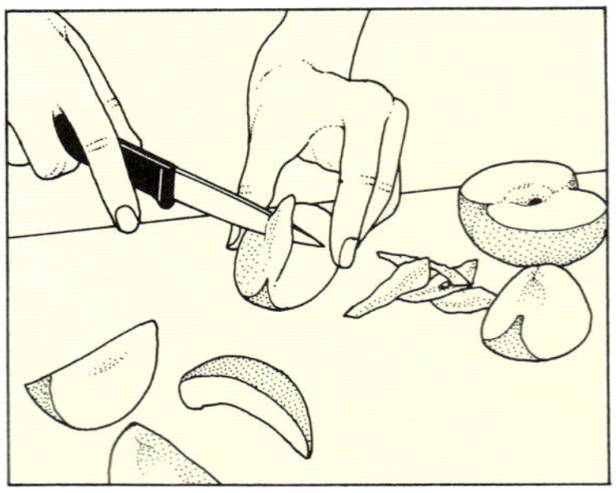

3 Peel the bananas and then slice them into thick chunks. Quarter and core the apples, but do not skin them.

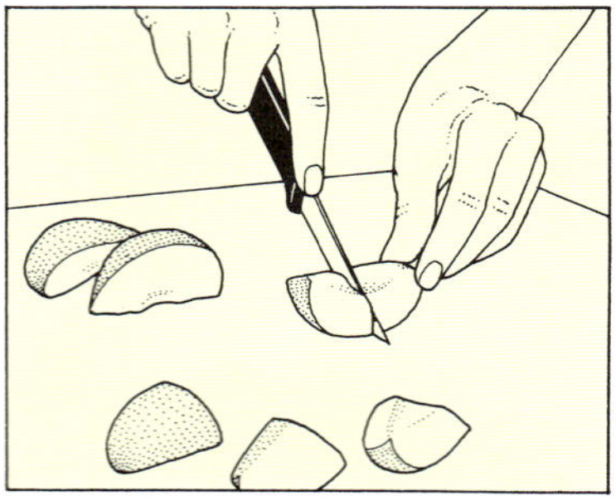

4 Cut each quarter in half crossways. Then put all the fruit together in a bowl. Mix together the orange rind and juice and the brandy or liqueur. Pour over the fruit, cover and leave for at least 30 minutes.

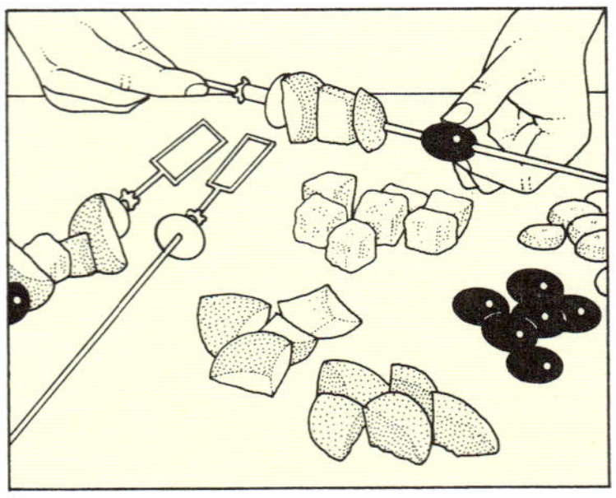

5 Thread the fruit on to kebab skewers, then brush with the melted butter. Place on the barbecue and grill for 10–15 minutes, turning and basting frequently during this time.

6 Meanwhile, make the dip. Whisk together the yogurt and 30 ml (2 tbsp) of the honey. Pour into a serving bowl and drizzle over the remaining 15 ml (1 tbsp) of honey. Garnish with a few fresh mint sprigs.

7 Serve the fruit kebabs as soon as possible after barbecuing, with the yogurt dip handed separately in a small bowl.

Menu Suggestion
Serve with Pasta, Prawn and Apple Salad (page 79) and Chilli Chicken (page 94).

Desserts

Fresh summer fruits – apricots, blackcurrants, cherries, peaches, raspberries and strawberries – make even the simplest of recipes taste wonderful. Ice-cool and refreshing they must be, and here's a mouthwatering selection for you to choose from. None take long to prepare, and most can be cooked ahead of time, so you can relax and enjoy yourself at the end of the meal.

FROSTED MINT CHEESECAKE

1.55* | ◻ ◻ £ | 436 cals

* plus 8 hours freezing and 45 minutes chilling; freeze after step 5

Serves 6

75 g (3 oz) butter or margarine
150 g (5 oz) caster sugar
100 g (4 oz) plain flour
225 g (8 oz) full fat soft cheese
142 g (5 oz) natural yogurt
75 ml (5 tbsp) mint-flavoured liqueur
30 ml (2 tbsp) water
7.5 ml ($1\frac{1}{2}$ tsp) gelatine
1 egg white
fresh mint, to decorate

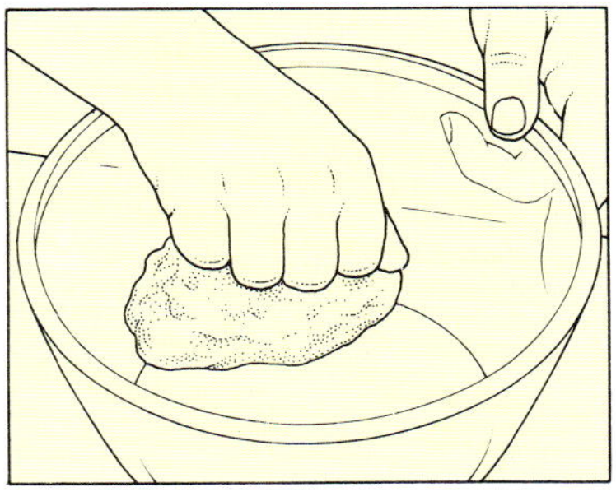

1 Make the shortbread mixture. Cream butter with 50 g (2 oz) caster sugar until smooth. Stir in the flour and knead the mixture until it is smooth.

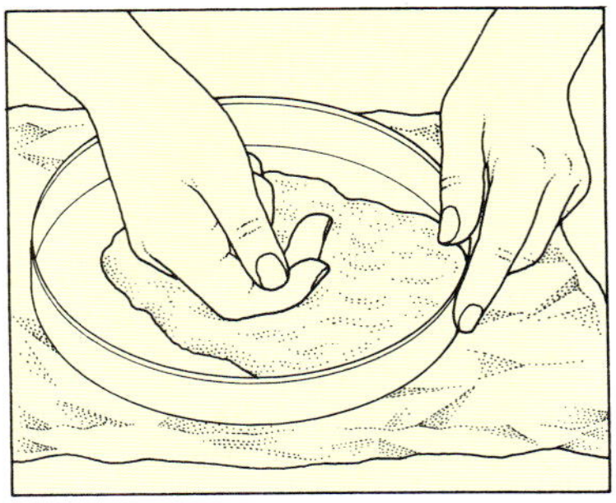

2 Press the shortbread mixture into the base of a 20.5-cm (8-inch) flan ring, placed on a foil-lined baking sheet. Bake in the oven at 180°C (350°F) mark 4 for 18–20 minutes; cool in ring.

3 Meanwhile, beat the cheese with a wooden spoon until smooth, gradually whisk in the yogurt, 25 g (1 oz) sugar and mint-flavoured liqueur.

4 Place the water in a bowl and sprinkle in the gelatine. Stand the bowl over a saucepan of hot water and heat gently until dissolved. Leave to cool slightly, then stir into the cheese mixture. Whisk the egg white until stiff, then fold into cheesecake mixture.

5 Pour the mixture over the shortbread base. Open freeze for about 8 hours or overnight, then ease off the flan ring. Wrap with foil when firm and return to the freezer until required.

6 About 1 hour before serving, remove the cheesecake from the freezer, and place on a serving plate.

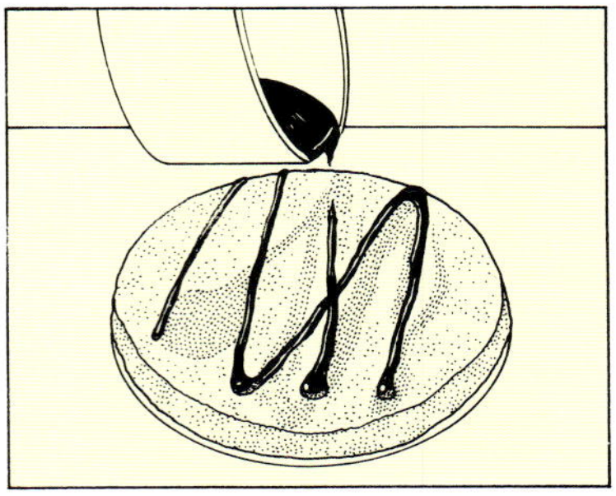

7 Warm the remaining sugar until it caramelises, then pour over the cheesecake in a lattice pattern. Place in the refrigerator for 45 minutes before serving. Decorate with mint.

Menu Suggestion
Serve with Artichokes à la grècque (page 9) and Devilled Duckling Salad (page 45).

COEURS À LA CRÈME

0.20* £ £ 325–487 cals

* plus overnight draining

Serves 4–6

225 g (8 oz) cottage cheese

25 g (1 oz) caster sugar

300 ml (10 fl oz) double cream

5 ml (1 tsp) lemon juice

2 egg whites, stiffly whisked

150 ml (5 fl oz) single cream, and fresh raspberries or strawberries, to serve

1 Press the cottage cheese through a nylon sieve into a bowl. Add sugar and mix well.

2 Whip the cream until stiff then add the lemon juice. Mix into the cheese and sugar mixture.

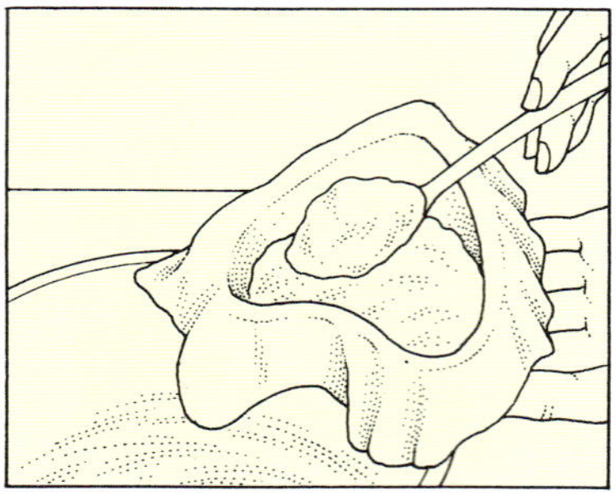

3 Line 4 or 6 small heart-shaped moulds with muslin (this is unnecessary if serving in the moulds). Fold stiffly whisked egg whites into cheese mixture. Spoon mixture into moulds. Drain overnight in refrigerator. Serve with cream and fruit.

Menu Suggestion
Serve with Asparagus Maltaise (page 22) and Smoked Chicken and Avocado Salad (page 29).

LATE SUMMER PUDDING

0.20* £ ✱ 271 cals

* plus overnight chilling

Serves 6

450 g (1 lb) mixed fruits (e.g. blackcurrants, blackberries, redcurrants, raspberries)

30 ml (2 tbsp) water

150 g (5 oz) sugar

100–175 g (4–6 oz) white bread, thinly sliced

whipped cream, to serve

1 Strig the blackcurrants. Hull the blackberries. Place the fruits in a colander and wash under cold running water.

2 Stir the water and sugar together and bring slowly to the boil, add the fruits and stew gently for 5–10 minutes, until they are soft but retain their shape.

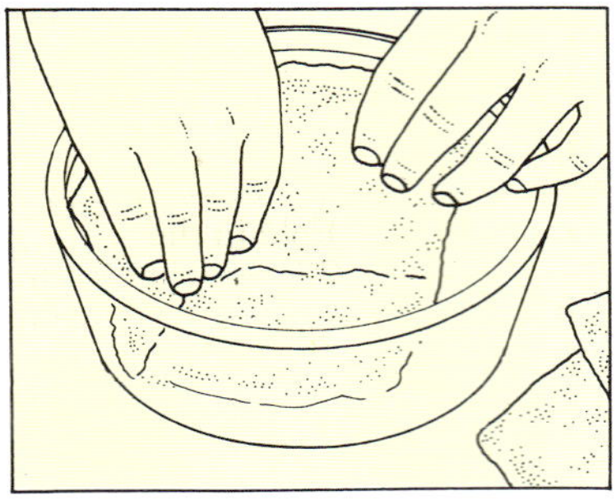

3 Cut the crusts from the bread and line the base and sides of a 900-ml ($1\frac{1}{2}$-pint) pudding basin with the slices so that there are no spaces between them.

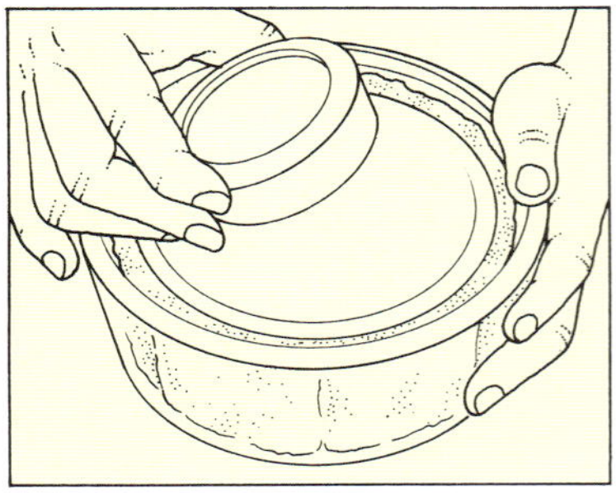

4 Pour in the fruit and completely cover with more slices of bread. Place a saucer with a weight on it on top of the pudding and refrigerate overnight. To serve, turn out on to a flat plate and serve with whipped cream.

Menu Suggestion

Serve with Salmon Mousse (page 16) and Salmagundy (page 56).

SUMMER PUDDING

Summer pudding – made with freshly picked red and black fruits – is *the* traditional English pudding for hot summer days. Served outside at a summer lunch party, with lashings of fresh whipped cream, nothing could be more perfect.

The combination of fruits for summer pudding is a matter of personal choice and availability. Traditionally, two fruits should be used, and these are usually redcurrants and raspberries, although these days blackcurrants, blackberries, loganberries and strawberries are also often included.

If you have some juice left over when putting the fruit into the bread-lined basin, save it until serving time. When you turn the pudding out onto its serving plate, you may find that some of the bread slices show white, in which case spoon over reserved fruit juice to cover any gaps.

EARLY SUMMER PUDDING WITH CHANTILLY CREAM

0.30* £ ✳* 451 cals*

* plus overnight chilling; freeze pudding only; calories include Cream

Serves 4

450 g (1 lb) mixed redcurrants, cherries and raspberries

30 ml (2 tbsp) water

150 g (5 oz) sugar

100–175 g (4–6 oz) white bread, thinly sliced

15 ml (1 tbsp) Kirsch

150 ml (5 fl oz) double cream

½ an egg white

15 g (½ oz) icing sugar

vanilla flavouring

1 Strig the redcurrants. Stone the cherries. Hull the raspberries. Place the fruits in a colander and wash under cold water.

2 Cook the fruits as indicated in step 2, opposite. Line the pudding basin with bread as indicated in step 3.

3 Add the fruit and liqueur and cover with more slices of bread. Place a saucer with a weight on it on top of the pudding; refrigerate overnight.

4 Lightly whip the cream. In a separated bowl, whisk the egg white until stiff. Fold in the whipped cream. Sift the icing sugar into the bowl and then fold in with a few drops of vanilla. Chill.

5 To serve, turn the pudding out on to a flat plate and serve with the chantilly cream.

Menu Suggestion
Serve with Potted Prawn Pâté (page 24) and Vitello Tonnato (page 40).

PEACH AND HAZELNUT GÂTEAU

1.15* £ £ ✱* 342 cals
* plus 2–3 hours chilling; freeze undecorated
Serves 8
175 g (6 oz) caster sugar
75 g (3 oz) plain flour, sifted
3 eggs
finely grated rind and juice of 1 lemon
75 g (3 oz) toasted hazelnuts, ground
300 ml ($\frac{1}{2}$ pint) water
700 g ($1\frac{1}{2}$ lb) medium peaches
300 ml (10 fl oz) whipping cream

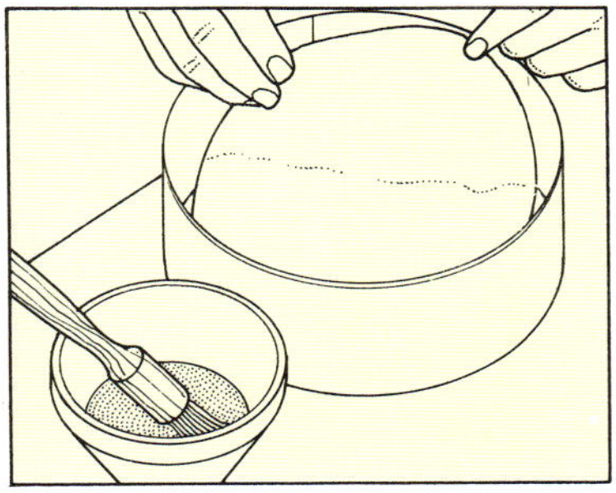

1 Grease a 23-cm (9-inch) round cake tin with unsalted butter or oil, then base-line it.

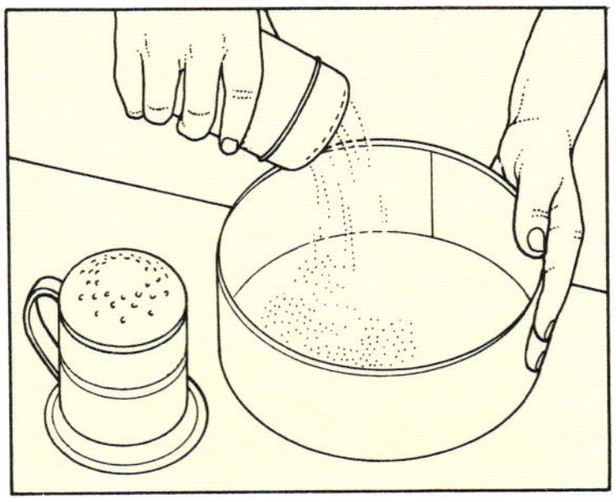

2 Dust with a little extra caster sugar and flour as a safeguard against the cake sticking.

3 Place eggs, 125 g (4 oz) sugar and lemon rind in a large deep bowl. Whisk vigorously until very thick and light. Fold the sifted flour lightly into the mixture with 50 g (2 oz) hazelnuts; spoon into tin and level the surface.

4 Bake in the oven at 180°C (350°F) mark 4 for about 35 minutes or until firm to the touch. Turn out and cool on a wire rack.

5 Make a sugar syrup from the water, remaining sugar and 30 ml (2 tbsp) lemon juice. Reserve two peaches to decorate. Skin and slice the remaining peaches and poach for 5–10 minutes until tender; drain.

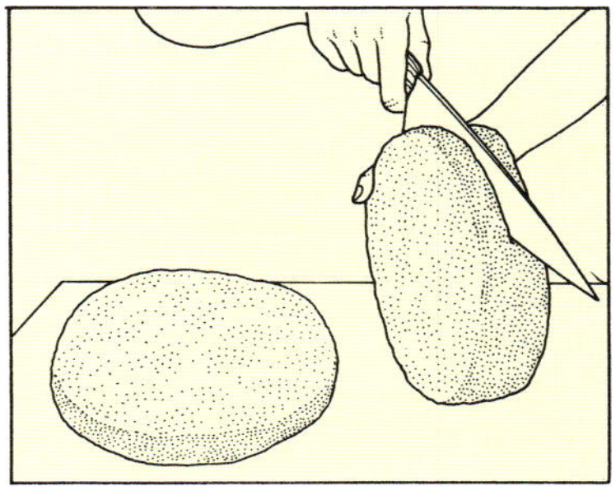

6 Split the gâteau into three, layer with the whipped cream and peaches, and refrigerate for 2–3 hours until required.

7 At serving time, slice the reserved peaches and use to decorate the gâteau together with reserved ground hazelnuts.

Menu Suggestion
Serve with Potted Prawn Pâté (page 24) and Coronation Chicken (page 49).

HAZELNUTS
It is sometimes difficult to buy ready-ground hazelnuts, although some good health food shops and large supermarkets may stock them. If difficult to obtain, buy shelled hazelnuts and toast them by putting them under the grill for a few minutes, shaking the grill pan constantly so that they toast evenly. After cooling, grind them finely in a nut mill or electric grinder.

STRAWBERRY AND ORANGE MOUSSE

0.45* £ £ 440 cals

* plus 2–3 hours chilling

Serves 6

700 g ($1\frac{1}{2}$ lb) fresh strawberries, hulled

finely grated rind and juice of 1 large orange

45 ml (3 tbsp) icing sugar

3 egg yolks and 2 egg whites

100 g (4 oz) caster sugar

45 ml (3 tbsp) water

15 ml (3 tsp) gelatine

300 ml (10 fl oz) double cream

150 ml (5 fl oz) single cream

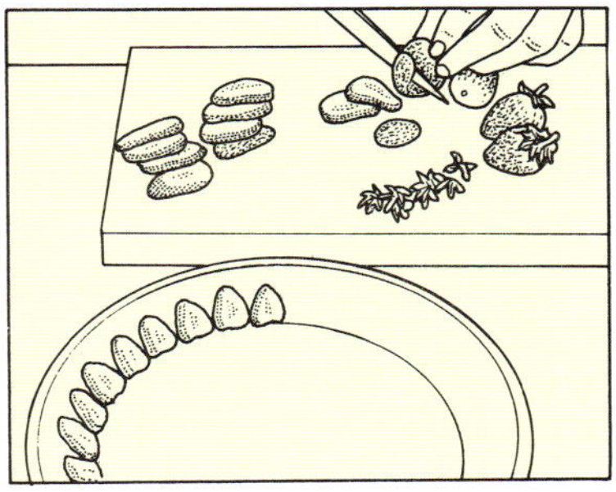

1 Thinly slice enough strawberries to line the sides of a 2.3-litre (4-pint) shallow glass dish.

2 Purée half the remainder in a blender or food processor with the finely grated orange rind, 75 ml (5 tbsp) juice and the icing sugar. Pass through a nylon sieve to give a very smooth texture. Reserve rest of strawberries for decoration.

3 Using electric beaters, whisk the egg yolks and caster sugar until thick and light. Then gradually whisk in the strawberry purée.

4 Place the water in a bowl and sprinkle in the gelatine. Stand the bowl over a saucepan of hot water and heat gently until dissolved. Leave to cool, then stir it into the mousse mixture.

5 Lightly whip the creams together. Fold one-third through mousse and keep the rest covered in refrigerator. Lastly, whisk the two egg whites and fold through the mixture. Turn carefully into the strawberry-lined glass dish, and refrigerate for 2–3 hours, until the mousse is set.

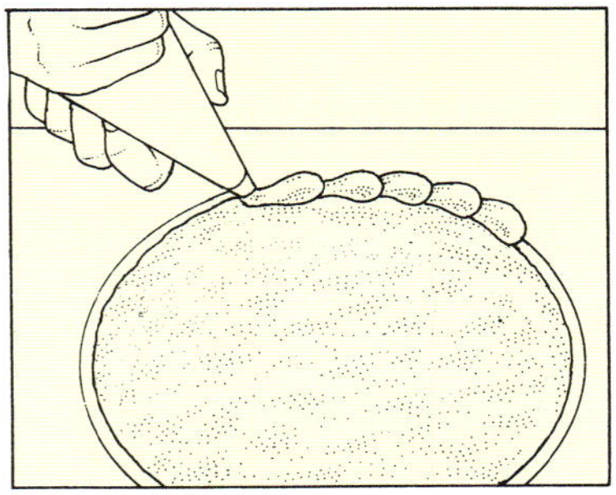

6 To serve, pipe the reserved cream on top of the strawberry and orange mousse and top with the remaining strawberries.

Menu Suggestion
Serve with Feta, Avocado and Tomato Salad (page 19) and Ceviche (page 50).

STRAWBERRIES
Strawberries and cream spell summer magic – and this beautifully decorated mousse literally makes your mouth water to look at it! The flavour of fresh orange complements strawberries perfectly, and the delicate texture of the mousse itself is irresistible.

BLACKCURRANT SORBET

0.30* £ ✳ 120 cals

* plus 6 hours freezing, 1 hour cooling and 30 minutes standing

Serves 6

450 g (1 lb) fresh blackcurrants, washed and strigged

100 g (4 oz) caster sugar

finely grated rind and juice of ½ a lemon

60 ml (4 tbsp) blackcurrant-flavoured liqueur (optional)

2 egg whites, stiffly whisked

fresh mint sprigs, to decorate

1 Cook the blackcurrants with 60 ml (4 tbsp) water until soft. Push through sieve to form purée.

2 Dissolve sugar in 300 ml (½ pint) water over low heat, add lemon rind; boil for 10 minutes. Cool for 1 hour. Add lemon juice; strain into bowl. Stir blackcurrant purée and liqueur, if using, into cooled syrup. Pour into a shallow freezer container and leave for 3 hours.

3 Transfer mixture to a chilled basin and break up with a fork. Fold in egg whites. Return to freezer for 3 hours. 30 minutes before serving, refrigerate to soften. Decorate with mint.

Menu Suggestion
Serve with Potted Shrimps (page 25) and Cold Beef in Soured Cream (page 34).

MIXED BERRY SORBET

0.30* £ ✳ 117 cals

*plus 6 hours freezing, 1 hour cooling and 30 minutes standing time

Serves 6

225 g (8 oz) strawberries

225 g (8 oz) redcurrants

150 ml (¼ pint) and 30 ml (2 tbsp) water

100 g (4 oz) caster sugar

150 ml (¼ pint) sparkling white wine

2 egg whites

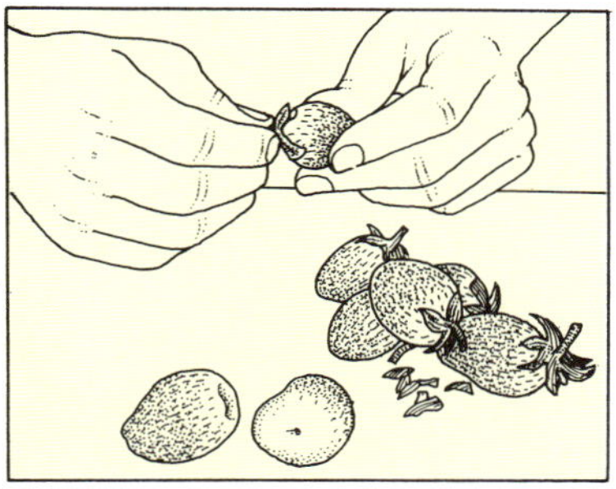

1 Hull the strawberries. Then remove the stalks from the redcurrants and place the fruit in a saucepan with 30 ml (2 tbsp) water. Cook for about 10 minutes until soft. Push the blackcurrants and strawberries through a sieve to form a purée.

2 Dissolve the sugar in 150 ml (¼ pint) water over low heat and boil gently for 10 minutes. Leave to cool for 1 hour.

3 Stir the wine and fruit purée into the cooled syrup. Pour into a shallow freezer container and leave for 3 hours.

4 Transfer frozen mixture to a chilled basin and break up with a fork. Whisk the egg whites until stiff and fold into the mixture. Return to the freezer for 3 hours. 30 minutes before serving, refrigerate to soften.

Menu Suggestion

Serve with Salmon Mousse (page 16) and Chef's Salad (page 31).

FRUIT SORBETS

Fresh strawberries and blackcurrants are specified here, although it is not absolutely essential to use these two fruits if they are not readily available. Frozen redcurrants can be used instead of fresh—and they need not be defrosted before using. Blackcurrants or even whitecurrants can be used as a substitute for the redcurrants, and raspberries, loganberries or blackberries as a substitute for the strawberries. As long as the fruit is unblemished and fully ripe, the sorbet is bound to look and taste good.

ALMOND AND CHERRY FLAN

1.25 £ 676 cals

Serves 6

225 g (8 oz) plain flour
225 g (8 oz) butter or margarine
2 eggs, separated
30–45 ml (2–3 tbsp) water
350 g (12 oz) fresh ripe black cherries, stoned
50 g (2 oz) caster sugar
125 g (4 oz) ground almonds
5 ml (1 tsp) almond flavouring
15 ml (1 tbsp) almond-flavoured liqueur (optional)
50 g (2 oz) self-raising flour
2.5 ml ($\frac{1}{2}$ tsp) baking powder
30 ml (2 tbsp) milk
25 g (1 oz) flaked almonds
thick pouring cream, to serve

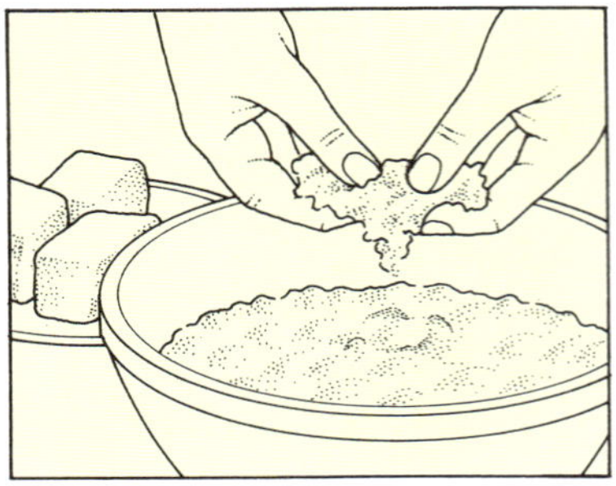

1 Place the plain flour in a large mixing bowl. Cut up and rub in 175 g (6 oz) butter until mixture resembles fine breadcrumbs. Bind to a firm dough with 1 egg yolk mixed with water.

2 Roll out the pastry, and use to line a 24-cm ($9\frac{1}{2}$-inch) flan dish. Bake blind in the oven at 200°C (400°F) mark 6 for 15–20 minutes until set but not browned; cool slightly.

3 Scatter the cherries over the pastry. Then cream the remaining butter and sugar well together and beat in ground almonds with the almond flavouring, liqueur, if using, and the remaining egg yolk. Fold in the self-raising flour and baking powder, sifted together, and lightly stir in the milk.

4 Whisk the two egg whites until they are stiff, and fold them into the creamed ingredients.

5 Spread over the cherries in the flan case and scatter the flaked almonds on top. Bake in the oven at 180°C (350°F) mark 4 for about 30 minutes. Serve warm with cream.

Menu Suggestion
Serve with Chicken Liver Pâté (page 21) and Salade Niçoise (page 60).

AMARETTO

Almond-flavoured liqueur—*amaretto*—a famous Italian liqueur, which comes from the town of Saronno near Milan in northern Italy, is said to be the best. Look for it in specialist off licences or Italian delicatessens with wine counters, and don't be confused between it and the little almond-flavoured macaroons called *amaretti*. The Italians are so fond of almonds that they even eat *amaretti* with *amaretto* after the coffee at the end of a meal!

HOT APRICOT SOUFFLÉ

1.15 £ 340 cals

Serves 4

450 g (1 lb) fresh apricots
30 ml (2 tbsp) water
40 g (1½ oz) butter
60 ml (4 tbsp) plain flour
150 ml (¼ pint) milk
50 g (2 oz) caster sugar
4 eggs, size 2, separated
15 ml (1 tbsp) apricot brandy
icing sugar, for dusting
single cream, to serve

1 Halve and stone the apricots. Then butter a 2-litre (3½-pint) soufflé dish. Stew apricots in water until soft. Rub fruit through a sieve. Discard skins.

2 Melt butter in a saucepan, stir in flour, then milk. Stir until smooth, then add apricot purée, bring to the boil, stirring, and simmer for 2 minutes.

3 Remove from heat and stir in sugar, egg yolks and liqueur. Whisk egg whites until stiff and fold into mixture.

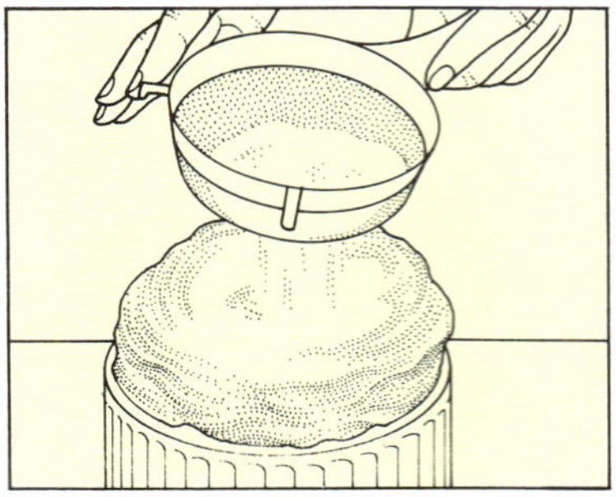

4 Turn the mixture into the soufflé dish. Bake in the oven for 45 minutes at 180°C (350°F) mark 4 until well risen. Dust with icing sugar and serve with cream.

Menu Suggestion
Serve with Crudités with Aïoli (page 26) and Pissaladière (page 30).

HOT CHERRY SOUFFLÉ

1.15 £ 351 cals

Serves 4

450 g (1 lb) fresh black or red cherries
30 ml (2 tbsp) water
40 g ($1\frac{1}{2}$ oz) butter
60 ml (4 tbsp) plain flour
150 ml ($\frac{1}{4}$ pint) milk
4 eggs, size 2, separated
50 g (2 oz) caster sugar
15 ml (1 tbsp) Kirsch
icing sugar, for dusting
single cream, optional

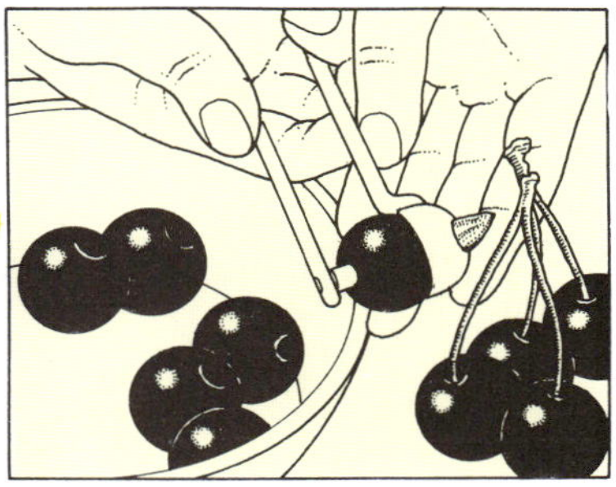

1 Remove the stones from the cherries. Put the cherries in a pan with the water and cook gently for 5–10 minutes until soft. Meanwhile butter a 2-litre ($3\frac{1}{2}$-pint) soufflé dish.

2 Either rub the fruit through a sieve or purée in a blender, or finely chop the fruit in a food processor.

3 Melt the butter in a pan, stir in the flour and cook gently for 1 minute, stirring. Remove pan from the heat and gradually stir in the milk. Bring to the boil and continue to cook, stirring, until the sauce thickens. Stir in the chopped cherries or purée.

4 Remove from the heat and stir in the sugar, egg yolks and liqueur. Whisk the egg whites until stiff and fold into the mixture.

5 Turn the mixture into the soufflé dish. Bake in the oven for 45 minutes at 180°C (350°F) mark 4 until well risen. Dust with icing sugar and serve with cream, if wished.

FRUIT BRANDIES

Kirsch is an *eau-de-vie*, or stone fruit brandy, in which the crushed kernels are included with the fruit juice—in this instance cherry. Other stone fruit brandies are *Mirabelle* (Mirabelle Plum); *Quetsch* (Switzen Plum); *Prune* (Plum); *Prunelle* (sloe).

ICED STRAWBERRY MERINGUES

0.20* £ £ ✻ 344 cals

* plus 1 hour cooling, 6–8 hours open freezing and 20–30 minutes standing before serving

Serves 6

225 g (8 oz) strawberries, hulled

25 g (1 oz) caster sugar

30 ml (2 tbsp) water

300 ml (10 fl oz) double cream

18 medium meringue shells, about 150 g (5 oz) total weight

30 ml (2 tbsp) brandy

double cream, to decorate (optional)

1 Place the strawberries (reserving 3 to decorate) in a small saucepan with the caster sugar and water. Cover the pan and heat gently for about 5 minutes until mushy, cool slightly.

2 Purée the pan ingredients in a blender or food processor and rub through a nylon sieve to remove any pips; allow the purée to cool for about 1 hour.

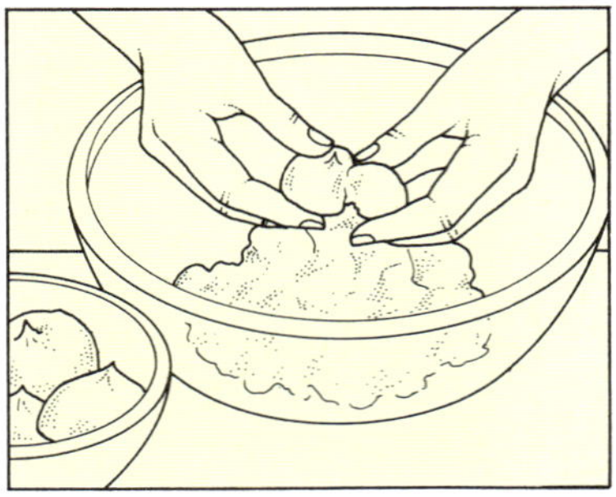

3 Lightly whip the cream in a large mixing bowl. Break each meringue shell up into three or four pieces.

4 Fold the pieces of meringue shell through the double cream together with the brandy and the cold fruit purée.

5 Spoon the mixture into six individual soufflé or ramekin dishes. Open freeze for 6–8 hours or overnight until firm, then wrap with foil and return to the freezer until required.

6 20–30 minutes before serving, transfer to the refrigerator. If wished, serve decorated with a whirl of cream and reserved strawberries, halved.

Menu Suggestion
Serve with Salmon Mousse (page 16) and Cyprus Stuffed Peppers (page 53).

STRAWBERRIES

If you have frozen strawberries or frozen strawberry purée in the freezer, this is the ideal dessert to use them for. You could even freeze some summer strawberries away specifically for making this dessert in wintertime. Whole strawberries do not retain their shape in the freezer because they have too high a water content, but as this recipe involves working the fruit to a purée before combining it with the meringues and cream, this will not matter – save your perfect whole strawberries for eating as they are.

Fresh Peach Ice Cream

0.15* £ ✳ 208 cals

* plus 5–6 hours freezing and 30 minutes standing before serving

Serves 6

350 g (12 oz) fresh ripe peaches
300 ml (½ pint) milk
grated rind and juice of 1 lemon
300 ml (10 fl oz) whipping cream
peach slices and fan wafers, to decorate (optional)

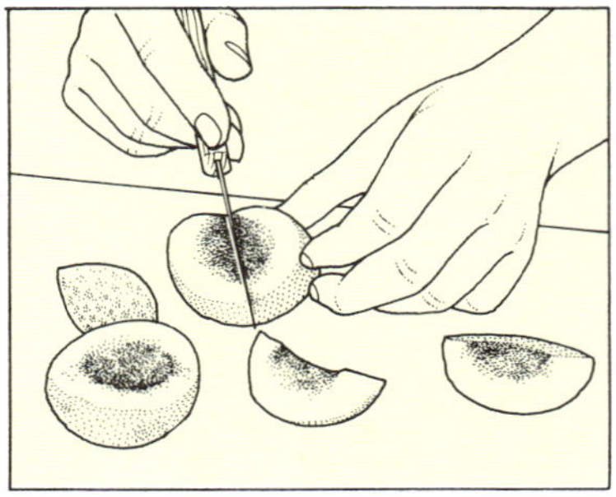

1 Using a sharp knife, quarter the peaches and remove the skins, discarding the stones.

2 Roughly slice the peaches into a blender or food processor, add the milk, lemon rind and juice and the cream. Blend well until the mixture is quite smooth.

3 Pour the mixture out into ice-cube trays (without divisions) or a shallow freezer container, freeze for about 2 hours until mushy in texture.

4 Turn into a large, chilled basin and mash with a fork. Return to the freezer for 3–4 hours to become firm.

5 About 30 minutes before serving, remove from the freezer and leave the ice cream to soften at room temperature. Serve decorated with peach slices and a fan wafer, if wished.

Menu Suggestion
Serve with Oriental Seafood Salad (page 11) and Pâté de Campagne with Black Olives (page 59).

USEFUL INFORMATION AND BASIC RECIPES

Eating Outdoors

Relaxed and informal, eating outdoors in hot sunny weather is one of the high spots of summer. Barbecues and picnics suit every large group and members of the family, so everyone can join in. If you are the host or hostess, make sure you give yourself time to enjoy yourself, too—the information in this chapter is designed with this in mind.

Eating outdoors can be an enjoyable experience as long as the weather is fine and the food is well planned for the occasion.

If eating outdoors on a terrace or patio, for example, choose 'fork foods' which do not need cutting or which can be easily managed on a lap, and organize the food and drink so that you are not continually rushing back and forth to the house.

PICNICS

Picnics will need even more careful planning. As well as planning eating and drinking utensils, you must remember rugs, groundsheets or picnic chairs to sit on, and also the food **must** be as tasty and interesting as possible within your limitations. Even the most informal picnic need not, for example, be based on sandwiches. Equally good picnic fare includes pies and patties, croquettes and rissoles, cubes of meat or firm fish, chicken portions and so on. Slices of a fairly firm cake, sweet biscuits and buns, plus fresh fruit are ideal desserts for eating with the fingers.

When packing food for a picnic, use small polythene bags for items such as cheese, cooked meats and solid salad ingredients. For more delicate foods such as quiches, pizzas, hard-boiled eggs and open flans, use cake tins or rigid polythene boxes and make sure that the foods are kept upright.

To transport food for picnics, the best choices are zip-up insulated (padded) bags or, even better, rigid polystyrene insulated boxes. To keep these bags and boxes cool, pack pre-frozen ice sachets or ice blocks in with the food.

For taking liquids on picnics, the vacuum flask is absolutely invaluable. The exceptions to the rule are Champagne, wines and fizzy drinks, which are best taken to picnics in the container in which they are purchased. When using a vacuum flask, always fill it as much as possible—any air trapped on the top will reduce the flask's insulating qualities. Do not, however, plan to keep food or liquids in a vacuum flask for more than 8 hours.

BARBECUES

When buying a new barbecue, concentrate on size. As a rough guide, it takes a barbecue grid diameter of at least half a metre (18 inches) to cook enough food for eight people at a time.

Make sure the unit is sturdy and stable, and that it offers some control over the positioning of the grid. A rotisserie spit is a handy optional extra for cooking whole chickens and joints of meat; aim for one that is battery- or electrically operated. A meat thermometer is another essential item for cooking large pieces of meat and poultry.

Long-handled barbecue tools are also essential: tongs, forks, slices and spatulas are the most useful for safe handling of food to and from the barbecue grid, and well-insulated oven gloves will provide added protection. A basting brush for brushing foods with oil or marinades, foil for wrapping certain foods, and absorbent kitchen paper for mopping up spills and wiping hands are also needed. A pair of bellows is a good idea for fanning reluctant flames and a bulb syringe for damping down those that get out of hand.

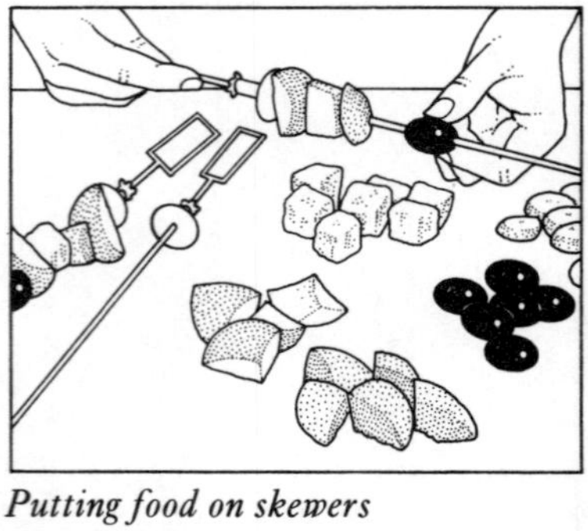

Putting food on skewers

Metal or wooden skewers are worth buying if you like kebabs, so, too, is a metal barbecue cage for cooking delicate items such as fish, which might disintegrate after over-handling.

Getting the fire ready Plan to start the barbecue fire 30–45 minutes before you want to begin cooking—the coals should be glowing red at night, lightly covered in white-grey ash in daylight. There must never be any flame while you are cooking. Charcoal or charcoal briquettes are the ideal fuel. Use proprietary charcoal lighters for lighting the barbecue; never use petrol, paraffin, methylated spirits or any other volatile fuel. To keep the charcoal at the right heat throughout the cooking time, always feed fresh charcoal on gradually from the outer edge, pushing a ring of fuel from the edge of the fire into the centre.

Lighting the fire

1 Arrange some firelighters in the bottom of the barbecue.

2 Pile the charcoal in a pyramid about 5–7.5 cm (2–3 inches) high over the top. (For a large joint, spread the charcoal in a single 2.5-cm [1-inch] layer.)

3 When the coals are burning strongly, spread them out in an even layer, then, just before you are ready to cook, put the grid in the position required so that it can heat up. To keep the charcoal at the right heat throughout the cooking time, always feed fresh charcoal on gradually from the outer edge, pushing a ring of fuel from the edge of the fire into the centre. Never throw charcoal directly on top of the fire—flames will leap up or you will have masses of unwanted smoke. Gentle heat is suitable for most foods, so feed the fire regularly and in small amounts—large quantities will reduce the heat too much and cause uneven cooking.

Any kind of food that can be fried or grilled is suitable for barbecuing. And barbecue cooking times can be calculated as the same as conventional grilling and frying times.

SANDWICHES

As soon as you have made sandwiches for a picnic, pack them in rigid polythene containers and seal them, or wrap them in cling film, foil or polythene bags, to keep them as fresh and moist as possible. The chart opposite gives some good ideas for fillings, but there are also many different types of bread and styles of sandwich to choose from.

For sandwiches made from conventional slices of bread, there are many ways in which you can ring the changes. Use one slice of brown bread and one of white in each sandwich for an interesting effect, or make double or triple deckers with 3 or 4 slices of bread and 2 or 3 different fillings (see right). Make rolled sandwiches by rolling up asparagus spears, ham slices or smoked salmon Swiss roll style in slices of bread from which the crusts have been removed. For pinwheels, spread slices of bread with a colourful filling, roll them up and refrigerate them. Just before serving cut each roll into thin slices. Toasted sandwiches if freshly made just before the picnic party departs, wrapped in foil and packed in an insulated box, are food for picnics on more chilly days. French bread sandwiches are hearty picnic fare. Omelette and salad is a traditional filling, or you could make a *pan bagna* (see page 56).

Pitta bread, when cut in half, reveals 'pockets' which are ideal for stuffing with the usual sort of sandwich ingredients, and with more substantial fillings such as spiced potato, lentils or vegetables.

Meat fillings

Cooked beef—sliced or minced with horseradish cream, mustard or soured cream
Corned beef with chopped watercress or celery
Minced lamb with soured cream and mint
Minced chicken with cottage cheese and pineapple
Minced pork and ham with cranberry sauce
Turkey with redcurrant jelly
Salami, tomato and cress
Pâté with walnuts and orange slices
Tongue with cream cheese and green peppers

Fish fillings

Salmon with chopped or sliced radishes
Smoked salmon with lettuce and lemon juice
Tuna with Russian salad
Shrimps with minced mussels
Crab (flaked) with avocado
Prawns, cottage cheese and green peppercorns
Herrings with sliced beetroot and soured cream
Rollmop herrings, mashed, with onion and tomato slices
Sardines with chopped watercress
Pilchards (mashed) with cottage cheese
Kippers with tomato and celery

Egg fillings

Egg mayonnaise with capers
Omelette (cold) cut into strips
Egg mayonnaise with avocado
Sliced egg with cream cheese and chives
Scrambled egg with bacon
Scrambled egg with watercress

Cheese fillings

Cheddar (grated) with chopped nuts and grated apple
Mashed Stilton with shredded spinach
Curd cheese with beansprouts
Danish blue with sliced grapes
Lymeswold or Blue Brie with orange slices
Cream cheese with chopped walnuts and olives
Cheddar cheese with fruit pickle
Cream cheese with grated carrots
Mozzarella and avocado
Brie and tomato
Camembert and cucumber
Feta, sliced onions and tomatoes
Caerphilly and mustard pickle
Edam with celery and chutney

Salad Ingredients

Fresh salad vegetables keep best in the crisper drawer of the refrigerator. Most will keep for up to a week if they are fresh to start with. Either keep them in rigid polythene containers or loosely wrapped in polythene bags, though celery and cucumber seem to keep most crisp if wrapped in cling film.

Many people still tend to think of salads as boring mixtures of raw, green 'rabbit' food. They need no longer be thought of in this way, however—especially in summer. The choice of foods that can be used is endless, with ingredients ranging from the usual lettuce, cucumber and tomato to exotic fruits and vegetables such as avocados, artichokes and mangoes, and cold cooked foods such as rice, pasta and spicy cooked meats.

Although the nutritional value of a salad will obviously vary according to its ingredients, there is no doubt that many salads are a high source of protein and vitamins. Fresh fruits and vegetables, especially valuable as roughage when eaten raw, contain high proportions of vitamin C. Extra goodness can be added with chopped nuts or grated cheese, or dressings based on yogurt.

Artichoke, globe: a thistle-like vegetable of which the heart (found below the leaves) is used, sliced, in salads. Buy artichokes with tightly closed leaves with no brown or dry edges. To obtain the heart, trim

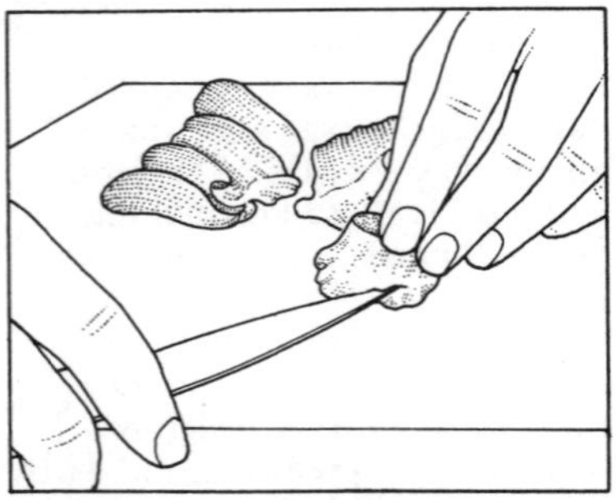

Trimming the base of globe artichoke

the base and snip off the leaf tops. Simmer in acidulated water for about 20 minutes until a leaf pulls away easily. Then pull away the leaves to reveal the hairy choke and cut this away with a sharp knife (see above). Finally, remove and slice the heart into the salad.

Asparagus: its delicately flavoured stalks may be white and thick or thin and green, in which case they are known as 'sprue'. Whatever the variety, choose firm, fresh-looking stalks. Asparagus must be cooked before serving cold in salads, either whole or cut into short lengths. First, scrape each

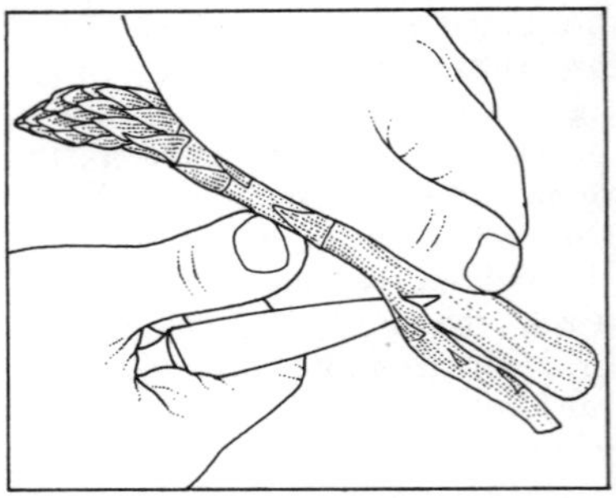

Trimming the woody parts from the asparagus stem

stalk with a sharp knife from tip to base, then trim off any woody parts at the stem base (see above). To cook, tie the stems in bundles (6–8 for thick stems; 12–15 for thin ones) and stand them upright in a special asparagus steamer or in a pan of boiling salted water filled so that the stems boil and the tops steam.

Aubergine: also called eggplant, or garden egg, this vegetable fruit usually has a shiny purple skin, although white and mottled purple-and-white varieties are also available. Aubergines can be fried, baked or simmered, then chilled to serve as a salad. When fresh, they should be firm and smooth with shiny skins. To prepare aubergines, trim and cut them into

Preparing aubergines

0.5-cm ($\frac{1}{4}$-inch) slices, then place them in a colander, sprinkled with salt (to remove their bitter flavour). Cover with a plate and leave to drain for 30 minutes. Rinse to remove any bitter juice, then dry.

Avocado: it may have a shiny green or bumpy brown skin, according to variety, but a ripe avocado always 'gives' slightly when pressed at the pointed end (see below). A hard, underripe avocado

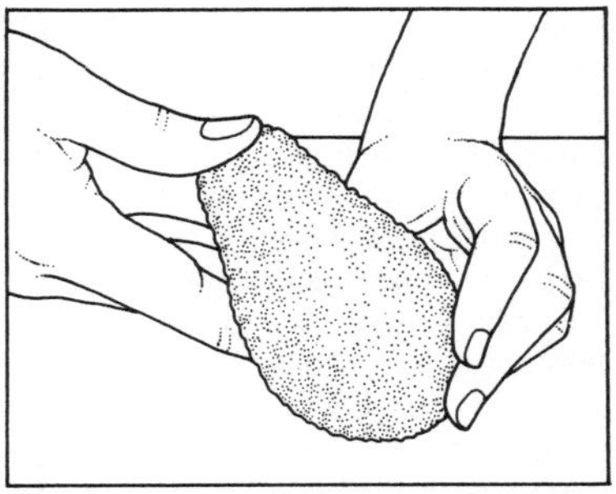

Testing avocados for ripeness

will ripen in 1–3 days if kept at room temperature or in about 1 week in the refrigerator. A good tip for ripening avocados is simply to keep them in a fruit bowl with other fruit. Fruit gives off ethylene gas which helps speed up the ripening process. To prevent discoloration, avocados should be added to salads at the last minute, or the flesh tossed in lemon juice.

Beans: there are three main types: broad, French and runner. *Broad beans:* choose smallish, full-looking pods. When very young and tender —no more than 5–7.5 cm (2–3 inches) long—the pods can be cooked in boiling salted water and eaten whole in salads. Pods any larger than this should be split and discarded, the beans removed and cooked lightly. For both cooked whole pods and beans, drain well then plunge in cold water and drain again before serving—this helps preserve both colour and flavour. *French beans:* excellent in salads, either whole or cut into pieces about 10 cm (4 inches) long. Avoid limp beans with brown patches. To prepare, top and tail the beans, then cook in boiling salted water until only just tender—they should have some 'bite'. Drain well, plunge into cold water and drain again, then dress at once, while still slightly warm. Leave to cool completely before serving. *Runner beans:* these should be eaten when young and fresh. Avoid large beans, which may well be too tough and stringy. Prepare by topping and tailing, then trimming any 'string' from the sides. Slice diagonally into pieces about 2 cm ($\frac{3}{4}$ inch) long, then cook and serve as for French beans.

Beansprouts: although they can theoretically be grown from any type of bean, the best-known are usually grown from mung beans. They are excellent in mixed salads. Beansprouts may be bought ready to use from oriental greengrocers and some large supermarkets and health food shops. Or grow them yourself at home: soak the beans or seeds in water overnight, then drain and place in a jam jar or a tray lined with damp absorbent kitchen paper (see below). Keep in

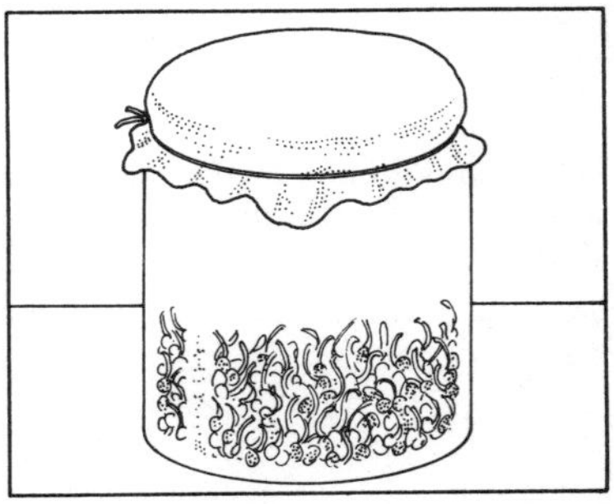

Growing beansprouts

a warm place (choose a dark place if you want pale sprouts, a light one for green sprouts) for about 5 days until the sprouts are about 7.5 cm (3 inches) long. Keep trays damp and rinse and drain the contents of jam jars daily. Before serving, simply rinse and drain. Do not bother to remove any remaining seed cases: these are highly nutritious.

Beetroot: this sweet-tasting crimson root is widely used in salads, and is often sold cooked and ready to use. Choose firm, smallish beets with crisp roots. Very small beets can be grated and eaten raw in salads, but all other types should be cooked before serving. To prepare the roots, trim any leaves to about 5 cm (2 inches) and wash carefully, taking care not to nick the skin or the beetroot will 'bleed' during cooking. Small beetroot should be boiled for about 30 minutes; larger, more woody ones for about 1$\frac{1}{2}$ hours (or pressure cooked at High pressure for 10–25 minutes). Drain, cool a little, then rub or peel off the skins. Add to salads at the last minute or other ingredients may pick up its red colour.

Broccoli and Calabrese: *Broccoli:* cauliflower-like, but with small, slim shoots bearing white or purple 'flowers'. When buying, look for strong stalks and heads. All types may be used in salads, either raw, or blanched by plunging into boiling, salted water for 5 minutes, then draining, refreshing in iced water and draining again. *Calabrese:* a type of broccoli which has medium to large heads with green 'flowers'. The heads should be closely packed together. Because the heads are very delicate, calabrese should be cooked like asparagus, with only the stems immersed in water (see Asparagus, opposite). To use in salads, cook until only just tender, drain carefully and dress while still warm.

Cabbage: many types are suitable for serving raw in salads. Sweet, pale green summer cabbages can be shredded and used raw in salads, and the darker leaves of spring cabbage can also be treated in the same way, though these should be used sparingly as they have rather a strong flavour. Both hard white cabbage and red cab-

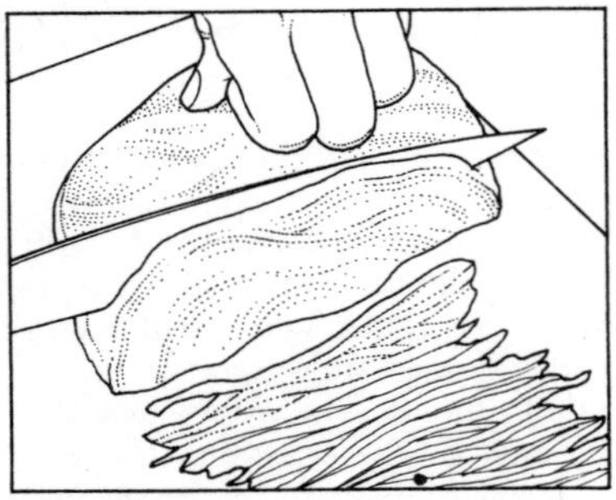

Making cabbage salad

bage are excellent shredded raw in salads (see above). Discard damaged outer leaves and thick, heavy stalks before shredding.

Cabbage, Chinese: also sold under the name of Chinese leaves, it looks like a large, rather pale long lettuce. Although it may be expensive, this vegetable goes a long way, and makes a beautifully crisp and unusual addition to any salad.

Carrot: the orange colour and crunchy texture of raw carrots make them good salad ingredients at any time of year, but the new, tender carrots of summer are especially delicious. Avoid ones that are soft or shrivelled. After trimming and scrubbing or scraping, tiny carrots can be served whole or cut into thin sticks, and it is often nice to leave a few feathery leaves on top of whole carrots if these are fresh. Larger carrots can be sliced, quartered or grated for salads.

Cauliflower: always choose firm, pure white heads for salads. To prepare, break the head or 'curd' into florets, then either serve them raw (the crunchy texture and almost 'peppery' flavour of raw cauliflower is excellent in salads) or, if you prefer, blanch them in boiling salted water for about 5 minutes. Drain, refresh in iced water, then drain again.

Celery: the white or greenish-white stalks are excellent in many salads, as are the chopped leaves. Celery should look firm and crisp. Much of it is sold ready-washed, and usually only needs rinsing before use, but celery that has not been treated in this way should be very thoroughly scrubbed under cold running water with a stiff vegetable brush. After preparing, chop or slice before adding raw to salads. Celery leaves (whole or chopped) make a pretty garnish.

Chicory: known to the French and Americans as endive. Tight, white torpedo-shaped chicory heads tipped with pale green are often available for salads at a time when other fresh salad ingredients are not so prolific; their slightly bitter flavour makes an unusual addition to any salad. They can be sliced, cut into quarters or separated into individual leaves (see below) before being added to

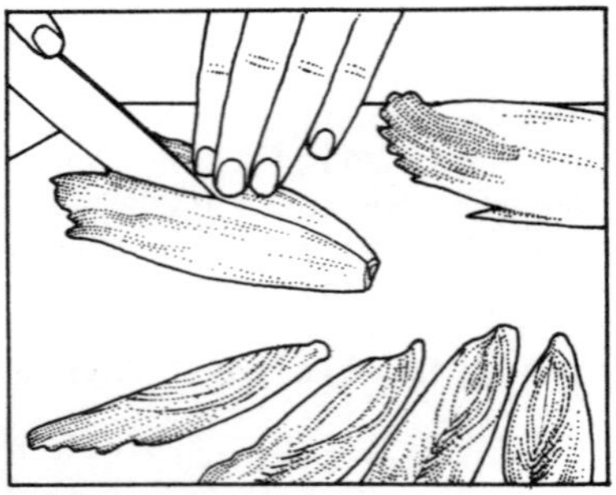

Preparing chicory

salads, and do not usually need washing: a wipe on the outside is all that is required.

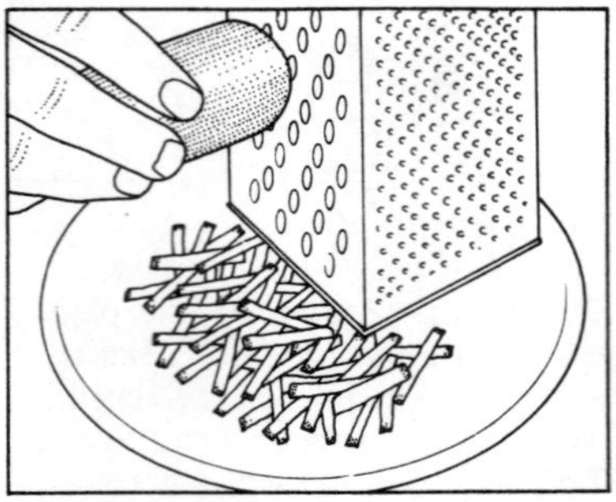

Grating courgettes

Courgette: also known as zucchini, this vegetable is a miniature marrow, with a firmer, fuller-flavoured flesh. The best courgettes are small and blemish-free. Courgettes can be used raw in salads, either grated or, if freshly picked, cut into slices. To use them cooked, cut them into 2.5 cm (1 inch) slices, blanch for 2–3 minutes in boiling salted water, drain, refresh in iced water and drain again.

Cucumber: one of the 'staple' salad vegetables, these are available in summer as (1) smooth-skinned hothouse varieties which do not necessarily have to be peeled before eating, and (2) outdoor ridge cucumbers whose skin must be removed before serving. Choose smallish cucumbers for salads as the larger ones tend to be tough. After preparing a cucumber by trimming it and peeling it if necessary (the skin can be taken off in strips for a decorative effect), it can be served at once cut into thin slices or wedges. To remove any bitter flavour, place slices of cucumber in a colander, sprinkle with salt and cover with a plate. Leave for 1 hour, then rinse and dry well. Another way to improve the flavour of a cucumber is to soak slices in wine vinegar flavoured with salt and a little sugar.

Dandelion: although a notorious garden weed, it has leaves which, when very pale and young, make a tender and interesting addition to salads. Do not use old dark green leaves, however: their peppery flavour is overwhelmingly strong. Pick the leaves as near to serving time as possible, then rinse and dry them and either serve them raw or blanch them in boiling water for 2–3 minutes.

Endive: the most common type of endive found in this country is the frizzy or curly endive, most expressively described by the French as *chicorée frisée*. Its frondy, wild-looking leaves and its unusual bitter flavour make it a very special salad ingredient. Prepare as for lettuce.

Fennel, Florence: looking rather like a squat version of celery topped with feathery leaves, this vegetable has a delicate aniseed flavour. The bulbs should be white or pale green—dark green ones are often slightly bitter. To prepare, trim the top and the base and remove any brown parts from the exterior.

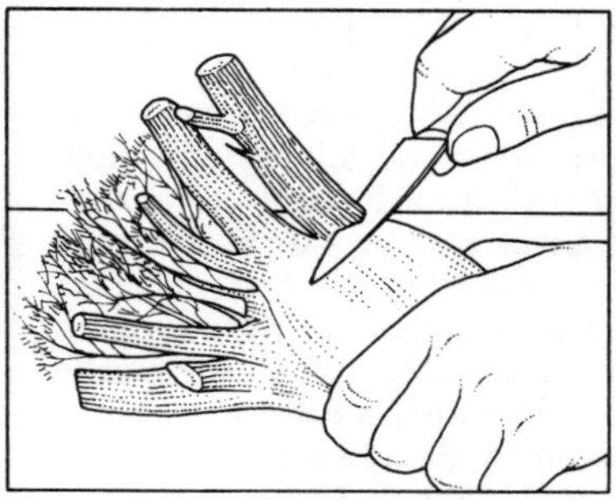

Trimming the top and base of fennel

Quarter or slice the fennel head and serve raw in salads. Snip the leaves on top as a garnish.

Garlic: because of its pungent flavour, it should be used sparingly in salads or it will swamp the other ingredients. For the mildest flavour, simply cut a peeled clove of garlic and rub it round the bowl in which the salad is to be served. Alternatively, make a *chapon* by rubbing the garlic on to a crust of bread or a slice of a French loaf (see below) and placing it in the

Preparing a chapon

base of the bowl before the salad is added. For a stronger flavour, add up to two crushed garlic cloves to the salad or dressing.

Kohlrabi: this root vegetable is a cross between a turnip and a cabbage; it can be either green or purple and has a mild turnip flavour. It can be eaten raw or cooked in salads according to taste; choose small vegetables no more than about 5 cm (2 inches) in diameter. To serve raw, trim off the leaf bases, then peel thinly and grate or slice thinly. To cook, steam or boil in salted water for about 20 minutes, then peel while still warm.

Leek: the best leeks to use for salads are mild-flavoured ones. Whole or sliced cold leeks coated in a vinaigrette dressing (page 143) are very popular as a salad starter, which is very quick, easy and inexpensive to make. If used in small amounts; finely chopped raw leeks can also be added to salads. To prepare, trim off and discard the coarse dark green tops and either use the remaining middle white sections whole or slice them into 2.5–5 cm (1–2 inch) lengths, then wash them very well to remove any grit. Cook them in boiling, salted water for 2–3 minutes only, then refresh in iced water and drain thoroughly before serving.

Lettuce: the green leaves of lettuce are the most popular and familiar of all salad ingredients. But there are so many varieties to choose from, especially if you grow your own crops, that lettuce need never be dull. Avoid drooping lettuces with brown or damaged patches. It is often a good idea to mix varieties in a salad to give a contrast in textures of soft, round lettuces and crisper varieties, which can be either round or long-leaved.

Prepare lettuce by trimming off the base, discarding any brown, wilted or damaged leaves, then washing leaves thoroughly under cold running water. Shake off any excess water, then pat dry in a tea towel, drain in a colander or salad basket or spin dry in a centrifugal dryer (see right, above). Serve the leaves whole, or tear them into

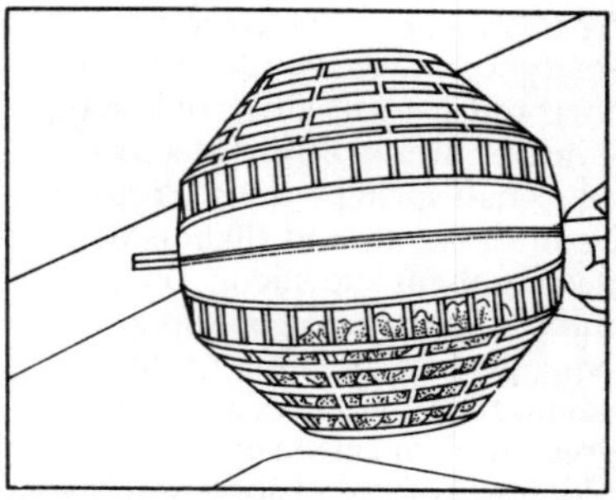

Draining lettuce in centrifugal dryer

pieces with your hands. They can also be finely shredded with a sharp knife if you prefer. If the lettuce is not to be served at once, or is a little limp, put it in a polythene bag and refrigerate for 30 minutes or more. Do not dress a lettuce salad until just before serving or it will lose its crispness.

Mushroom: raw button mushrooms are excellent in salads, but the larger, flat mushrooms are not a suitable choice. To prepare, trim the mushroom stalks and wipe but do not peel the caps—much of the food value of a mushroom is in its skin. Quarter the mushrooms or slice them thinly before adding them to the salad. Remember that once they have been mixed with a dressing they tend to discolour quickly and release a lot of liquid which may spoil the appearance of a dish—so always add them at the last moment.

Mustard and cress: sold in punnets, but easy to grow at home from seed, mustard and cress has a good flavour but is best used as a salad garnish rather than a major ingredient. Snip the shoots near their base, then place in a colander and wash under cold running water to remove any seeds. Drain well, then scatter on a salad or arrange in small bunches.

Onion: of the many different types of onion available, many have uses in salads. Choose clear, firm onions with dry skins. The best types for eating raw are the sweet-flavoured

Spanish onions (the largest of all the types and easily identified by their red-brown skins), red onions (with vermilion skins), shallots and small spring onions. Prepare Spanish onions and shallots by peeling them and slicing them thinly. Trim spring onions at their base, peel off any limp or discoloured outer leaves and trim the green tops to within about 5 cm (2 inches) of the white onion base.

Peas: fresh shelled peas give a true taste of summer to a salad. Look for crisp, young pods. If the peas are very small they may be eaten raw; if larger, cook them in boiling salted water for 5–10 minutes then drain, refresh in cold water and drain again. The exact cooking time will depend on the size of the peas. Frozen peas should be cooked according to package instructions before they are used in salads. *Mange-tout peas:* this type of pea has edible pods. Also known as snow or asparagus peas, they should be cooked before using in salads unless they are exceptionally young and tender. To prepare, top and tail the pods (see below), removing any 'strings' from the sides, then steam for 5 minutes or boil for 2 minutes. Drain, refresh; add to salad.

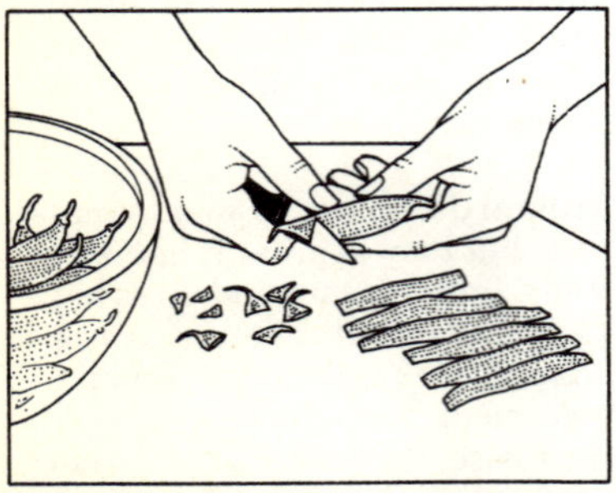

Topping and tailing pods

Potato: new potatoes make excellent salad ingredients because they stay firm after boiling and keep their shape. Simply wash them well, then scrub or scrape. Boil them in their skins, then leave whole, if small, or dice if larger and immediately toss in chosen dressing and herbs. Leave for at least 1 hour for flavours to develop before serving. Fresh new potatoes in their skins are rich in vitamin C, so never peel before cooking.

Radicchio: a red-leaved Italian variety of chicory which is used in the same way as lettuce. Remove any damaged or discoloured outer leaves, then wash and slice thinly and add to a salad.

Radish: the strong, rather peppery taste of the radish adds 'bite' to a salad while its skin, which is usually crimson, adds colour. All the preparation a radish needs is trimming and washing. It may be sliced or left whole, or for a salad garnish may be vandyked or made into 'lilies' (see page 141).

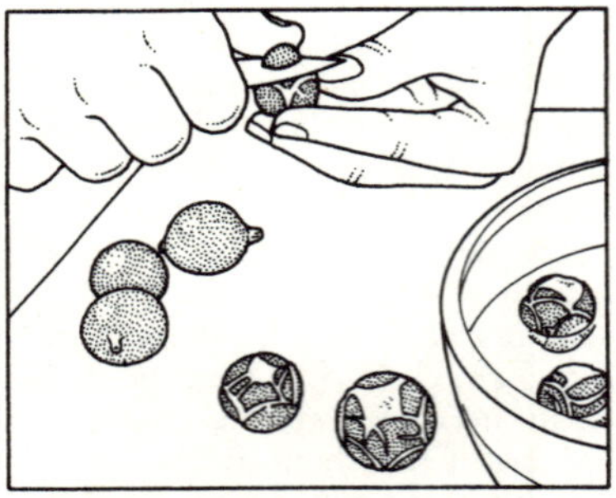

Making a radish 'rose'

Sorrel: the medium to dark green leaves of sorrel look similar to spinach, but have a sharp, lemony flavour, and should be used sparingly in salads. To prepare, wash leaves well, then pull off stalks and large midribs. Shred finely.

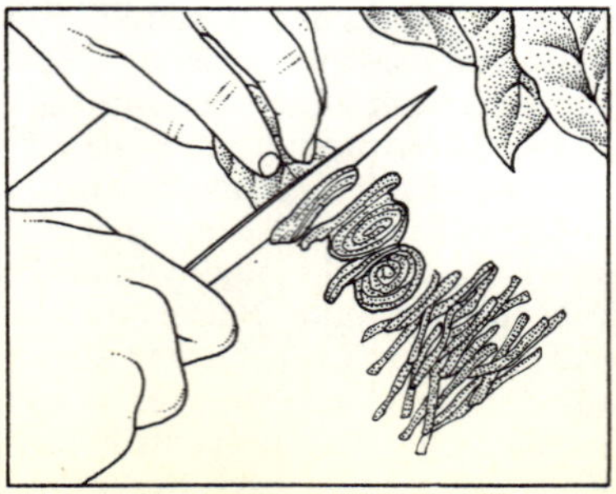

Shredding sorrel

Spinach: the best type to use raw in salads is the pale green summer type, which has a delicate flavour. Choose and prepare as for sorrel, above. Winter and perpetual spinach have a stronger flavour, and are best used sparingly with other vegetables.

Sweetcorn: choose medium-sized cobs with plump kernels. They must be removed from their cobs and cooked for use in salads. To prepare, stand cob upright, then cut downwards close to the cob, starting at the centre and turning it as you work (see below). Then turn cob other way up and repeat. Cook the corn in boiling water for 5–10 minutes until tender, but do not add salt during cooking or it will toughen. Drain, cool and serve.

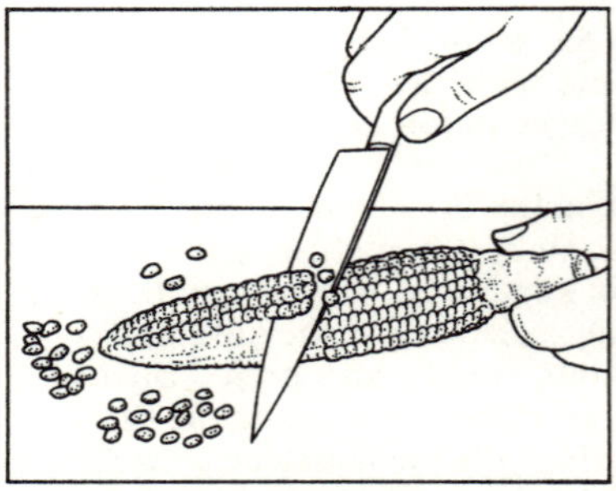

Removing kernels from corn cob

Sweet pepper: also known as capsicum, it is available in many colours. All types can be used raw in salads. To chop or cut into strips, first cut pepper in half, remove core, seeds and pith, then chop or cut as desired. For pepper rings, cut top off carefully—it should come away with core and seeds attached. Remove remaining seeds and pith, then cut flesh into rings.

Tomato: all the many varieties from the tiny cherry tomato to the huge beefsteak varieties are a natural choice in salads. Choose firm, unblemished fruits. To use in salads, wipe with a damp cloth, then slice, halve or quarter.

Summer Fruit

Apple: although all kinds can be used to add colour and flavour to salads, eating apples are generally preferable, as cooking apples can sometimes be too tart. There are many varieties—red and green, sweet and tart, or crisp- or soft-textured. When using them in salads, choose a variety that will provide a contrast (in texture, flavour and colour) with the other ingredients you are using. Whatever the variety, buy firm, well-coloured fruit. To use, quarter and core the apples and peel them if you wish—but bear in mind that the skin adds colour and is also the part of the fruit which provides roughage. Slice, dice or grate apples to add to salads but always toss them immediately in lemon juice or dressing to prevent any discoloration, or, alternatively, add them to a salad at the last moment.

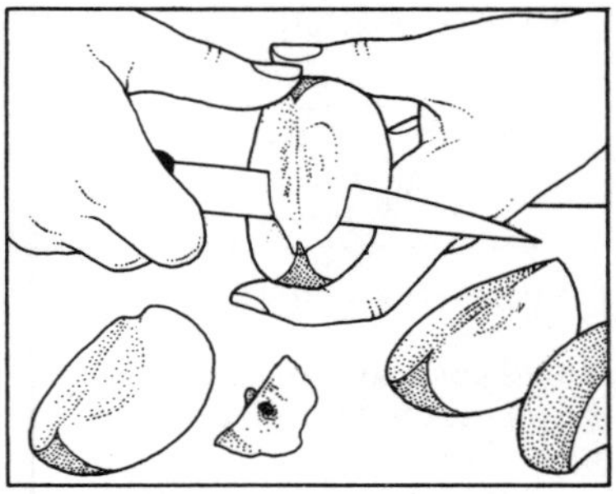

Preparing apples

Apricot: fresh apricots add colour and a sharpish taste to salads. To use, halve and stone them before adding. Sweeter canned apricots should be thoroughly drained before use in salads.

Banana: peeled and sliced, they add sweetness and a tropical look and flavour to a salad; they combine particularly well with beansprouts and dates. They should be tossed immediately in lemon juice after preparation or they will quickly discolour. Add them to salads just before serving.

Dried Fruit

The sweetness of dried fruit makes a welcome contrast to the more usual savoury ingredients of a salad. A handful of raisins, sultanas or currants peps up the bland flavour of a cabbage-based salad, for example, and dates and prunes are the perfect complement to any salad containing cheese or bananas; dried apricots go well with the rather bitter flavour of chicory and endive—they are also superb with mayonnaise-based dressings.

Before adding any dried fruit to a salad, make sure to remove all stones for easy eating. If you are in a hurry, soaking is not absolutely necessary so long as you cut the fruit up small.

Grapefruit: there are yellow-skinned and pink-tinged varieties, of which the latter are slightly sweeter. Whichever is used, choose fruits that feel heavy and have unblemished skins. The acidity and high vitamin C content of grapefruit makes it an excellent salad ingredient. To prepare, peel (see Orange) and slice, removing pith and membrane and working in a bowl to collect juice. Alternatively, halve the fruit, cut round the inside of the pith and remove flesh in segments (see below). Cut away flesh from between membrane 'spokes', again working over a bowl to collect the juice, and use collected juice in dressing, instead of lemon juice or vinegar.

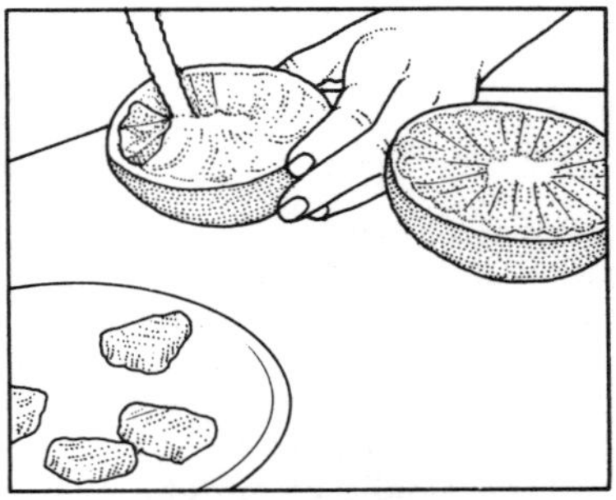

Segmenting a grapefruit

Grapes: both white (green) or black varieties are suitable. Avoid bruised fruits. To prepare, wash and dry. Leave seedless grapes whole. Halve other types and remove seeds before adding to salads.

Kiwi fruit: also known as Chinese gooseberry, it is the size and shape of an egg, and has brown, hairy skin beneath which is a juicy green flesh containing black seeds arranged in a circle. The flavour is rather like a melon with a hint of strawberry. Kiwi fruits are imported and therefore expensive to buy, but their unusual and attractive appearance makes them very useful in salads. To prepare, peel thinly with a small, sharp knife, then slice carefully into rings.

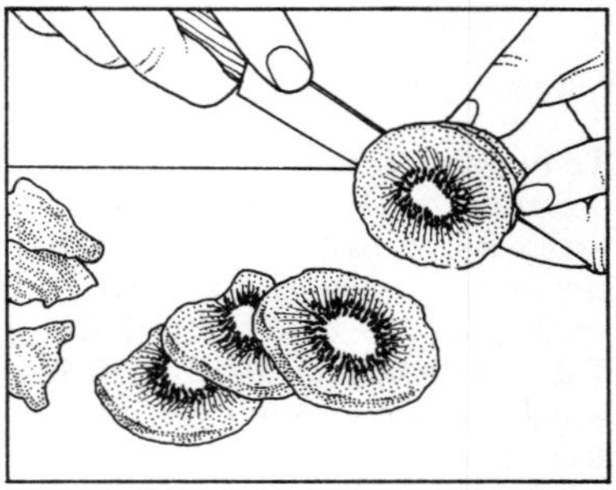

Slicing Kiwi fruit

Mango: a tropical fruit about the size of a large pear and with a peach-pineapple flavour, it can be either yellow or orange. Choose by their softness, and avoid fruits with an unpleasant pungent smell. To prepare, peel skin in sections, then slice flesh down to large stone. Save juice and use in dressing.

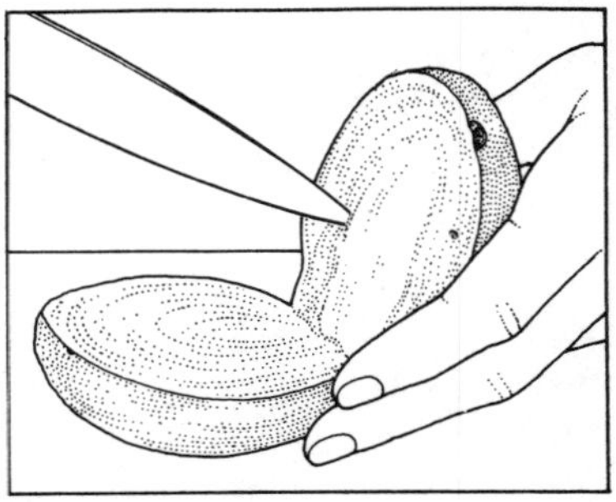

Slicing a mango

Melon: from the red flesh of the watermelon to the pale green of ordinary melons, they all make good salad ingredients. Choose fruits that feel heavy and yield when pressed at the stem end.

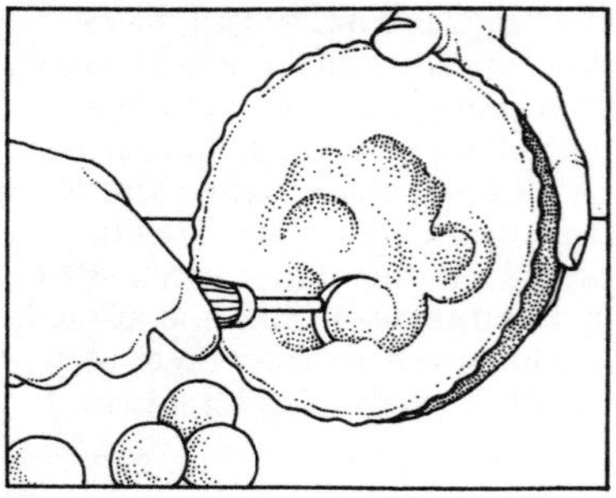

Scooping out melon flesh

To prepare, cut in half, remove the pips, then scoop out the flesh with a melon baller. Alternatively, cut away the skin with a sharp knife, then dice or slice the flesh. Take care when refrigerating salads which contain melon: cover the salad bowl tightly with cling film or other foods in the refrigerator will take on the melon's flavour.

Orange: its colour, sweetness and high vitamin C content makes it an attractive addition to salads. Buy firm fruits that are heavy for their size and have smooth, unblemished skins. To prepare, peel using a serrated knife and cutting away all the pith and just a little of the flesh. Slice into rings, removing the centre core of pith, or separate into segments, then remove membrane.

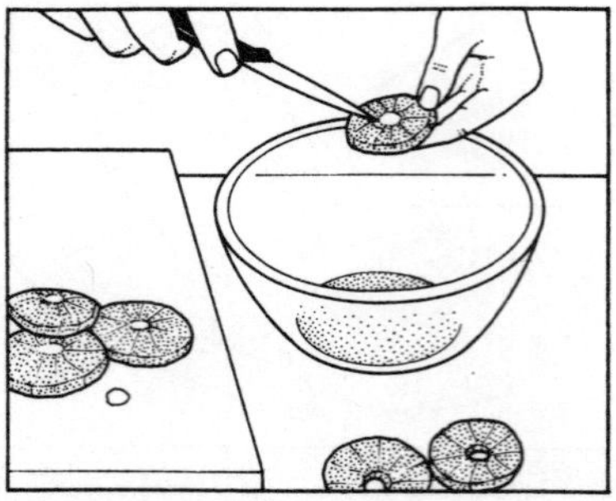

Removing the pith from oranges

Pawpaw: also known as papaya, it can be used successfully in salads. Choose unblemished fruit and prepare by halving the fruit and removing pips (see below) and skin.

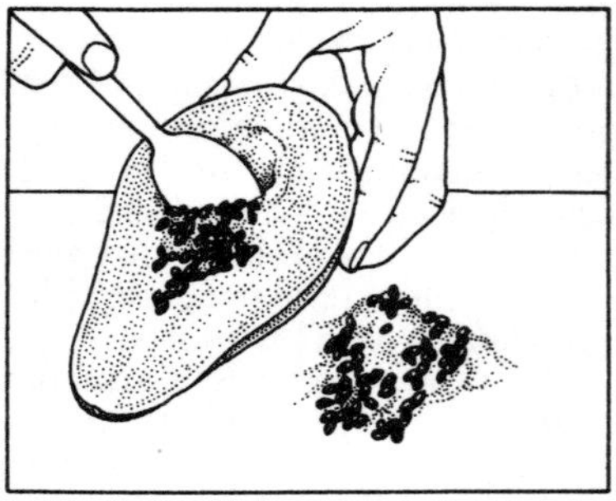

Removing pips from pawpaw

Peach: fresh peaches, halved or quartered and stoned, are excellent salad ingredients. Avoid bruised and over-soft fruits. To peel, plunge them into boiling water for 1 minute, then peel off the skin with a sharp knife or by hand.

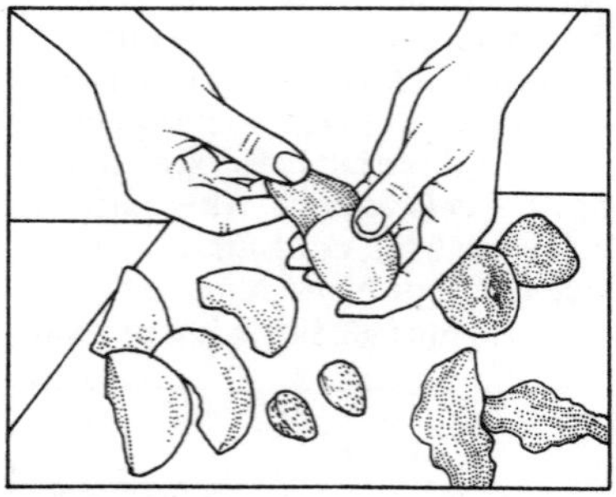

Peeling peaches

Remember that there is always a risk that the flesh may become damaged or discoloured in the process. Canned peaches can also be used—the type canned in natural juice being the best. Drain them well and use some of the juice in the salad dressing. Peaches canned in heavy syrup may be used, but should first be rinsed then drained and patted dry.

Pear: ripe dessert varieties may be used in salads, and they go well with nuts (especially walnuts) and any salad dressed with blue cheese dressing. Avoid bruised or over-ripe fruit. To prepare, peel, quarter and core, then slice or dice. Toss immediately in lemon juice and use soon after preparation.

Pineapple: the sweet-sour taste of the fresh fruit gives an exotic interest to a salad, used in rings or chopped. Choose a ripe pineapple by pulling a leaf from its top—this

Testing pineapple ripeness

should come away easily. Prepare the pineapple by slicing off the top and the base, then cutting the fruit lengthways into quarters or eighths. Cut out the woody core from each section, then cut the flesh from the skin (see below). Do not cut too close to the skin or you will be left with a lot of

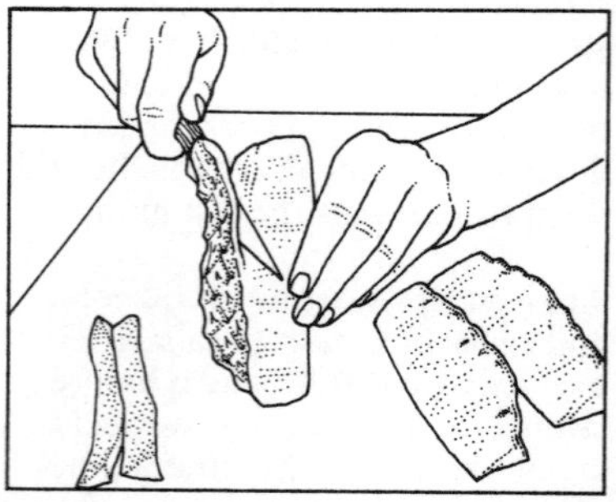

Cutting pineapple skin from flesh

whiskery 'eyes' in the flesh. Chop or slice the flesh, and add it to the salad. Save any juice for the dressing. Make pineapple rings by cutting the skin from the whole fruit, slicing it, then removing cores with a small cutter. Drained, canned pineapple may also be used.

PULSES

Pulses, which include dried peas, beans and lentils, are extremely valuable salad ingredients. Not only do they add colour and variety of texture and flavour, but they are also a valuable and inexpensive source of protein. They are also quite high in carbohydrates, however, and their inclusion in a salad will therefore automatically give it a higher calorie rating.

For the cook, the greatest disadvantage of using pulses is the fact that most of them need soaking for 8 hours or overnight before cooking. (Exceptions are varieties of split lentils and mung beans.)

If you are planning to use pulses in a recipe and have forgotten to soak them, you can use the 'hot soak' method: place them in a saucepan, cover with cold water, then bring them very gradually to the boil. Allow them to boil hard for about 3 minutes, then leave them to soak, tightly covered, for about 1 hour. (An even quicker alternative is to use drained, canned pulses.) After soaking, pulses should be rinsed and drained before being cooked in fresh, cold water. Salt should be added after, not during, cooking, to prevent the pulses from becoming tough. Use the chart below as a guide to cooking times, but remember that red kidney beans must be allowed to boil hard for the first 10 minutes to destroy poisonous substances.

To cut down on lengthy cooking times pulses can be pressure cooked (see below for times). Allow at least 1 litre (2 pints) cold water for every 450 g (1 lb) dry weight of pulses, but make sure the cooker is no more than half full.

Bring the water to the boil, add the pulses and bring back to the boil, uncovered, stirring. Skim off any scum, cover and cook at High (15-lb) pressure for the required time. Reduce pressure slowly after cooking or the pulses may block the cooker's vent. When cooked, drain well and leave to cool. They are best dressed with a vinaigrette while still warm. Herbs and spices make excellent complements to pulses: try cumin, coriander, caraway, chilli, basil, marjoram or tarragon.

COOKING DRIED PULSES

Type	Appearance	Cooking time	Pressure cooking time at high (H) pressure
Aduki beans	Round, red, very small	30–60 minutes	10 minutes
Black beans	Kidney-shaped, black, shiny	1½ hours	20 minutes
Black-eye beans	Small, kidney-shaped, pale cream with black spot or 'eye'	45–60 minutes	20 minutes
Butter beans	Large, flattish, kidney-shaped, pale cream	1½ hours	25 minutes
Cannellini beans	White, like long haricots	1 hour	20 minutes
Chick peas	Round with pointed top, ivory with a reddish tinge	1½–2 hours	20 minutes
Flageolet beans	Kidney-shaped, pale green	1 hour	20 minutes
Foule (ful) beans	Dull brown, round, thick skins	1–1¼ hours	20 minutes
Haricot beans	Kidney-shaped, pale cream	1–1½ hours	20 minutes
Lentils	Small and red or green or larger and greenish brown, round, flattish	1 hour	15 minutes
Mung beans	Round, green, very small	40 minutes	5 minutes
Red kidney beans	Kidney-shaped, crimson red	1–1½ hours (boil for first 10 minutes)	20 minutes
Rose cocoa or borlotti beans	Long, pink with dark red flecks	1 hour	20 minutes
Soya beans	Small, round, ivory, become elongated when soaked	3–4 hours	35–40 minutes
Split peas	Small, green or yellow, round	45–60 minutes	15 minutes

PASTA, RICE AND GRAINS

It is easy to turn a light salad into a more substantial dish by adding pasta, rice or grains, or by making these the basis of the salad. Nuts, seeds and olives add texture, colour and flavour, as well as nutritive value.

PASTA

Both fresh and dried pasta are now widely available at supermarkets and delicatessens: choose plain egg pasta; wholewheat; green, spinach-based; pink, tomato-flavoured; and even speckled with basil. Allow about 50 g (2 oz) pasta per person in a main course salad. For every 225 g ($\frac{1}{2}$ lb) pasta, bring 2.3 litres (4 pints) cold water to the boil, with 15 ml (1 tbsp) salt. When the water boils, swirl in 10 ml (2 tsp) oil to prevent the pieces sticking together and add the pasta. Bring back to the boil, then lower the heat and simmer until it is *al dente*, that is, until it is tender but still has some 'bite' to it. Allow about 10–15 minutes for dried pasta (the exact cooking times vary from one brand to another, so consult packet instructions if necessary); 3–4 minutes only for fresh pasta.

When the pasta is cooked, drain it well, then cool it quickly by plunging it into cold water. Drain it again very thoroughly. If the pasta is not to be used at once, toss it in a little oil, to prevent the pieces sticking together, then refrigerate, covered, until required—it will keep for up to 1 week. Otherwise, immediately mix with a dressing and flavourings of your choice—both mayonnaise and vinaigrette-based types go well with pasta.

RICE

Long-grain varieties are generally the best in salads as round-grain rice tends to be rather too sticky and glutinous. Brown rice has a nuttier flavour than white rice, and is better for you because it contains more fibre, but it does take much longer to cook.

Allow about 2.3 litres (4 pints) water for every 225 g ($\frac{1}{2}$ lb) white or 175 g (6 oz) brown rice. Bring the water to the boil with 20 ml (4 tsp) salt per 2.3 litres (4 pints) water, plus the juice of half a lemon, if liked, to add extra flavour, or a pinch of saffron or ground turmeric for a yellow colour. Add the rice, bring the water back to the boil, then give one good stir to loosen the grains. Reduce the heat and simmer for about 15 minutes for white rice or 40 minutes if brown—again, as with pasta, until it is tender but still has a 'bite'. Once the rice is cooked, drain it at once in a sieve, then run cold water through it to cool it quickly. It can then be kept, covered, in the refrigerator, for up to 1 week until needed (as with pasta, stirring in a little oil helps to keep the grains separate), or used at once. Flavour the dressing as you prefer, but remember that curry spices are as good in a rice salad as they are in traditional curry and rice dishes.

PASTA SHAPES

For salads, select from the types of pasta illustrated. As a rule, avoid the very small types, such as soup pasta, also the large tubes of cannelloni and sheets of lasagne. Stuffed pasta, however, makes a good, substantial salad ingredient. Consult packet for cooking times—they are invariably longer than for unstuffed types.

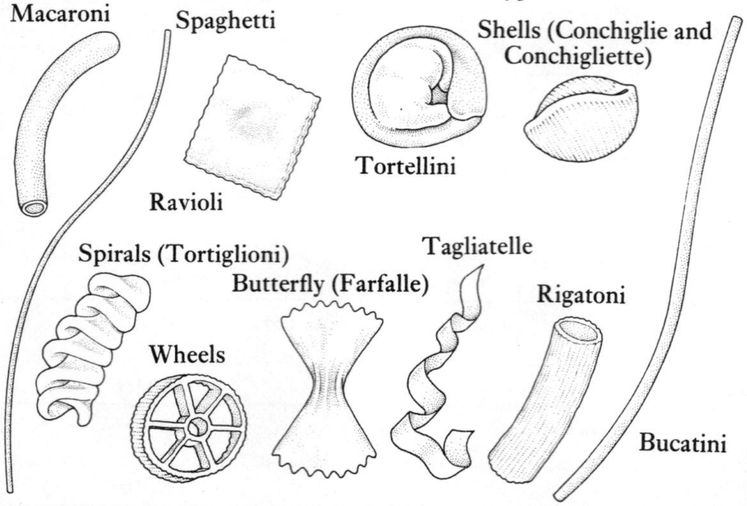

GRAINS

Cooked millet and wheat grains can be used in salads in the same way as rice or pasta. Millet is cooked in at least three times its volume of boiling water for 20 minutes, while whole wheat is soaked in cold water overnight then boiled for about $1\frac{1}{2}$ hours (or pressure-cooked for 25 minutes) until tender. Bulghar, bulgur or burghul wheat (pre-cooked cracked wheat which needs no cooking) is soaked in cold water for 30 minutes, then drained and spread on a clean tea towel. Squeeze out excess moisture, mix with a dressing and flavourings and set aside for 30 minutes before serving.

NUTS, OLIVES AND SEEDS

Nearly all nuts make a tasty addition to salads and can be added whole or chopped. Similarly, sunflower, poppy, caraway, sesame and melon seeds all add variety. Stoned green or black olives are also ideal in salads.

HOW TO MAKE SALAD GARNISHES

It's just as important with a salad as any other dish to garnish it and make it look as appealing and fresh as possible. If you're in a hurry you can add a quick finishing touch by simply sprinkling grated cheese over the top of a salad—Red Leicester or a blue cheese such as Stilton give a good splash of colour, for example. A handful of nuts and raisins or toasted sunflower or sesame seeds also adds interest to the top of a salad, so too does sieved egg yolk and white sprinkled over separately in bands of different colour. Crumbled crisply grilled bacon or crushed crisps add texture, whereas slices of citrus fruit or slices of hard-boiled egg add colour. And don't forget to use fresh herbs in the summertime—just a sprig or two or a sprinkling of chopped leaves can make all the difference.

Some garnishes take a little more time and trouble, plus advance preparation, but none of them are difficult. Here are a few ideas to give you inspiration.

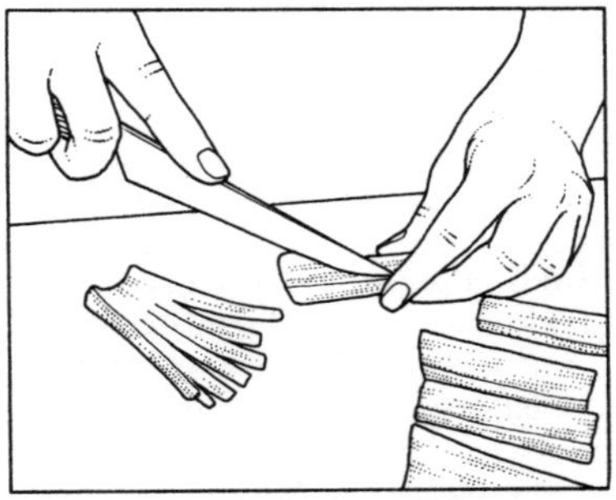

Celery curl: cut a celery stick into strips about 1 cm ($\frac{1}{2}$ inch) wide and 5 cm (2 inches) long. Make cuts along the length of each, close together and to within 1 cm ($\frac{1}{2}$ inch) of one end. Leave in iced water for 1–2 hours until fringed strips curl. Drain well.

Crimped cucumber: run the prongs of a fork down the sides of a cucumber to remove strips of peel, then slice the cucumber thinly in the usual way—each slice will have an attractive deckled edge.

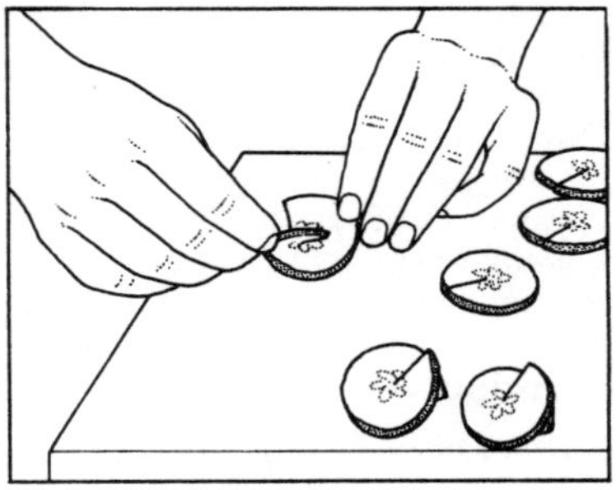

Cucumber cone: cut a piece of cucumber into thin slices. Make a cut in each slice from the centre to the outer edge, then wrap one cut edge over the other to form a cone.

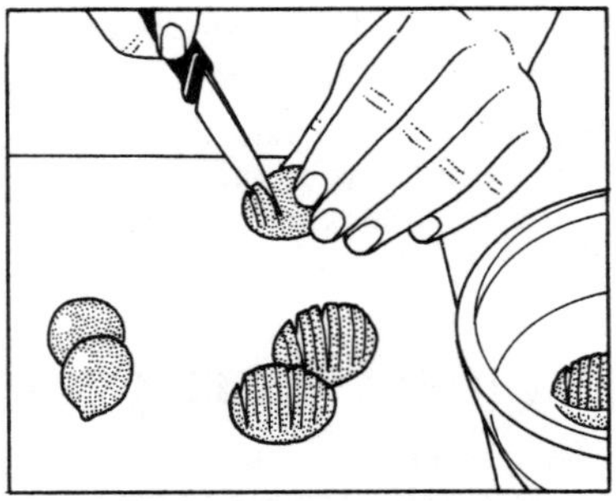

Radish fan: cut a narrow slice from the top or stalk end of a well-shaped radish. Make five or six deep cuts at intervals along the length of the radish, without cutting right through. Place in iced water for 1–2 hours and leave to open out like a fan.

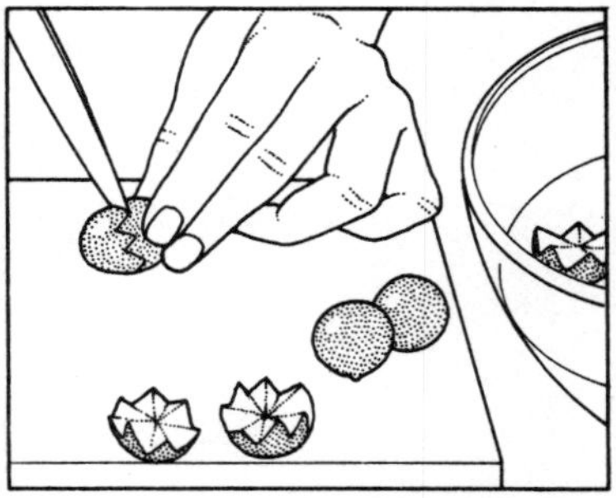

Radish waterlily: prepare as for radish fan (below left), making 4–8 small deep cuts rather than the thin snips, crossing one another across the centre at the root end. Place in iced water for 1–2 hours.

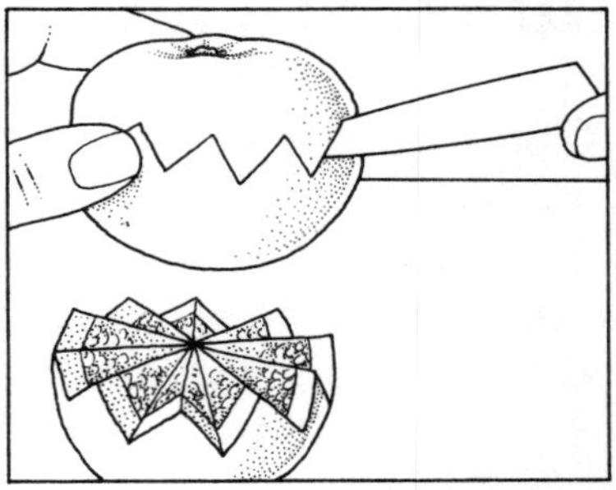

Tomato waterlily: using a small, sharp-pointed knife, make a series of V-shaped cuts around the middle of a firm tomato, cutting right through to the centre. Carefully pull the halves apart.

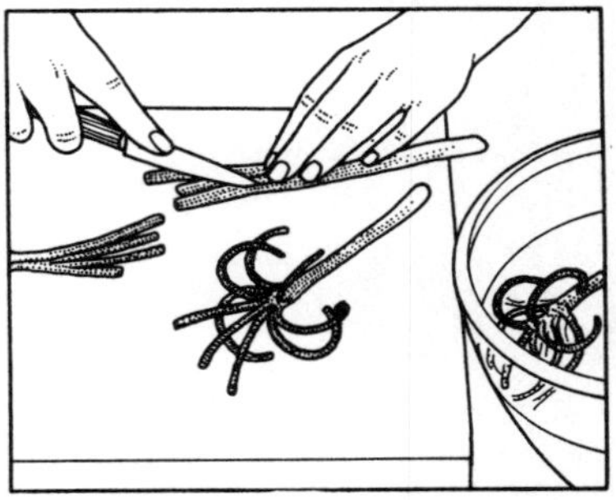

Spring onion curl: trim the root end and all but 5 cm (2 inches) of the leaves from a bunch of spring onions. Skin the onions and then cut the green leaves two or three times lengthways. Place in cold water for 1–2 hours until the green leaves curl up tightly.

Sauces, Dressings and Stocks

Good-quality oils and vinegars are essential for well-flavoured dressings, so don't buy cheap ones, as they'll prove to be a false economy. Supermarkets and delicatessens stock an ever-increasing variety, which will help you ring the changes with different flavours.

OILS

Edible oils are produced from nuts, seeds and beans. The following are best for dressings.

Corn oil: also called maize oil; made from sweetcorn. Use in dressings for a bland flavour.

Groundnut oil: also known as peanut or arachide oil. A pale, bland oil which can be mixed with olive oil to make it go further.

Hazelnut oil: an expensive oil with a delicate, nutty flavour. 'Stretch' it with any bland oil. Keeps in the refrigerator for only about 6 months, once opened.

Olive oil: main producers are France, Italy, Greece and Spain. Virgin oil (labelled as such), is the best, it is dark green and has a strong, rich flavour and aroma. Paler oils, though inferior to virgin oil, are good in salads and usually cheaper. Other types are oil from a second crushing of olives, which is weaker in colour, taste and aroma, and second-grade oil—the poorest in quality.

Safflower oil: a nutty-flavoured, pale, light oil with a high polyunsaturated fat content. Use to 'stretch' stronger oils.

Sesame seed oil: a heavy oil with a rich amber colour and deliciously nutty flavour. Use sparingly.

Soya bean oil: a heavy-textured oil with a strong flavour.

Sunflower oil: a pale, light oil with a mild flavour and a high polyunsaturated fat content. Use on its own or to 'stretch' stronger oils.

Vegetable oil: a blended oil from the seeds of different plants. The cheapest of oils, not noted for fine flavour.

Walnut oil: one of the most expensive oils. Like hazelnut oil, once opened it keeps in the refrigerator for no longer than 6 months. Superb with green salads.

VINEGARS

In addition to wine vinegars and cider vinegar, which are the best for dressings, an increasing range of unusually flavoured vinegars is now available. Try making the following at home, then seal with airtight, vinegar-proof lids.

Herb vinegar: Place sprigs of fresh herbs in bottles, add wine vinegar, cover and leave in a cool place for 6 weeks. Strain, pour into bottles and seal.

Fruit vinegar: Place washed raspberries, blackberries or blackcurrants in a bowl and break up slightly. For each 450 g (1 lb) fruit, pour in 600 ml (1 pint) distilled malt or white wine vinegar. Cover and leave for 3–4 days, stirring occasionally. Strain and add 450 g (1 lb) sugar to each 600 ml (1 pint). Boil for 10 minutes, cool, strain, pour into bottles and seal.

Garlic vinegar: Place three skinned and sliced garlic cloves in a warm bottle. Add 600 ml (1 pint) boiled distilled malt vinegar; cool. Seal and leave in a cool place for 6 weeks. Strain, re-bottle and seal.

GUIDELINES TO GOOD SALADS

- Allow just enough dressing to cling to the leaves or other salad ingredients, but no more.
- Dress leafy salad vegetables just before serving. Dress cooked vegetables and pulses while warm and leave to marinate to allow time to absorb the flavour.
- To toss the salad at the table, mix the dressing in the bottom of the bowl, cross the servers over it and pile the salad loosely on top—then you can toss salad and dressing together without spilling either.
- For freshness, serve and toss salad in a chilled bowl.

Vinaigrettes

BASIC VINAIGRETTE

Makes 135 ml (9 tbsp)

90 ml (6 tbsp) olive oil
45 ml (3 tbsp) wine vinegar, cider vinegar or lemon juice
2.5 ml (½ tsp) sugar
2.5 ml (½ tsp) wholegrain, Dijon or French mustard
salt and freshly ground pepper

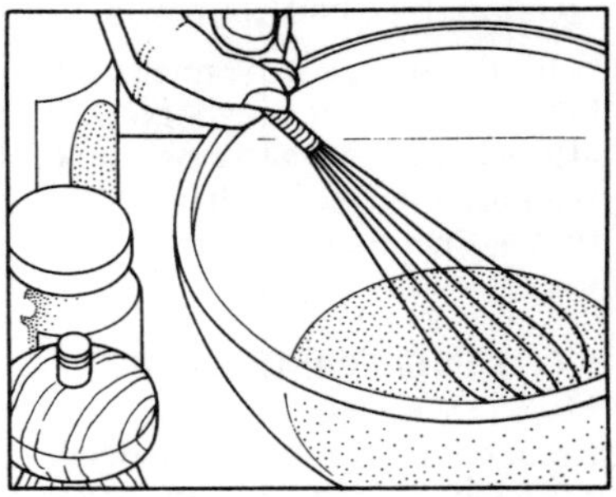

1 Place all the ingredients in a bowl or screw-topped jar and whisk or shake together.

2 Before use, whisk or shake the dressing again, as otherwise the oil separates out on standing.

Note: If a recipe calls for 150 ml (¼ pint) dressing, add an extra 15 ml (1 tbsp) oil.

VARIATIONS

Fresh herb vinaigrette: add 15 ml (1 tbsp) chopped fresh parsley or 15 ml (1 tbsp) chopped fresh mint or 10 ml (2 tsp) chopped fresh chives.

Mustard vinaigrette: add an extra 15 ml (1 tbsp) mustard.

Curry vinaigrette: add 5 ml (1 tsp) curry powder.

Blue cheese vinaigrette: add 25 g (1 oz) blue cheese, crumbled.

Garlic vinaigrette: add 2 garlic cloves, skinned and crushed.

Not suitable for freezing

Other Dressings

AVOCADO DRESSING

Makes about 300 ml (½ pint)

ripe avocado
15 ml (1 tbsp) lemon juice
30 ml (2 tbsp) mayonnaise (see page 145)
30 ml (2 tbsp) single cream
salt and freshly ground pepper

Halve, stone, peel and slice the avocado. Place in a blender or food processor with the remaining ingredients and blend at high speed until velvety smooth. Check the seasoning.

Not suitable for freezing

SOURED CREAM DRESSING

Makes 150 ml (¼ pint)

142 ml (5 fl oz) soured cream
30 ml (2 tbsp) white wine vinegar
¼ small onion, skinned and finely chopped
2.5 ml (½ tsp) sugar
5 ml (1 tsp) salt
freshly ground pepper

Mix together the soured cream, vinegar, onion and sugar. Season with salt and freshly ground pepper and mix again thoroughly.

Not suitable for freezing

SLIMMERS' YOGURT DRESSING

Makes 150 ml (¼ pint)

142 g (5 oz) natural yogurt
15 ml (1 tbsp) vegetable oil
5–10 ml (1–2 tsp) white wine or cider vinegar
5 ml (1 tsp) wholegrain mustard

Mix all the ingredients well together and chill before serving.

Not suitable for freezing

WALNUT DRESSING

Makes 225 ml (8 fl oz)

small slice wholemeal bread
40 g (1½ oz) walnuts
10 ml (2 tsp) lemon juice
1 garlic clove, skinned
salt and freshly ground pepper
200 ml (7 fl oz) olive oil

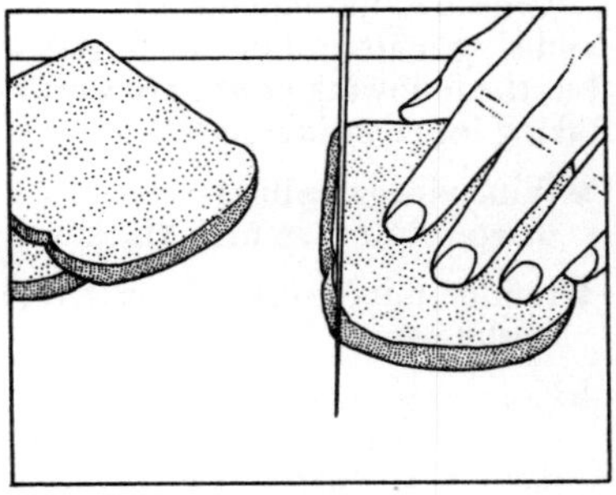

1 Remove the crusts from the slice of bread and soak it in cold water for a few minutes. Squeeze out the excess moisture.

2 Place the bread in a blender or food processor. Add the walnuts, lemon juice, garlic and seasoning and blend the ingredients at high speed until the mixture is very finely ground.

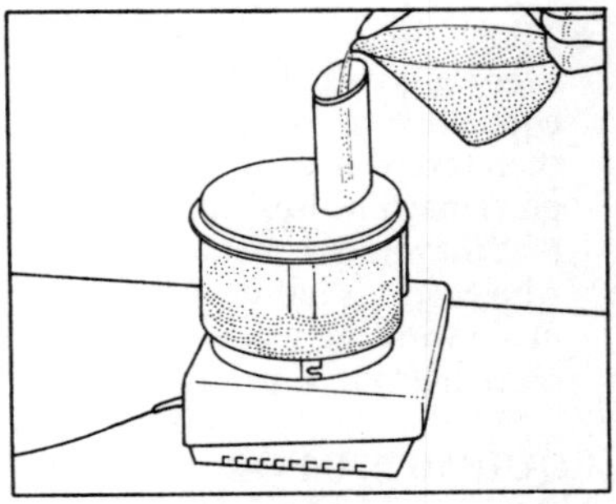

3 Gradually add the oil through the funnel, while the machine is still running, until it is all incorporated. Check the seasoning and stir well before use.

Not suitable for freezing

MAYONNAISE

INGREDIENTS

Good-quality ingredients are essential for mayonnaise to taste at its best—so take care in your selection of oil and vinegar and don't skimp on cost or all your efforts will be in vain.

Choice of ingredients is obviously a matter of personal taste, but the following points are worth taking into consideration:

- Wine vinegar will give a less sharp result than malt vinegar.
- Lemon juice gives a distinctive, fresh tang.
- Corn or groundnut oil is a wise choice because of its fairly bland flavour. It will not override the other flavours of the seasonings you add, or the food which with the mayonnaise is to be served.
- Olive oil, apart from its high cost, gives a strong flavour (and also a thicker texture), which can mask the flavour of the food with which the mayonnaise is to be served. Don't, therefore, use olive oil to make mayonnaise to serve with delicately flavoured foods such as shellfish and eggs.
- Allow 150 ml (¼ pint) oil for every egg yolk. 1 whole egg is equivalent to 2 egg yolks, and therefore will make 300 ml (½ pint) mayonnaise, but remember that mayonnaise made with whole eggs is lighter than that made with egg yolks—and is more likely to separate.

EQUIPMENT FOR MAKING MAYONNAISE

The classic French way to make mayonnaise is in a mortar and pestle, but if you do not have one of these, you can use an ordinary mixing bowl and a wooden spoon or fork. A balloon or rotary whisk can be used to make the task easier or, if you have one, an electric whisk.

An electric blender or food processor can also be used for greater speed, although you will probably have to make a 300-ml (½-pint) quantity in order for the blades of the machine to be covered. This method is more successful when mayonnaise is made from whole eggs rather than just the egg yolks.

Put the eggs in the bottom of the goblet with the seasonings and half the vinegar or lemon juice. Start the machine running (on slow speed if your machine has a variable speed control), then add the oil gradually through the hole in the top of the blender goblet or food processor funnel. When all the oil has been added, add the remaining vinegar or lemon juice and taste and adjust the seasoning.

RULES FOR SUCCESS

- All ingredients *must* be at room temperature. Never use eggs straight from the refrigerator or oil from a cold larder as this is bound to result in curdling. If necessary, warm the bowl and utensils before starting to mix the ingredients.
- After mixing the egg with the dry ingredients (see opposite), start to add the oil only *a drop at a time*. This may seem very time-consuming and tedious, but if you try to hurry up this process you will have a disaster on your hands. (The oil and the moisture in the egg do not mix naturally, but beaten vigorously a drop at a time the oil breaks down into small droplets which are coated by the protein molecules in the yolk to form an emulsion.)
- Once the emulsion is formed, you can start to add the oil in a thin, steady stream, *but keep beating vigorously* or the oil could still form a separate layer and the mixture curdle.
- If the mayonnaise becomes too thick before all the oil is added, thin it down by beating in 5 ml (1 tsp) of the vinegar or lemon juice which is to be beaten in at the end (see opposite), *then* continue adding the oil.

HOW TO RESCUE CURDLED MAYONNAISE

If your mayonnaise curdles during—or after—making, don't panic and don't throw it away. There are several ways to rescue it so that you need not waste ingredients. Beat the curdled mayonnaise into one of the following:

5 ml (1 tsp) hot water
5 ml (1 tsp) Dijon mustard
5 ml (1 tsp) vinegar or lemon juice
1 egg yolk
30 ml (2 tbsp) bottled mayonnaise

Add the curdled mayonnaise a little at a time, beating vigorously after each addition to make sure it is all incorporated. When the mixture is smooth, continue adding the oil, a drop at a time.

STORING HOMEMADE MAYONNAISE

Commercial varieties of mayonnaise have a long shelf life because they contain emulsifiers, stabilizers and preservatives. Homemade mayonnaise obviously has none of these, and the freshness of the eggs affects its keeping qualities—it will keep for 3–4 days at the most at cool room temperature, or up to 1 month in a screw-topped glass jar in the refrigerator. Always allow mayonnaise to come to room temperature and whisk vigorously before serving. Homemade mayonnaise will not freeze.

MAYONNAISE

Makes 150 ml ($\frac{1}{4}$ pint)

1 egg yolk
5 ml (1 tsp) Dijon mustard
2.5 ml ($\frac{1}{2}$ tsp) salt
1.25 ml ($\frac{1}{4}$ tsp) freshly ground pepper
2.5 ml ($\frac{1}{2}$ tsp) sugar
15 ml (1 tbsp) white wine or cider vinegar or lemon juice
about 150 ml ($\frac{1}{4}$ pint) corn or groundnut oil

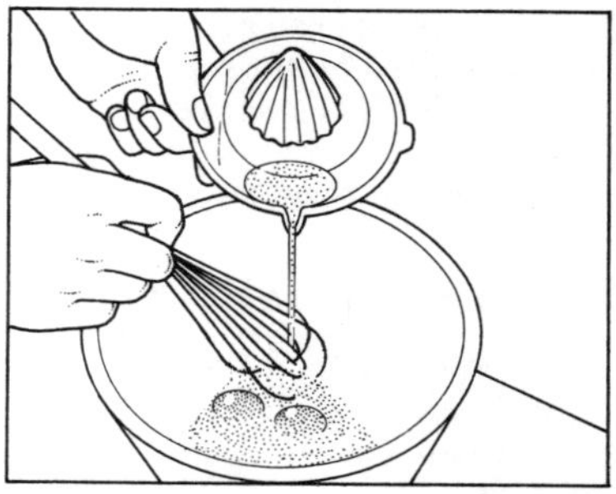

1 Put the egg yolk into a bowl with the mustard, seasoning, sugar and 5 ml (1 tsp) of the vinegar or lemon juice.

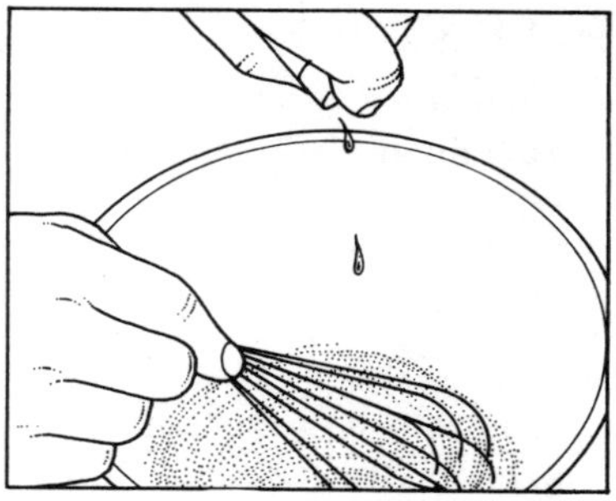

2 Mix thoroughly, then add the oil, *drop by drop*, stirring briskly with a wooden spoon the whole time, or whisking until sauce is thick.

3 Add a little more vinegar or lemon juice if sauce is too thick. When all the oil has been added, add the remaining vinegar or lemon juice gradually and mix thoroughly.

Thinning mayonnaise
Thin mayonnaise down with a little warm water, single cream, vinegar or lemon juice just before serving. Add the extra liquid slowly—too much will spoil the consistency.

VARIATIONS

These are made by adding the following ingredients to 150 ml ($\frac{1}{4}$ pint) mayonnaise.

Caper mayonnaise: add 10 ml (2 tsp) chopped capers, 5 ml (1 tsp) chopped sweet peppers (also known as pimientos) and 2.5 ml ($\frac{1}{2}$ tsp) tarragon vinegar.

Celery mayonnaise: add 15 ml (1 tbsp) chopped celery and 15 ml (1 tbsp) chopped fresh chives.

Cucumber mayonnaise: add 30 ml (2 tbsp) and finely chopped cucumber.

Herb mayonnaise: add 30 ml (2 tbsp) chopped fresh chives and 15 ml (1 tbsp) chopped fresh parsley.

Piquant mayonnaise: add 5 ml (1 tsp) tomato ketchup, 5 ml (1 tsp) chopped stuffed olives and a pinch of paprika.

Tomato mayonnaise: add half tomato, skinned and diced, 1 spring onion, chopped, and 5 ml (1 tsp) white wine vinegar or lemon juice.

Lemon mayonnaise: add the finely grated rind of 1 lemon and use lemon juice instead of vinegar.

Curry mayonnaise: add 5 ml (1 tsp) curry powder to the egg yolk mixture before adding the oil.

Green mayonnaise: blanch 3 large spinach leaves quickly in boiling water, drain and chop finely. Add to the mayonnaise with 15 ml (1 tbsp) chopped fresh parsley and 30 ml (2 tbsp) chopped fresh chives.

Watercress mayonnaise: add one quarter of a bunch of watercress, very finely chopped, to 150 ml ($\frac{1}{4}$ pint) lemon mayonnaise.

THOUSAND ISLAND DRESSING

Makes 150 ml ($\frac{1}{4}$ pint)

150 ml ($\frac{1}{4}$ pint) mayonnaise
15 ml (1 tbsp) chopped stuffed olives
5 ml (1 tsp) finely chopped onion
1 egg, hard-boiled, shelled and chopped
15 ml (1 tbsp) finely chopped green pepper
5 ml (1 tsp) chopped fresh parsley
5 ml (1 tsp) tomato purée

Mix all the ingredients together until well combined.

Not suitable for freezing

TARTARE SAUCE

Makes 150 ml ($\frac{1}{4}$ pint)

150 ml ($\frac{1}{4}$ pint) mayonnaise
5 ml (1 tsp) chopped fresh tarragon or chives
10 ml (2 tsp) chopped capers
10 ml (2 tsp) chopped gherkins
10 ml (2 tsp) chopped fresh parsley
15 ml (1 tbsp) lemon juice or tarragon vinegar

Mix all the ingredients well, then leave the sauce to stand for at least 1 hour before serving.

Serve with fish.

Not suitable for freezing

BLUE CHEESE DRESSING

Makes about 350 ml (12 fl oz)

150 ml ($\frac{1}{4}$ pint) mayonnaise
142 ml (5 fl oz) soured cream
75 g (3 oz) blue cheese, crumbled
5 ml (1 tsp) wine or cider vinegar
1 garlic clove, skinned and crushed

Mix all the ingredients well together. Allow to stand for several hours.

Not suitable for freezing

STOCKS AND SAUCES

A good stock is the basis of any soup or sauce and homemade stock is best of all. Ready-made stock preparations, in the form of bouillon cubes, save time in an emergency, but they can be rather salty. Sauces and chutneys add interest to all types of summer food. Some, like mint sauce, have an affinity with certain types of dish, others, like mayonnaise or tomato sauce, can be used with a variety of foods.

CHICKEN STOCK

Makes 1.1–1.4 litres (2–2½ pints)

carcass and bones of a cooked chicken
1.4–1.7 litres (2½–3 pints) water
onion, skinned and sliced
1 carrot, peeled and sliced
1 stick celery, washed, trimmed and sliced
bouquet garni (optional)

1 Break down the carcass and bones of the cooked chicken, and make sure to include any skin and chicken scraps.

2 Put in a pan with the water, onion, carrot, celery and the bouquet garni, if using.

3 Bring to the boil, skim and simmer, covered, for 3 hours. Or pressure cook at High (15-lb) pressure for 45–60 minutes.

4 Strain the stock thoroughly, discarding the flavouring vegetables, and leave to cool. When cold, remove all traces of fat.

BEEF STOCK

Makes about 1.4 litres (2½ pints)

450 g (1 lb) shin of beef, cut into pieces
450 g (1 lb) marrowbone or knuckle of veal, chopped
1.7 litres (3 pints) water
bouquet garni
1 onion, skinned and sliced
1 carrot, peeled and sliced
1 stick celery, washed, trimmed and sliced
2.5 ml (½ tsp) salt

1 To give a good flavour and colour, brown the bones and meat in the oven (exact temperature not important) before using.

2 Put in a pan with the water, bouquet garni, vegetables and salt. Bring to the boil, skim and simmer, covered, for 5–6 hours. Or pressure cook on High (15-lb) pressure for 1–1¼ hours using 1.4 litres (2½ pints) water. If using marrowbones, increase the water to 1.7 litres (3 pints) and cook the liquid for about 2 hours.

3 Strain the stock thoroughly, discarding the vegetables, and leave cool. Remove fat.

BEARNAISE SAUCE

Makes about 200 ml (⅓ pint)

30 ml (2 tbsp) tarragon vinegar
45 ml (3 tbsp) wine vinegar
15 ml (1 tbsp) finely chopped onion
2 egg yolks
10 ml (2 tsp) water
100 g (4 oz) butter, softened
salt and freshly ground pepper

1 Put the vinegars and the onion into a saucepan. Boil gently until the liquid is reduced by about one third. Cool and strain.

2 Put the egg yolks, reduced vinegar liquid and the cold water into a double saucepan or a bowl standing over a pan of gently simmering water. Whisk until thick and fluffy.

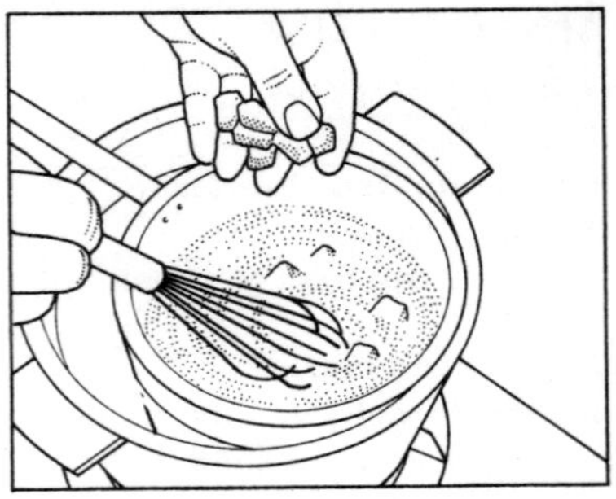

3 Gradually add the butter, a tiny piece at a time. Continue whisking until each piece has been absorbed by the sauce and the sauce itself has thickened. Season with salt and pepper. Serve with grilled or roast meats.

HOLLANDAISE SAUCE

Makes about 300 ml (½ pint)

5 ml (1 tsp) lemon juice
5 ml (1 tsp) wine vinegar
15 ml (1 tbsp) water
3 white peppercorns
½ small bay leaf
4 egg yolks
225 g (8 oz) butter, softened
salt and freshly ground pepper

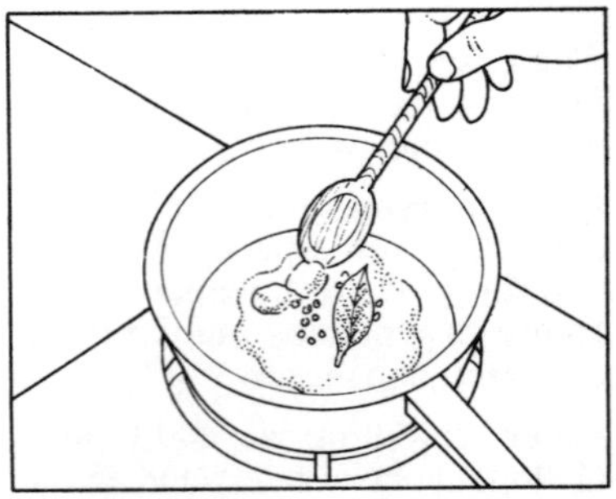

1 Put the lemon juice, vinegar, water, peppercorns and bay leaf into a saucepan. Boil gently until the liquid is reduced by half. Leave aside until cold and then strain thoroughly.

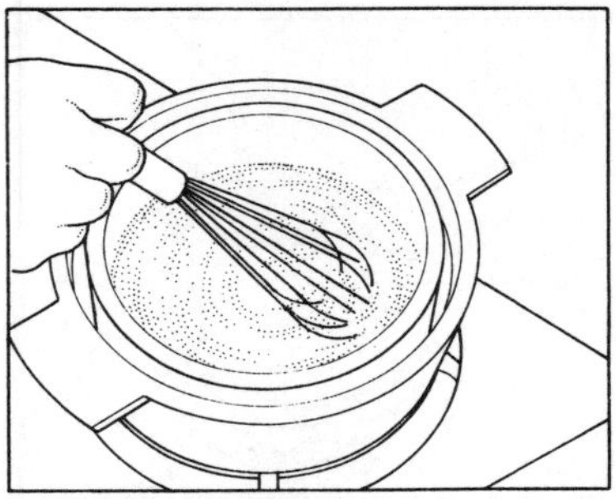

2 Put the egg yolks and reduced vinegar liquid into a double saucepan or a bowl standing over a pan of gently simmering water. Whisk until thick and fluffy.

3 Gradually add the butter, a tiny piece at a time. Continue whisking until each piece has been absorbed by the sauce and the sauce itself is the consistency of mayonnaise. Season with salt and pepper, and serve immediately. Serve with fish, egg, chicken and vegetable dishes

WHITE SAUCE

Makes 300 ml (½ pint) pouring sauce
15 g (½ oz) butter
15 g (½ oz) plain flour
300 ml (½ pint) milk
salt and freshly ground pepper

1 Melt the butter in a saucepan. Add the flour and cook over low heat, stirring with a wooden spoon, for 2 minutes. Do not allow the mixture to brown.

2 Remove the pan from the heat and gradually blend in the milk, stirring after each addition to prevent lumps forming.

3 Bring to the boil slowly and continue to cook, stirring all the time, until the sauce comes to the boil and thickens.

4 Simmer very gently for a further 2–3 minutes. Season the sauce with salt and freshly ground pepper.
Serve with fish, poultry, ham, bacon, egg and vegetable dishes

VARIATION

Coating sauce: follow the White Sauce recipe above, but increase butter and flour to 25 g (1 oz) each.

Cheese sauce: follow the recipe for White sauce or Coating sauce above. Before seasoning with salt and pepper, stir in 50 g (2 oz) finely grated Cheddar cheese, 2.5–5 ml (½–1 tsp) prepared mustard and a pinch of cayenne pepper.

TOMATO RELISH

Makes about 1.4 kg (3 lb)
1.4 kg (3 lb) tomatoes, skinned and sliced
450 g (1 lb) cucumber or marrow, peeled, seeded and roughly chopped
50 g (2 oz) salt
2 garlic cloves, skinned and finely chopped
1 large red pepper, cored, seeded and roughly chopped
450 ml (¾ pint) malt or cider vinegar
15 ml (1 tbsp) mustard powder
2.5 ml (½ tsp) ground allspice
2.5 ml (½ tsp) mustard seeds

1 Layer the tomatoes and cucumber or marrow in a bowl, sprinkling each layer with salt. Cover and leave overnight.

2 Next day, drain and rinse well and place in a large saucepan. Add the garlic and pepper.

3 Blend the vinegar with the spices, stir into the pan and bring slowly to the boil. Boil gently for about 1 hour, stirring occasionally, until the mixture is soft.

4 Spoon the relish into preheated jars and cover immediately with airtight and vinegarproof tops to seal completely.
Store for 3–4 months before use

PLUM CHUTNEY

Makes about 2.25 kg (4½ lb)
30 ml (2 tbsp) pickling spice
900 g (2 lb) plums, halved, stoned and chopped
225 g (8 oz) red tomatoes, skinned and chopped
900 ml (1½ pints) malt or cider vinegar
450 g (1 lb) onions, skinned and chopped
450 g (1 lb) cooking apples, peeled, cored and chopped
450 g (1 lb) carrots, trimmed, peeled and diced
100 g (4 oz) sultanas
450 g (1 lb) demerara sugar
15 ml (1 tbsp) salt

1 Tie the pickling spice in a piece of muslin. Place all the ingredients in a pan together with the muslin bag.

2 Bring to the boil and simmer for about 2½ hours, stirring occasionally, until thick. Remove the muslin bag.

3 Spoon the plum chutney into preheated jars and cover immediately with airtight, vinegar-proof tops.

MINT SAUCE

Makes about 300 ml (½ pint)
100 g (4 oz) chopped fresh mint
225 g (8 oz) sugar
300 ml (½ pint) vinegar

1 Put the mint into dry, wide-necked jars. Dissolve the sugar in the vinegar, stirring with a wooden spoon, and bring to the boil. Leave until cold.

2 Pour the cooled liquid over the mint and seal the jars to make them airtight. To serve, lift out sufficient mint with a wooden spoon, together with a little of the liquid. Put into a jug or sauce boat and add a little fresh vinegar.
Serve with lamb

Dressing a crab

Most fishmongers sell dressed crab, or will dress a crab for you while you wait – usually at no extra cost. But there are times – particularly on holiday – when you will need to dress a freshly caught crab yourself. It's not difficult to do, simply follow the step-by-step instructions. You'll find it far more satisfying serving crab you've dressed yourself than one which you have bought.

DRESSING A CRAB

1 medium (900 g/2 lb) uncooked crab
water
salt
1 bay leaf
15 ml (1 tbsp) lemon juice

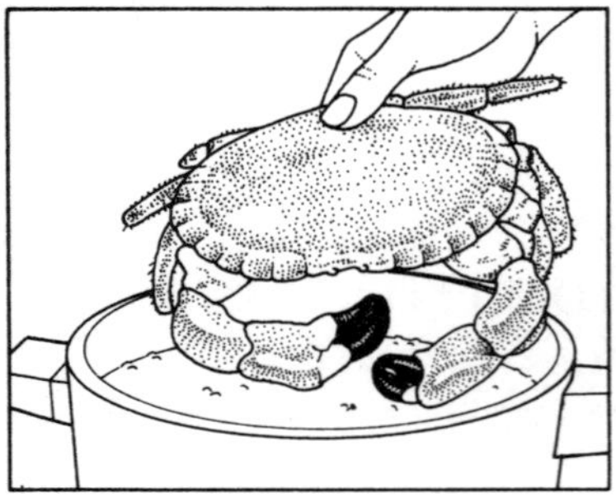

1 Place the crab in a large saucepan in cold, salted water. Add the bay leaf and lemon juice. Bring slowly to boiling point and boil fairly quickly, covered, for 10–20 minutes. Allow the crab to cool in the water.

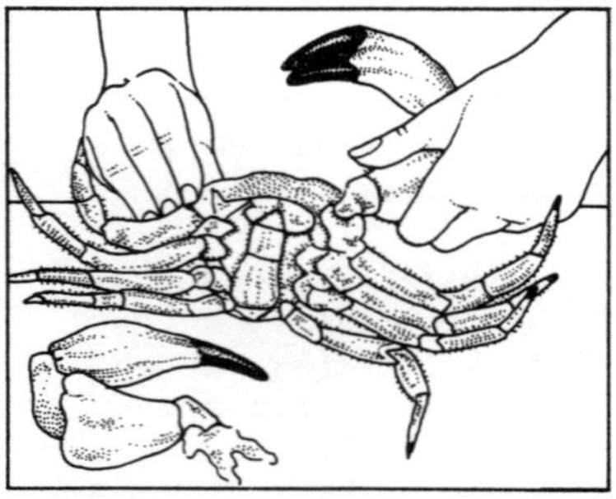

2 Place the crab on its back on a large chopping board. Take a claw firmly in one hand, holding it as close to the body of the crab as possible. Twist it off, steadying the body with the other hand.

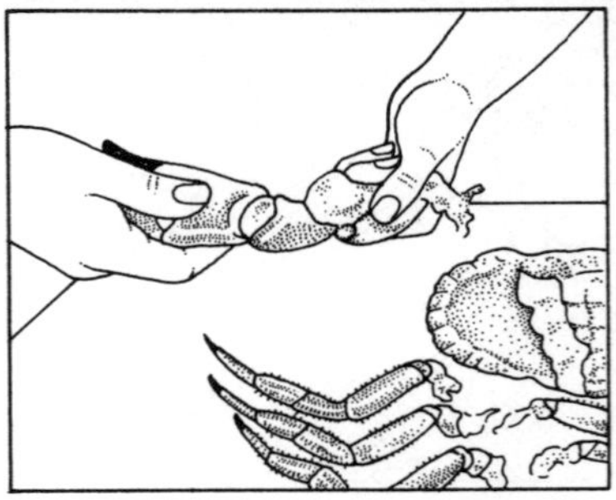

3 Remove the other claw and the legs in the same way. Snap the claws of the crab in half by bending them backwards at the natural joint. This maybe a little difficult.

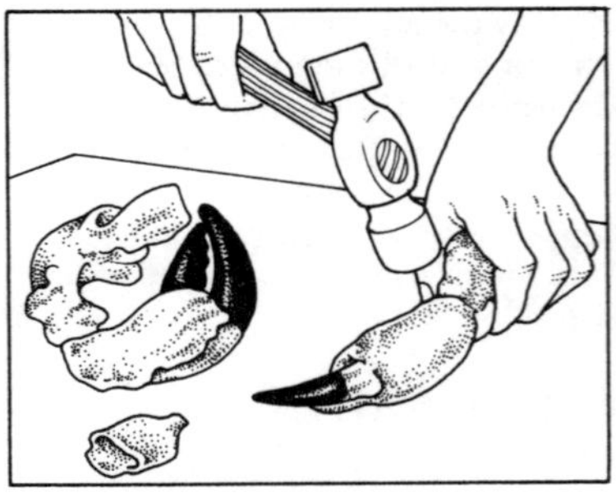

4 Hold the claws at the top end and, with a hammer or heavy weight, tap the shell smartly on the rounded edge to crack the claws open. Try not to shatter the shell during this process. Repeat with second claw.

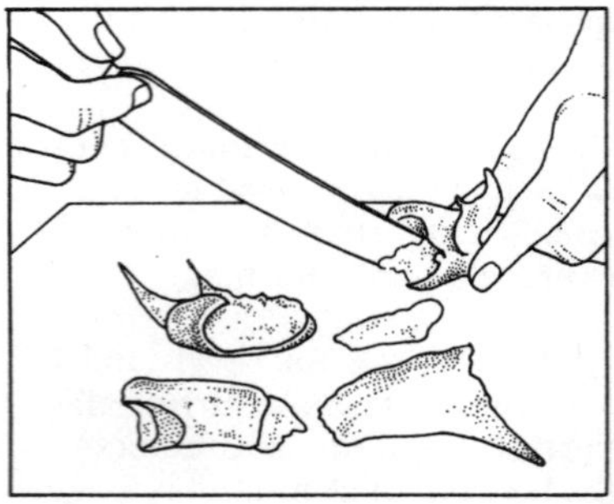

5 Using a blunt knife, ease the white meat out of the claws. Keep the blade as close to the edges of the shell as possible.

6 Using a teaspoon handle or skewer, reach well into the crevices to make sure all the white meat is removed. Discard any membrane.

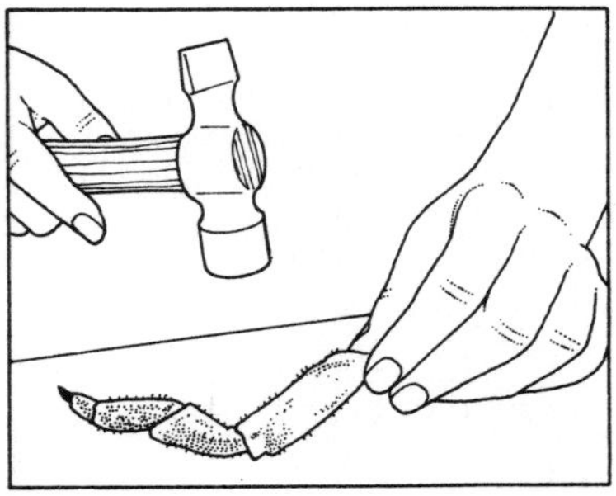

7 Crack the larger legs open and scrape out the white meat with the teaspoon handle or a skewer. Keep the small legs for decoration. Reserve all the scooped-out white meat in one bowl.

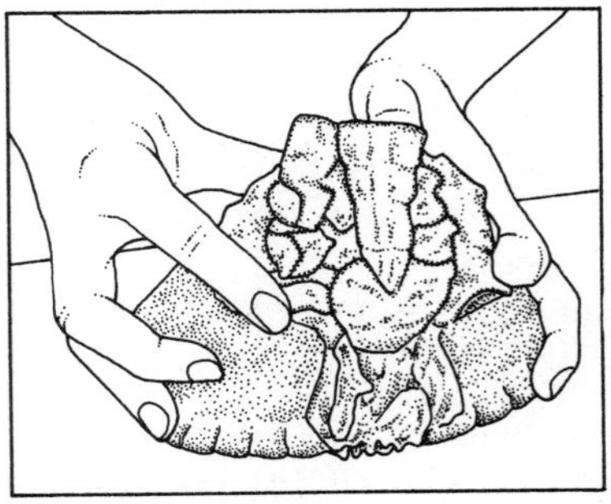

8 Place the crab on its back with the tail flap towards you, head away from you. Hold the shell firmly and press the body section upwards from beneath the tail flap and ease out with your thumbs until the body is detached.

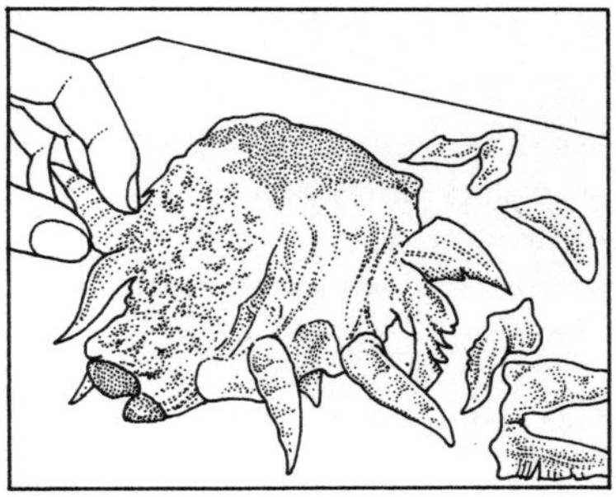

9 Pull off the inedible, grey feather-like gills (known as dead men's fingers) from the body section and discard them.

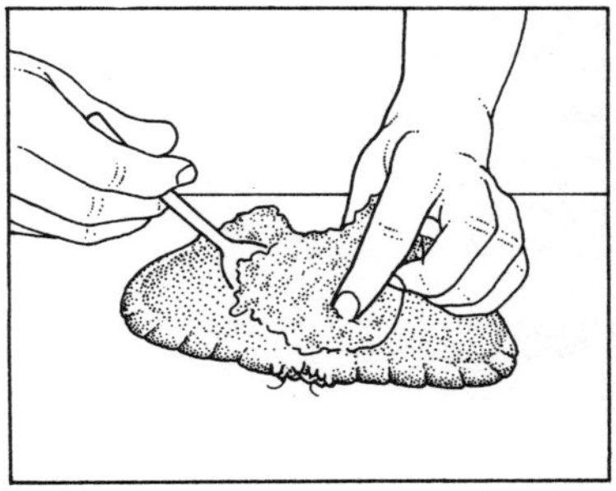

10 Use a spoon to remove stomach bag and mouth which are attached to the back shell. If the bag breaks, make sure you remove all the greenish or grey-white matter.

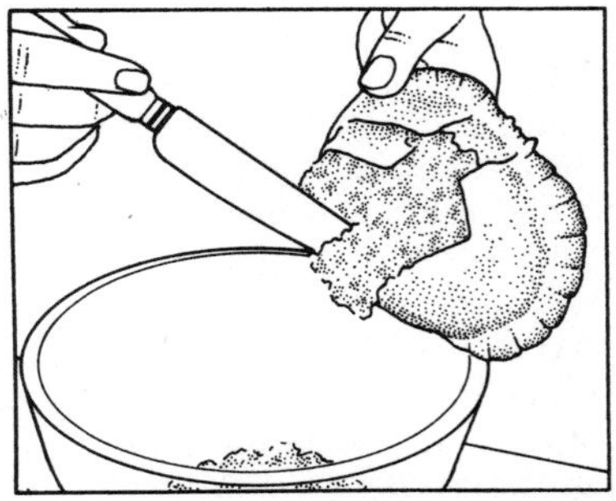

11 Ease the brown meat out of the shell, running a knife around the edge to bring it out smoothly. Put in another bowl.

12 Discard any membrane and scrape out corners with the handle of a teaspoon. Keep brown and white meat in separate basins.

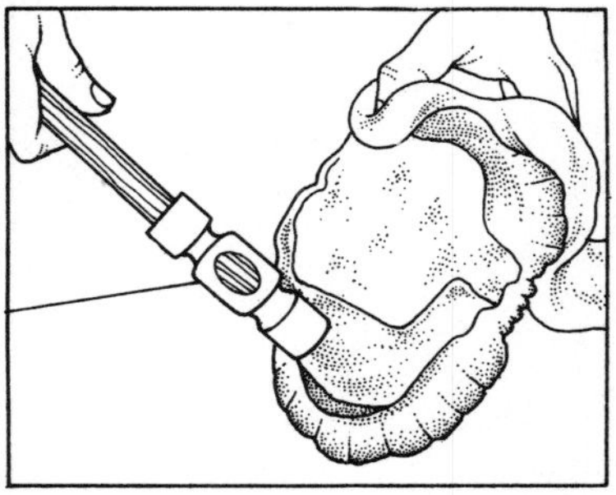

13 Protect your hand with a cloth. Hold the shell firmly and tap with the hammer just inside natural line of shell until inner shell breaks smoothly away.

14 Scrub the shell well under cold running water. Then dry the empty shell on absorbent kitchen paper and rub the outside lightly with oil.

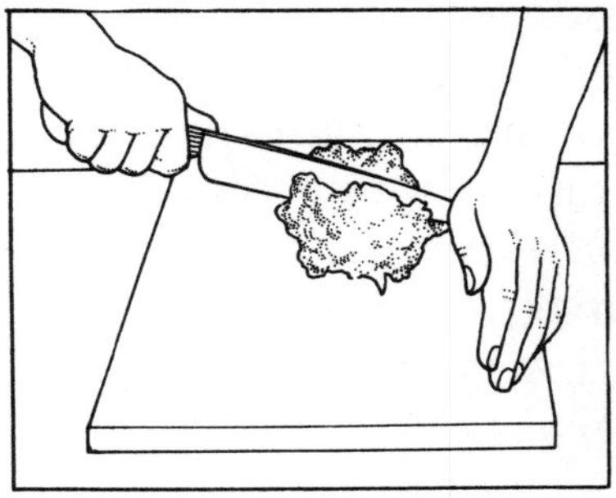

15 Place the body on its back on the board. Cut through the body to divide it in two.

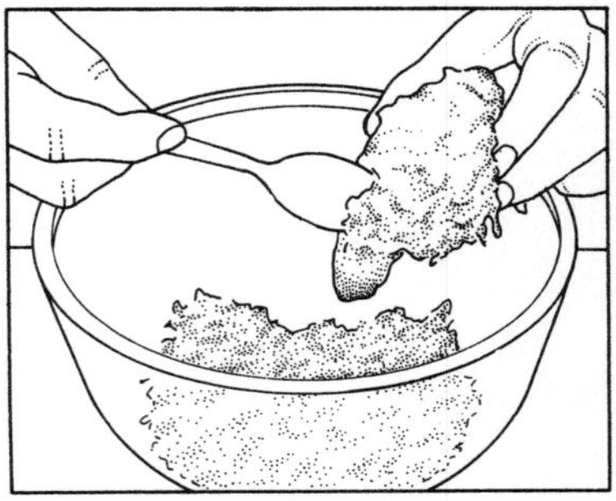

16 Spoon any creamy brown meat out into the bowl with the rest. Discard the body pieces. Complete dressing the crab as indicated on page 42.

Drinks

Here's a selection of drinks recipes for you to make at home. Summer punches and cups, home-made lemonade, iced tea and coffee – all reminiscent of long, hot summer days. Drinks to relax with – simplicity itself to make, and far nicer to drink than the commercial varieties. Get mixing right away!

ICED COFFEE

Serves 4–6

50 g (2 oz) ground coffee
900 ml (1½ pints) water
sugar, to taste
ice cube and whipped cream, to serve

Make some strong black coffee. While it is still hot, add sugar to taste. Cool and chill. To serve, pour into glasses, add an ice cube and top with whipped cream.

ICED TEA

Serves 4–6

25–35 ml (5–7 tsp) China tea
900 ml (1½ pints) water
crushed ice
sugar, to taste
lemon slice, to serve

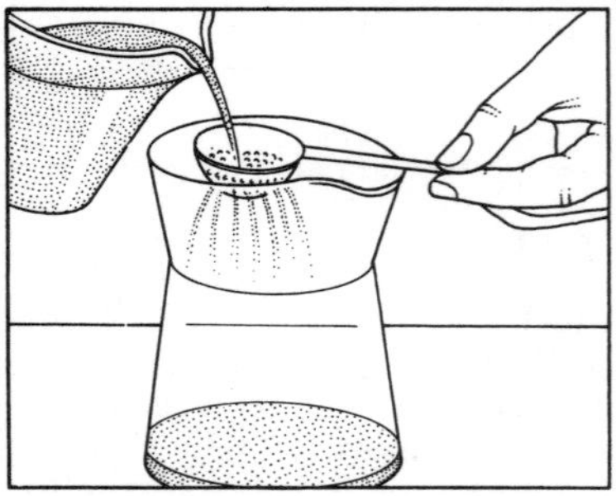

Make China tea in the usual way and strain into a jug. Add sugar to taste and chill. Serve in glasses which have been half filled with ice and a slice of lemon. Add a sprig of mint, if liked.

MILK SHAKES

Mix chilled milk with strong coffee, chocolate powder, fruit juice or syrup, or use a special milk shake flavouring; blend until frothy either with a rotary whisk or in an electric blender.

For an ice-cold milk shake, add 15–30 ml (1–2 tbsp) ice cream to each glass before serving.

ICE CREAM SODA

1 glass soda water per person
15 ml (1 tbsp) ice cream per person

Whisk the soda water and ice cream together with a rotary whisk until frothy or blend them at maximum speed for 1 minute in an electric blender. Pour into a large glass and serve at once.

ICED BANANA SHAKE

Makes 300 ml (½ pint)

300 ml (½ pint) milk
banana, peeled and mashed
30 ml (2 tbsp) ice cream

Whisk all the ingredients together with a rotary whisk until frothy, or blend at maximum speed for 1 minute in an electric blender or food processor. Pour the shake into a large glass.

COFFEE MILK SHAKE

Make as above, using 150 ml (5 fl oz) milk, 150 ml (5 fl oz) black coffee and 30 ml (2 tbsp) ice cream.

PINEAPPLE CRUSH

Serves 8

539-ml (19-fl oz) can pineapple juice
juice of 1 orange
juice of 1 lemon
sugar
1.1 litres (2 pints) ginger ale, chilled
pineapple sage or mint, to garnish (optional)

Combine the fruit juices, sweeten to taste and chill. Just before serving, add the ginger ale. Garnish with the sage, if liked.

SALT LASSI (Yogurt drink)

Serves 4–6

- 284 g (10 oz) natural yogurt
- 900 ml ($1\frac{1}{2}$ pints) water
- 3.75 ml ($\frac{3}{4}$ tsp) salt
- a little freshly ground pepper
- 3.75 ml ($\frac{3}{4}$ tsp) ground cumin seeds
- chopped fresh mint (optional)
- crushed ice, to serve

1 Place all the ingredients except the crushed ice in a blender or food processor and mix at high speed for 2–3 minutes.

2 To serve, add some crushed ice to individual glasses, pour the prepared lassi on top.

SWEET LASSI

Prepare salt lassi as above, but omit the salt, pepper and ground cumin seeds, and add 10–15 ml (2–3 tsp) sugar instead.

'STILL' LEMONADE

Makes about 1.1 litres (2 pints)

- 3 lemons
- 175 g (6 oz) sugar
- 900 ml ($1\frac{1}{2}$ pints) boiling water

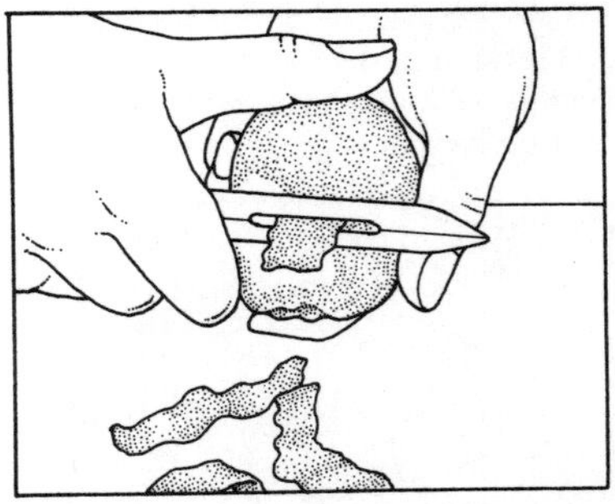

1 Wash the lemons and peel off the rind thinly with a potato peeler. Put rind and sugar into a basin and pour on the water.

2 Cover and leave to cool, stirring occasionally. Add the juice of the lemons and strain the lemonade. Serve chilled.

SUMMER PUNCH

Serves 18–20

- 3 bottles medium white wine, chilled
- $\frac{3}{4}$ bottle dry sherry
- 60 ml (4 tbsp) Grand Marnier
- 4 small bottles tonic water
- crushed ice
- 3 cucumber slices, a slice of apple and a fresh mint sprig per jug, to garnish

1 Mix the wine, sherry, orange-flavoured liqueur and tonic in one or more jugs and chill the liquid before serving.

2 To serve, add crushed ice and garnish with the cucumber, apple and mint.

BRANDY CIDER CUP

Makes about 2 litres ($3\frac{1}{2}$ pints)

- 600 ml (1 pint) weak China tea
- 50 g (2 oz) sugar
- juice of 2 oranges
- 90–120 ml (6–8 tbsp) brandy
- 1 litre ($1\frac{3}{4}$ pints) cider
- lemon, thinly sliced

Infuse the tea and strain it on to the sugar in a bowl. Cool and add the orange juice and brandy. Just before serving add the cider and decorate with the lemon slices.

SANGRIA

- 3 pints red wine
- bottle Champagne or sparkling white wine
- 60 ml (4 tbsp) brandy
- 15 ml (1 tbsp) Cointreau
- juice of 1 lemon
- assorted fruit—1 sliced orange and lemon
- bananas, apples and grapes (without skin or pips)

Let mixture stand for 2 or 3 hours to allow flavours of the fruits to be thoroughly absorbed. Serve the sangria well iced.

WHITE WINE CUP

Makes about 3.7 litres ($6\frac{1}{2}$ pints)

- crushed ice
- 3 bottles white wine
- $\frac{3}{4}$ bottle dry sherry
- 60 ml (4 tbsp) curaçao
- 4 'splits' tonic water
- 3 slices of cucumber, a slice of apple and a sprig of borage per jug

Mix all the ingredients together in one or more jugs and chill before serving.

PINEAPPLE CIDER CUP

Makes about 5.5 litres (10 pints)

- 4.5 litres (8 pints) dry cider
- 600 ml (1 pint) soda water
- orange
- lemon
- 340-g (12-oz) can pineapple pieces, drained
- 12 maraschino cherries
- 150 ml ($\frac{1}{4}$ pint) dry sherry
- sprigs of mint, to decorate

1 Chill the cider and the soda water in the bottles. Pare the orange and lemon rind free of all the white pith and put in a bowl with the pineapple pieces, cherries, sherry, orange juice and lemon juice and chill.

2 Just before serving, pour the cider and soda water over this mixture and decorate with sprigs of fresh mint.

Freezing Summer Produce

Summer is the peak time of year for fruit and vegetables and, whether you grow your own in the garden or have access to cheap supplies from a local farm or market, if you own a freezer it should be the busiest time of year for stocking up.

Freezer owners can take advantage of gluts and bargain bulk buys so that when dreary autumn and winter comes they can enjoy the luxury of out-of-season produce without having to pay the earth.

How to Freeze Vegetables

Most vegetables freeze successfully unless they have a very high water content such as cucumbers or Jerusalem artichokes. Only freeze the very youngest and freshest of produce —ideally all vegetables should be frozen just as they reach maturity.

PREPARATION

The only disadvantage to freezing vegetables is the amount of time you need to set aside for preparation, before you can actually put them in the freezer, so when you have lots of vegetables to freeze, allow yourself plenty of time. All vegetables must be fully prepared, that is scrubbed or peeled, with roots, leaves and damaged parts removed. Vegetables in the pod should be podded before freezing (except in the case of mangetouts and very young broad beans which can be frozen whole). The blanching of vegetables is recommended (see below) and, although time-consuming, is well worth the trouble in the long run because it increases the storage life of vege-

HOW TO BLANCH VEGETABLES

Blanching is a scalding process which halts enzyme activity in vegetables. Though not absolutely essential, it is advisable. Enzymes are naturally present in food; they are not harmful, but if they are not halted in this way, they will continue to work during storage in the freezer and after a period of time will cause the vegetables to lose colour, flavour and texture and, most important of all, ascorbic acid (vitamin C). Obviously the blanching process itself causes loss of ascorbic acid, but this is only slight compared with the amount which would be lost during storage if the vegetables are not blanched.

Short-term storage In times of glut and/or when you are too busy to blanch vegetables before freezing they can be frozen unblanched, but in this case storage times will be shortened by as much as one-quarter. Plan to use these vegetables as soon as you possibly can after freezing. Special blanching sets are available which are worth buying if you freeze a lot of vegetables, otherwise use a large saucepan and a colander or wire basket.

1 Bring 3.6 litres (6 pints) *unsalted* water to the boil in the pan, place 450 g (1 lb) vegetables in the basket and immerse in the boiling water. Bring the water back to the boil immediately, then blanch the vegetables for the recommended length of time (see chart pages 154–6).

2 Have ready a large bowl of iced water. Immediately the blanching time is up, remove the basket from the boiling water. Quickly plunge the basket of vegetables into the water and leave until the vegetables are cold (cooling time is usually the same as scalding time).

3 Remove the basket from the water, drain the vegetables, then tip them out onto a clean tea towel or absorbent kitchen paper. Dry, then pack immediately to avoid discoloration.

tables in the freezer and also maintains their fresh quality. For example, a notable change in the eating quality of unblanched Brussels sprouts can be detected after only 3 days; in broad beans after 3 weeks; in runner beans after 1 month; in peas after 6 months.

One plus point with blanching which cuts down on time is that the same blanching water doesn't have to be renewed with every batch of vegetables —the same water can be used six or seven times, and by doing so you will in fact achieve a build-up of vitamin C in the blanching water and less loss of minerals, though the iced water for cooling after blanching should be renewed with each batch.

PACKING VEGETABLES FOR THE FREEZER

Vegetables can be packed in either rigid polythene containers or freezer-proof polythene bags, whichever is most convenient for you. Vegetables such as peas, beans and sweetcorn are best frozen as free-flow packs in polythene bags so that they do not stick together as one solid mass and you can use as many or as few as you like. Open-freeze them on trays before packing in this way (see open-freezing method for fruit, right).

THAWING AND COOKING VEGETABLES

Always cook vegetables from frozen to avoid overcooking (this is especially important when they have been blanched before freezing). Plunge then into a minimum amount of boiling salted water (about 300 ml (½ pint) water) and 2.5 ml (½ tsp) salt to every 450 g (1 lb) vegetables.

Alternatively, frozen vegetables can be cooked in a covered pan with butter, seasoning and herbs; or added to soups and stews without prior cooking.

HOW TO FREEZE FRUIT

All fruits are suitable for freezing, either whole or sliced, mashed or puréed to a pulp. Possible exceptions are bananas, which can only be frozen if mashed to a purée and combined with other ingredients, and pomegranates, which are too watery. As with vegetables, it is only worth freezing top-quality produce. Ideally, fruits should be frozen just at the point when they become ready for eating, but slightly over-ripe fruits can still be used for purées.

PREPARATION

Rinse all fruits (except for soft fruits) in ice-cold water, a few at a time, then drain. If slicing fruits which are likely to discolour, drop them into a bowl of acidulated water during preparation.

PACKING FRUIT FOR THE FREEZER

There are four ways of packing fruit for the freezer. Use only the methods recommended for each individual type (see chart, pages 156–8) or you will have disappointing results.

Dry pack method Suitable for small, whole fruits with perfect, undamaged skins which are not likely to discolour: examples are blackberries, cherries, currants, gooseberries and strawberries. Fruits frozen in this way can become mis-shapen through freezing together in a solid mass and are best used in pies and preserves where perfect shape is not important.

To dry pack: pick over fruits; wash, then dry. Pack in rigid containers.

Open-freezing method Recommended for small whole fruits or pieces of fruit which need to keep their shape during storage: examples are apple slices, cherries, and strawberries which are used in open tarts and flans or as decorations for desserts and cakes.

To open-freeze: pick over fruits, prepare as necessary (see chart, pages 156–8), then spread out on a tray. Freeze until solid, then remove and pack in rigid containers or freezer bags for free-flow packs.

Dry sugar pack method This method helps soft, juicy fruits retain their shape and texture during freezing; ideal for berries which produce a sweetened juice on thawing—perfect for mousses, fruit salads, or for serving with cream or ice cream.

To make a dry sugar pack: put a layer of fruit in the bottom of a rigid container, then sprinkle with caster sugar. Repeat layers to fill container, leaving 2 cm (¾ inch) headspace.

Sugar syrup pack method Best for non-juicy fruits which have a low vitamin C content and stone fruits which discolour easily (such as apricots, peaches and pears).

When preparing fruits, make sure you have enough syrup to make it a day in advance and refrigerate overnight.

To make sugar syrup: dissolve the sugar in the water by heating gently. Bring to the boil, then remove from the heat, strain, cover and cool. Allow 300 ml (½ pint) syrup for every 450 g (1 lb) fruit.

Prepare fruit quickly (see chart, pages 156–8), place in rigid containers and immediately pour over cold sugar syrup, leaving 2 cm (¾ inch) headspace.

THAWING AND COOKING FRUIT

If the fruit is served raw, thaw in unopened container and eat chilled. Stone fruits frozen in a sugar syrup should be kept submerged when thawing—open the container just before serving or fruits will discolour.

Thawing times for fruit

In a refrigerator	6–8 hours
At room temperature	2–4 hours

Dry packs and dry sugar packs thaw more quickly than sugar syrup packs. For quick, emergency thawing, place the container in a bowl of slightly warm water for 30 minutes–1 hour. If fruit is cooked, thaw until pieces are just loosened. Cook as for fresh fruit, but if it is packed in sugar or sugar syrup, decrease or omit sugar.

VEGETABLE	PREPARATION	PACKAGING AND STORAGE TIME	THAWING
Artichoke, Globe	Remove outer leaves and stalks. Trim tops and stems. Wash. Blanch in water with lemon juice for 5–7 mins. Drain and cool upside down.	Pack in rigid containers. 6 months	Cook from frozen in boiling salted water for approx. 7 mins according to size.
Asparagus	Cut off woody ends. Scrape off fibrous scales. Grade into thick and thin stems. Wash. Blanch thin stems 2 mins, thick 4 mins. Drain and cool.	Tie into small bundles. Pack bundles tips to stalks in rigid containers, separating them with freezerproof non-stick paper. 9 months	Cook from frozen to avoid over-cooking. Plunge into boiling salted water and cook for 2 mins according to size.
Aubergine	Peel if liked. Slice into 2.5 cm (1 inch) rounds or dice. Sprinkle with salt, leave 30 mins. Rinse and drain. Blanch 3–4 mins. Drain and cool.	Pack in layers in rigid containers, separating layers with freezerproof non-stick paper. 12 months	Thaw in unopened containers until just beginning to soften, then use as fresh.
Avocado	Will not freeze whole, so prepare in pulp form. Peel and mash with 15 ml (1 tbsp) lemon juice to each avocado.	Quickly pack pulp in rigid containers. Seal and freeze immediately to prevent discoloration. 2 months maximum	Thaw in unopened containers for approx. 2 hrs. Use as soon as possible or flesh will discolour.
Bean (Broad/French/ Runner)	Broad: Shell and blanch 3 mins. French: Trim ends and blanch 2–3 mins; runner: Slice thickly and blanch 2 mins. Drain and cool.	Pack in usable quantities in freezer-proof polythene bags, or open-freeze and pack as free-flow packs. 12 months	Cook from frozen in boiling salted water: broad beans 3–5 mins; French and runner 5–7 mins.
Beetroot	Only freeze small whole beetroot. Boil in water with 5 ml (1 tsp) vinegar 5–10 mins until tender. Drain and rub off skins. Cool.	Pack in rigid containers either whole or in slices. 6 months maximum	Thaw in unopened containers at room temperature approx. 4 hrs. Use in salads or heat through as a hot vegetable.
Broccoli (Calabrese or green sprouting)	Remove outer leaves and trim stem. Divide into sprigs and remove woody stalks. Wash in salted water. Blanch thin sprigs 3 mins, medium 4 mins, thick 5 mins. Drain and cool.	Pack sprigs of similar size in rigid containers, alternating heads. 12 months	Cook from frozen in boiling salted water 3–7 mins according to size.
Cabbage (hard green/red/ white)	Remove outer leaves. Wash. Shred. Blanch 1½ mins. Drain and cool.	Pack in usable quantities in freezer-proof polythene bags. 6 months	Cook from frozen in a little salted water with a knob of butter for 5 mins.
Carrot	Scrub or scrape. Leave whole if young, otherwise slice or dice. Blanch whole carrots 3 mins, slices and dice 2 mins. Drain and cool.	Pack in usable quantities in freezer-proof polythene bags or open-freeze and pack as free-flow packs. 12 months	Cook from frozen in boiling salted water 3–5 mins according to size. Slices and dice can be added frozen to casseroles and soups.
Cauliflower	Only freeze the head as individual florets, approx. 5 cm (2 inches) in diameter. Blanch 2–3 mins according to size with 15 ml (1 tbsp) lemon juice to each 600 ml (1 pint) water. Drain and cool.	Open-freeze and pack as free-flow packs. 6 months	Cook from frozen in boiling salted water 4–6 mins according to size.
Celery	Scrub separated stalks and cut into 5 cm (2 inch) lengths. Blanch 3 mins. Drain and cool.	Pack in usable quantities in freezer-proof polythene bags. 9 months	Use frozen in casseroles and soups, etc, or thaw at room temperature 2–4 hrs and use in made-up cooked dishes.
Courgette	Do not peel. Leave small, young courgettes whole or halve lengthways. Cut large courgettes into 1 cm (½ inch) slices. Blanch whole courgettes 2 mins, halves and slices 1 min. Drain and cool.	Pack in usable quantities in freezer-proof polythene bags or open-freeze and pack as free-flow packs. 6 months	Thaw in bags 2 hrs at room temperature then use as fresh. Slices can be added frozen to casseroles, soups and made-up cooked dishes.
Fennel	Trim off frondy top. Cut bulb lengthways into quarters. Blanch 3 mins. Drain and cool.	Pack in usable quantities in freezer-proof polythene bags. 6 months	Cook from frozen in boiling salted water 7 mins, or leave in bags at room temperature until soft enough to slice, then use in dishes.

VEGETABLE	PREPARATION	PACKAGING AND STORAGE TIME	THAWING
Fresh herbs	Only freeze freshly gathered herbs. Wash only if absolutely necessary and shake dry. Separate into sprigs; then strip off leaves, or chop leaves finely (but not bay, rosemary, sage and thyme). To increase storage leave on sprigs. Blanch 1 min. Drain and cool.	Pack sprigs in freezerproof polythene bags or rigid containers; keep all one kind together or combine them in *bouquets garnis*. Pack whole and chopped leaves in ice cube trays, fill with water, open-freeze until solid then remove from trays and pack together in freezerproof polythene bags. 6 months (9 months for blanched)	Use sprigs from freezer for cooking, either whole or by crumbling leaves with fingers. Add frozen cubes of herbs to cooked dishes, or thaw 1 hr at room temperature and use as fresh.
Garlic	Only freeze whole bulbs—do not separate into cloves.	Wrap bulbs individually in foil or cling film, then pack several cloves together in a freezerproof polythene bag. Overwrap. 3 months maximum	Break individual cloves from frozen whole bulb and thaw approx. 2 hrs at room temperature before using as fresh.
Kohlrabi (small roots only)	Cut off leaves. Peel. Slice or dice. Blanch 1½–2 mins. Drain and cool.	Open-freeze and pack as free-flow packs. 12 months	Steam from frozen 10–12 mins, or stir-fry from frozen, or thaw 2–4 hrs and deep-fry in batter.
Leek	Remove green tops, roots and outer leaves. Cut into 1 cm (½ inch) slices and wash thoroughly. Blanch 3 mins. Drain and cool. Or sauté 4 mins in butter or oil and cool.	Pack in usable quantities in polythene bags. 6 months	Use frozen in made-up cooked dishes.
Marrow	Peel. Cut into chunks, discarding seeds. Blanch 2 mins. Drain and cool.	Pack in rigid containers. 6 months	Steam from frozen 2 mins.
Mushroom (only small button)	Wipe clean (do not wash or peel). Trim stalks. Sauté in butter 1 min. Cool.	Open-freeze and pack as free-flow packs. 3 months	Sauté from frozen in butter.
Onion	Peel small pickling onions and leave whole. Peel large onions, then slice or dice. Blanch whole onions 2 mins, slices or dice 1 min. Drain and cool.	Open-freeze whole onions and pack as free-flow packs. Pack slices and dice in usable quantities in freezerproof polythene bags. Overwrap. 3 months	Use frozen in casseroles, etc, or thaw in bags 2 hrs at room temperature, then use as fresh.
Pea (including mange-tout)	Freeze only very young peas. Shell and blanch 1 min, shaking basket to distribute heat evenly. Drain and cool. Top and tail mange-touts. Blanch 30–60 secs.	Open-freeze and pack as free-flow packs. 12 months	Cook shelled peas from frozen 4 mins in boiling salted water, or add frozen to casseroles and soups, etc. Sauté frozen mange-touts in butter for few minutes only.
Pepper, sweet (capsicum)	Wash and dry. Halve, then remove core, seeds and stalk. Leave as halves, or slice or dice. Do not blanch.	Open-freeze and pack as free-flow packs. 6 months	Add frozen to casseroles, soups and other cooked made-up dishes. Thaw halves in bags 2 hrs at room temperature, then stuff as fresh.
Potato (new)	Only freeze small, even-sized potatoes. Scrape. Cook in boiling salted water until just tender. Drain and cool.	Pack in usable quantities in freezerproof polythene bags. 12 months	Steam from frozen with butter and mint. Take care not to overcook.
Spinach (including sorrel and Swiss chard)	Wash individual leaves thoroughly and remove thick stalks. Leave whole or tear. Blanch 2 mins. Drain and cool. Purée if liked.	Pack in usable quantities in polythene bags. 12 months	Cook from frozen in a heavy pan with butter and seasonings until thawed.
Sweetcorn	Only freeze young corn. Remove silks and husks. Trim stalks. Blanch whole corn-on-the-cob 4–8 mins according to size. Drain and cool. Kernels can be stripped off cob with a sharp knife, if liked.	Wrap cobs individually in foil or cling film, then open-freeze and pack together in freezerproof polythene bags. Open-freeze kernels and pack as free-flow packs. 12 months	Thaw whole cobs overnight in refrigerator, then boil in unsalted water with a little sugar 5 mins or until tender. Cook kernels from frozen 4 mins in boiling water, or add frozen to casseroles, soups, etc.

VEGETABLE	PREPARATION	PACKAGING AND STORAGE TIME	THAWING
Tomato	Whole and halved tomatoes can be frozen, but as they can only be used in cooking, they are most useful frozen as a purée: skin and core, simmer 5 mins then purée through sieve or in blender.	Pack whole tomatoes in usable quantities in freezerproof polythene bags. Pack halves in rigid containers, separating layers. Pack purée in rigid containers, leaving headspace. 12 months	Thaw whole tomatoes 2 hrs at room temperature, then use as fresh in cooking. Grill halves from frozen. Thaw purée at room temperature until usable consistency.
Turnip	Only freeze small, young turnips. Trim and peel. Slice or dice. Blanch 2½ mins. Drain and cool. Or cook 10 mins until tender, then drain and mash.	Open-freeze slices and dice and pack as free-flow packs. Pack mashed turnip in rigid containers, leaving headspace. 12 months	Cook slices and dice from frozen 5 mins in boiling salted water. Or add frozen to casseroles, soups, etc. Reheat frozen mashed turnip in a double boiler.

FRUIT	PREPARATION	PACKAGING AND STORAGE TIME	THAWING
Apple	Peel, core and slice. Keep in water with lemon juice added (to prevent discoloration). Blanch cooking apples 1 min. Drain and cool. Can also be cooked to a purée—cool before packing.	Immediately pack drained slices in rigid containers or freezerproof polythene bags. Pack purée in rigid containers, leaving headspace. 12 months (8 months for apple purée)	Thaw in unopened containers 1 hr at room temperature. Or use from frozen in pies, puddings and sauces, etc.
Apricot	Prepare quickly to avoid discoloration. Peel whole fruit after plunging into boiling water 30 secs. Leave fruit whole or cut in halves or slices. Or cook to a purée with or without sugar and cool.	Pack whole fruit, halves and slices in rigid containers in sugar syrup made from 450 g (1 lb) sugar to 1.1 litres (2 pints) water plus 20 ml (4 tsp) lemon juice. Immerse fruit by placing crumpled paper under lid of container. Pack purée in rigid containers, leaving headspace. 12 months	Thaw in unopened containers 3–4 hrs in refrigerator, then use as soon as possible to avoid discoloration. Or use from frozen in cooked pies and puddings, etc. Fruit frozen in syrup can be poached in syrup after thawing.
Avocado	SEE CHART FOR VEGETABLES		
Bilberry (or Blueberry)	Wash and drain thoroughly. Leave whole or crush lightly with 100 g (4 oz) sugar to 450–700 g (1–1½ lb) fruit.	Whole fruit: dry pack; or open-freeze and pack as free-flow packs; or pack in rigid containers with sugar syrup made from 900 g (2 lb) sugar to 1.1 litres (2 pints) water, leaving headspace. Pack crushed fruit in rigid containers. 12 months	Thaw in unopened containers 2½ hrs at room temperature. Poach fruit in syrup after thawing.
Blackberry	Pick over and remove stalks. Wash only if absolutely necessary. Leave whole, or cook with a little water and sugar to taste, then purée if liked. Cool.	Whole fruit: dry pack; or open-freeze and pack as free-flow packs; or dry sugar pack allowing 100–175 g (4–6 oz) sugar to 450 g (1 lb) fruit. Pour cooked and puréed fruit into rigid containers, leaving headspace. 12 months	Tip dry and dry sugar packs into a bowl and thaw approx. 2 hrs at room temperature. Thaw purée in container overnight in refrigerator, or heat from frozen in heavy pan.
Cherry	Remove stalks. Wash and dry. Remove stones. Leave raw, or poach in water until tender. Cool.	Whole sweet cherries: dry pack; or open-freeze and pack as free-flow packs; or dry sugar pack allowing 100 g (4 oz) sugar to 450 g (1 lb) fruit. Pack sour cherries in rigid containers with sugar syrup made from 450 g (1 lb) sugar to 1.1 litres (2 pints) water plus 2.5 ml (½ tsp) ascorbic acid, leaving headspace. Pack poached cherries in rigid containers, leaving headspace. 12 months (raw); 8 months (poached)	Thaw raw and poached cherries in unopened package 3 hrs at room temperature. Use immediately package is opened or fruit will discolour.

FRUIT	PREPARATION	PACKAGING AND STORAGE TIME	THAWING
Currant (black/red/ white)	Remove stalks. Wash and dry fruit. Top and tail. Leave whole or crush lightly with sugar to taste. Or cook with a little water and sugar to taste, then purée or sieve if liked. Cool.	Whole currants: dry pack; or open-freeze and pack as free-flow packs; or pack in rigid containers with sugar syrup made from 700 g (1½ lb) sugar to 1.1 litres (2 pints) water, leaving headspace. Pack crushed, cooked and puréed fruit in rigid containers, leaving headspace. 12 months	Cook from frozen or thaw in containers 1–2 hrs at room temperature.
Damson	Wash and dry fruit. Do not freeze whole as skins will toughen. Halve fruit and remove stones. Or cook with a little water and sugar to taste, then sieve to remove skins and stones. Cool.	Pack halves in rigid containers with sugar syrup made from 450 g (1 lb) sugar to 1.1 litres (2 pints) water, leaving headspace. Pack purée in rigid containers, leaving headspace. 12 months.	Thaw halves in syrup 2½ hrs at room temperature, then poach until tender. Thaw purée in containers 1 hr at room temperature or cook from frozen.
Fig	Wipe or wash gently to avoid bruising. Remove stems. Peel if liked.	Wrap unpeeled figs individually in foil then pack together in freezerproof polythene bags. Pack peeled figs immediately in rigid containers with sugar syrup made from 225 g (8 oz) sugar to 1.1 litres (2 pints) water, leaving headspace. 12 months	Thaw in bags or containers approx. 2 hrs at room temperature then use as fresh.
Gooseberry	Wash. Top and tail if freezing as dry sugar pack, in syrup sugar or as stewed whole fruit. Leave raw or cook with a little water and sugar to taste, then sieve if liked.	Whole raw gooseberries: dry pack; or open-freeze and pack as free-flow packs; or dry sugar pack allowing 100–175 g (4–6 oz) sugar to 450 g (1 lb) fruit; or pack in rigid containers with sugar syrup made from 700 g (1½ lb) sugar to 1.1 litres (2 pints) water leaving headspace. Pour cooked and puréed fruit into rigid containers, leaving headspace. 12 months	Rub off tops and tails from frozen dry and free-flow packs, then cook from frozen. Cook dry sugar and sugar syrup packs from frozen or thaw in containers 2½ hrs at room temperature, then cook. Thaw cooked and puréed fruit in containers 2½ hrs at room temperature.
Grape	Leave seedless varieties whole, in bunches if liked. All other grapes should be peeled, halved and seeded.	Whole grapes and bunches: open-freeze and pack as free-flow packs. Halves: pack in rigid containers with sugar syrup made from 450 g (1 lb) sugar to 1.1 litres (2 pints) water, leaving headspace. 12 months	Thaw in bags or containers approx. 2 hrs at room temperature.
Mango	Only freeze ripe (not green) fruit. Peel and slice, discarding stone.	Immediately pack sliced flesh in rigid containers with sugar syrup made from 700 g (1½ lb) sugar to 1.1 litres (2 pints) water plus 20 ml (4 tsp) lemon juice, leaving headspace. 12 months	Thaw in unopened containers 1–2 hrs at room temperature, then use as soon as possible while still slightly chilled—to avoid discoloration.
Melon (Cantaloupe and Honeydew varieties—not Watermelon)	Only freeze perfectly ripe fruit. Cut in half, remove seeds and fibres. Cut flesh into pieces or use a melon baller to make even-sized balls.	Dry sugar pack allowing 100–175 g (4–6 oz) sugar to 450 g (1 lb) fruit, or pack in rigid containers with sugar syrup made from 450 g (1 lb) sugar to 1.1 litres (2 pints) water, leaving headspace. 12 months	Thaw in unopened bags or containers 1–2 hrs at room temperature, then serve chilled to preserve firm texture as much as possible.
Pawpaw (Papaya)	Peel. Halve lengthways. Scoop out and discard seeds. Slice flesh thinly. Purée ripe fruit with sugar and lemon juice to taste, if liked.	Freeze unripe slices in savoury dishes, e.g. casseroles. Freeze ripe slices as for mango above. Pour purée into rigid containers, leaving headspace. 12 months	Thaw slices as for mango above. Thaw purée in unopened containers overnight in refrigerator.

FRUIT	PREPARATION	PACKAGING AND STORAGE TIME	THAWING
Peach (including nectarine)	Prepare quickly to avoid discoloration. Fruit must be peeled before freezing: peel firm fruit as for apricot above, ripe fruit by holding under cold running water and rubbing off with fingers. Halve fruit and remove stones. Leave as halves or slice.	Pack halves and slices in rigid containers with sugar syrup made from 450 g (1 lb) sugar to 1.1 litres (2 pints) water plus juice of 1 lemon, leaving headspace. Pour purée into rigid containers, leaving headspace. 12 months	Thaw in unopened containers 3–4 hrs in refrigerator, then use as soon as possible to avoid discoloration. Fruit frozen in syrup can be poached in syrup after thawing.
Pear	Prepare quickly to avoid discoloration. Cooking pears: peel, core and leave whole, or cut into halves or quarters. Immediately poach in water, sugar and flavourings or spices until just tender. Cool. Dessert pears: peel. Cut into halves or quarters, removing cores. Brush with lemon.	Cooking pears: pack in rigid containers with cooking liquid, leaving headspace. Dessert pears: immediately pack in rigid containers with sugar syrup made from 700 g (1½ lb) sugar to 1.1 litres (2 pints) water, leaving headspace. 12 months	Thaw in unopened containers 2½ hrs at room temperature, then use as soon as possible to avoid discoloration. Poached pears can be reheated gently in cooking liquid after thawing.
Pineapple	Only freeze ripe fruit. Peel and core. Cut flesh into rings or chunks. Flesh can also be crushed, with or without sugar.	Dry pack rings and chunks, interleaving layers with freezerproof paper; or pack in rigid containers with sugar syrup made from 450 g (1 lb) sugar to 1.1 litres (2 pints) water, leaving headspace. Pack crushed pineapple in rigid containers, leaving headspace. 12 months	Thaw in unopened containers 2½ hrs at room temperature.
Plum (including greengage)	Wipe clean and remove stalks. Halve and remove stones. Leave as raw halves or poach until tender in sugar syrup made from 450 g (1 lb) sugar to 1.1 litres (2 pints) water plus 2.5 ml (½ tsp) ascorbic acid. Cool. Halves can also be cooked in a little water with sugar to taste, then sieved and cooled.	Pack raw halves in rigid containers with sugar syrup made from 700 g (1½ lb) sugar to 1.1 litres (2 pints) water plus juice of 1 lemon, leaving headspace. Pack poached plums in rigid containers with cooking liquid, leaving headspace. Pour purée into rigid containers, leaving headspace. 12 months	Thaw raw and poached halves as for pear above. Thaw purées in unopened containers overnight in refrigerator.
Raspberry (including loganberry)	Do not wash. Hull. Leave whole if perfect, otherwise crush or purée with or without sugar according to future use.	Whole fruit: dry pack; or open-freeze and pack as free-flow packs; or dry sugar pack allowing 100 g (4 oz) sugar to 450 g (1 lb) fruit. Pack crushed and puréed raspberries in rigid containers, leaving headspace. 12 months	Thaw whole and crushed fruit in unopened bags or containers 2 hrs at room temperature. Serve whole fruit chilled to preserve shape and texture as much as possible. Thaw purées in unopened containers overnight in refrigerator.
Rhubarb	Trim off leaves and root ends. Wash and dry stalks. Cut into 2.5 cm (1 inch) lengths. Blanch 1 min. Drain and cool. Rhubarb can also be poached in water with sugar and flavourings or spices until just tender. Cool and purée, if liked.	Blanched rhubarb: open-freeze and pack as free-flow packs; or dry sugar pack, allowing 100–175 g (4–6 oz) sugar to 450 g (1 lb) fruit. Poached rhubarb: pack in rigid containers with cooking liquid, leaving headspace. Puréed rhubarb: pour into rigid containers, leaving headspace. 12 months	Use uncooked rhubarb from frozen in pies and other puddings, allowing extra cooking time. Thaw poached rhubarb in container 3 hrs at room temperature then reheat gently in cooking liquid. Thaw puréed rhubarb in container overnight in refrigerator.
Strawberry	Do not wash. Hull, then slice, crush or purée. (Whole strawberries do *not* freeze successfully.) Add sugar to taste to crushed and puréed fruit.	Pack slices in rigid containers with sugar syrup made from 700 g (1½ lb) sugar to 1.1 litres (2 pints) water, leaving headspace. Pack crushed and puréed fruit in rigid containers, leaving headspace. Add 2.5 ml (½ tsp) ascorbic acid. 12 months	Thaw sliced and crushed fruit in containers 1–2 hrs at room temperature. Serve slices chilled to preserve shape and texture as much as possible. Thaw purées in unopened containers overnight in refrigerator.

INDEX